DOING RESEARCH IN EDUCATION

Doing Research in Education

A Beginner's Guide

edited by

DECLAN FAHIE AND SHANE D. BERGIN

UNIVERSITY COLLEGE DUBLIN PRESS
PREAS CHOLÁISTE OLLSCOILE BHAILE ÁTHA CLIATH
2022

First published 2022
by University College Dublin Press
UCD Humanities Institute, Room H103,
Belfield,
Dublin 4

www.ucdpress.ie

Text and notes © Declan Fahie and Shane D. Bergin, 2022

ISBN 978-1-910820-81-0 pb

All rights reserved. No part of this publication may be reproduced, stored in a retrieval system, or transmitted in any form or by any means, electronic, photocopying, recording or otherwise without the prior permission of the publisher.

CIP data available from the British Library

The right of Declan Fahie and Shane D. Bergin to be identified as the editors of this work has been asserted by them

Typeset in Dublin by Gough Typesetting Limited, Dublin
Text design by Lyn Davies
Printed in Scotland on acid-free paper
by CPI Antony Rowe, Chippenham, Wiltshire.

Contents

Acknowledgements		viii
Preface by Declan Fahie (University College Dublin) and Shane D. Bergin (University College Dublin)		ix
List of Contributors		xvii
1	Where to Begin: Choosing and Refining Your Research Question *Declan Fahie, School of Education, University College Dublin, Shane D. Bergin, School of Education, University College Dublin and Rachel Farrell, School of Education, University College Dublin*	1
2	Ethical Research: The Foundation of Good Practice *Aisling M. Leavy, Department of STEM Education, Mary Immaculate College, Limerick*	13
3	Doing a Literature Review *Rory Mc Daid, Marino Institute of Education, Dublin, Ireland*	30
4	Quantitative Research Methods *Aibhín Bray, School of Education, Trinity College Dublin, Joanne Banks, School of Education, Trinity College Dublin and Ann Devitt, School of Education, Trinity College Dublin*	45
5	Using Qualitative Research Methods in Education Research *Aoife M. Lynam, School of Education, Hibernia College; Conor Mc Guckin, School of Education, Trinity College Dublin and Mary Kelly, School of Education, Hibernia College.*	64
6	Researching Children and Other 'Vulnerable' Groups *Audrey Bryan, Dublin City University Institute of Education, Dublin, Ireland*	82
7	Historical Research in Education *Tom O'Donoghue, Graduate School of Education, The University of Western Australia and Judith Harford, School of Education, University College Dublin, Ireland*	95
8	The 'Method' of Philosophy? Thinking, Reading, and Writing *Áine Mahon and Emma Farrell, School of Education, University College Dublin*	111
9	Using Technology in Your Research Project *Enda Donlon, Institute of Education, Dublin City University, Ireland*	128
10	Taighde trí Ghaeilge (Doing Your Research through Irish) *Clíona Murray, Scoil an Oideachais agus Niall Mac Uidhilin, Acadamh na hOllscolaíochta Gaeilge, OÉG*	144

| 11 | Practitioner Research | 164 |

Emma Farrell, School of Education, University College Dublin,
Shane D. Bergin, School of Education, University College Dublin and
Declan Fahie, School of Education, University College Dublin

| Index | | 177 |

Dedication

This book is dedicated to all of our students; past, present and future.

Acknowledgements

We would like to express our sincere gratitude to each of the authors who contributed to this book. Without their scholarship, professionalism, and good humour, this book would not have been possible. We also wish to acknowledge the courtesy and patient assistance of Noelle Moran and Orla Carr from UCD Press. Special thanks, too, for our Head of School, Associate Professor William Kinsella, for his support.

Finally, we are both eternally grateful to Vincent and Emma – for their love, their encouragement, and their forbearance.

Declan & Shane
November 2022

Preface

This book is a step-by-step guide for novice researchers towards successfully completing a research dissertation/thesis within the field of education. The fundamentals of research are examined comprehensively, and the book is designed to ground the practical advice and instructions within contemporary educational scholarship, as well as pointing towards further reading and resources. All authors are research-active academics and draw upon their considerable experience in their respective chapters. Each author has supervised many students in completing their theses, education projects, and dissertations and fully understand the practicalities/challenges encountered by the novice researcher/student.

Every chapter represents a discreet methodological or research paradigm and is underpinned by ethical research behaviours. The aim of the book is to provide the reader (practicing teachers, student teachers or those involved/interested in the informal education sector) with all the information required to successfully complete their undergraduate or Masters-level research project in education. While the guidance this book offers is applicable to students conducting education research anywhere in the world, particular attention is given to researching educational issues in Ireland, where completing a research thesis is a requirement of all initial teacher education programmes.

The book is divided into 11 chapters each of these focuses on one, discrete, aspect of doing research. Chapter 1, by Fahie, Bergin and Farrell, focuses on the initial challenge of identifying and refining a research question. This is followed by Aisling Leavy's chapter on the importance of ethical behaviour within research. Chapter 3 highlights the importance of a well-researched literature review, while Chapters 4 and 5 interrogate the practicalities of undertaking research using qualitative and quantitative methodologies, respectively. These chapters are by Bray, Banks, and Devitt (Chapter 4) and Lynam, McGuckin and Kelly (Chapter 5). In Chapter 6, Audrey Bryan writes of the particular attention students must give to issues associated with researching vulnerable groups (including children). Tom O'Donoghue and Judith Harford discuss the importance of historical research methodologies within educational scholarship, while in Chapter 8, Mahon, and Farrell champion the appropriateness of different philosophical methodologies. Enda Donlan follows this in Chapter 9 where he offers practical guidance on how to best employ technology to optimise the research process. Acknowledging the Irish context of this book, Chapter 10, by Murray and Mac Uidhilin, looks at the challenges and rewards of researching education through Irish – ag déanamh taighde trí ghaeilge. Finally, Chapter 11 by Farrell, Bergin and Fahie offers clear guidance on engaging in reflexive research, which places the researcher/practitioner at the centre of the research process.

This guidebook is designed to complement, rather than replace, research methods lectures offered in colleges and universities for novice researchers. In this regard, we advise all students to follow the instructions of their own lecturer/advisor carefully, particularly in respect of scope, word count, formatting, citation style, structure etc. of their dissertation. While each institution will have their own particular guidelines for students conducting education research, those of us working and studying within them share a common commitment to scholarship and research within education. Virtually every education degree in Ireland involves students conducting research. While the depth of treatment will be determined by the weight the respective thesis module holds in your programme, doing research and writing your thesis will see you join a community of scholars – a community that may empower you to better understand and shape the future of education.

The following section offers some general advice that will help you as you start your research project or thesis. Take some time to carefully read each of the points highlighted below.

Mindset

Conducting education research – be that as a novice or experienced practitioner – can be extremely rewarding. Nevertheless, it is important to acknowledge the very real challenges associated with it too. While for many novices, the open-ended, creative nature of research can seem exciting, for others it may seem a far-cry from the more structured education they are used to (and good at!). Regardless of your mindset, recognise that you are a novice researcher and be open to the advice of those who are expert. The role of your thesis advisor is critical in this regard, as they are charged with actively supporting their student(s) towards overcoming their fears, pursuing their passions, and completing a thesis which truly represents, both, their ability and their commitment to a chosen course of study.

If, for whatever reason, you are concerned about your capacity to conduct education research, we wish to assure you that you would not be the first person to think this way! We hope this book will help you think about the process of doing research and that it will encourage you to be brave while engaging enthusiastically with the whole research process.

Relationship with your Thesis Advisor

You will be assigned a research advisor who will counsel on your research and on the writing of your thesis. This is a professional relationship that requires work on your part. At the beginning, it would be wise for you to learn what your advisor expects of you and how they would like you to interact with them. For example, your supervisor may have dedicated office hours when you can make an appointment to seek advice or support. You may also be allocated a specific time to meet with your supervisor to discuss the progress of your research. You should also discuss how best to share documents and data – Chapter 9 may help inform these discussions.

Use the time with your advisor well. Prior to each meeting, make note of any questions or problems you wish to discuss. If you would like them to offer feedback on written work you have completed, be sure to check when they would expect it to be submitted. Be honest in this relationship and ask for help if you need it, as problems can often be solved relatively easily if they are raised in time. Whatever you do, do not 'go to ground' and ignore contact from your supervisor. Problems will not go away, and you may need to have frank conversations with your supervisor.

While ethical issues relevant to your research will be examined to ensure participants are protected, you must also be mindful of your own care and well-being. Remember that as a novice researcher, you have your thesis advisor to help you deal with any dilemmas that arise. Pay particular attention to advice they may have around field work and the (often informal) protocols that ensure data is collected safely and with appropriate consent (e.g., if you are collecting data in your school, it might be important to brief the principal and keep them informed).

Research, by nature, is uncharted territory. Your supervisor's role is to guide you and offer advice. They will advise on almost all aspects of your work but ultimately, the research work you complete should be led by you. In our experience, student researchers who excel are those who, through on-going conversations with their advisers, show they fully understand the task assigned to them. This involves being well-read, creative, authentic, and organised. It also involves the capacity to listen deeply to what their supervisor tells them and reflect upon what that means for their work. Mindful that an explicit example might better to describe what we mean here, we'd point to the following scenario – where a student presents initial findings from their fieldwork to their supervisor. The supervisor asks the student to compare how they analysed their data to arrive at findings with the approaches taken in the literature. One student might respond by outlining the similarities and differences and just leave it at that. A second student might also compare and contrast the approaches but then will consider the implications for their work. It is this capacity to critique and apply learning that makes the second student's work stand out. Perhaps you might be thinking it is unfair of the supervisor not to explicitly tell the student what they wished them to do – this is a common response. We would, in turn, point again to the need for students to understand the task being asked of them – to do research, which means being creative, analytical, etc. In summary, it is essential that you understand what is being asked of you in your research module. Core to that understanding is you listening to the guidance your supervisor gives you and applying it to your practice.

Read the guidelines

While your thesis module may carry more weight than any other on your course, it is still a module and as such will come with clearly defined learning outcomes and details on how you will be assessed. As with any other module, you must carefully consider what you're being asked to do. It is our experience that students come to their thesis modules with numerous preconceived notions about what's expected of them and what research involves.

Each college or university will have its own rules and requirements in terms of the structure of the thesis i.e., the shape of the dissertation, how long it is, the citation style, what needs to be included in each chapter, how it must be formatted etc. It is really important that you are clear about these guidelines and that you strictly adhere to them. Remember, the structure/formatting of the thesis is, in itself, often a criterion for awarding marks by your supervisor.

Student Workload

While most universities and colleges consider research projects/theses as 'capstone' assessments (a final assessment of your academic programme), the number of ECTS (European Credit Transfer System) credits associated with these modules will differ from programme to programme. The number of credits is directly linked to expected student workload which, for a research project or thesis, is an indicator of the depth of engagement expected of you. Your institution will have defined learning outcomes for the research module you are taking, make sure you read them and are confident in your understanding of what is being expected/required of you.

Research is, by design, novel. While your supervisor will have experience from their own work, as well as through guiding many other students, the work you are doing is new. This means that unforeseen events are inevitable.

The effective researcher is practical in responding to these. For example, a student who might have planned to analyse ten datasets for their project only to find the time taken to do each one is far beyond their initial estimate, may have to consider adjusting their sample size. Another example could be that a student who has designed a questionnaire for children realises they have to clarify what a keyword in the questionnaire means for the children to complete it. Regardless of what you are researching, you will hit a bump. It is essential that when you do, you get in touch with your supervisor and talk to them about ways to move forward.

Ethics

Before you begin your research work, you must ensure that you are fully compliant with the ethical guidelines for your university or college. Chapter 2 will expand on the basis for these guidelines. Regardless of the requirements of your institution's ethical guidelines, it is of critical importance that you act with sensitivity and transparency at all times – particularly when researching vulnerable groups like children (see Chapter 6 for more). This applies equally if your research topic is such that it is considered exempt from a full application for ethical approval. It is important that you act responsibly when gathering, analysing, and presenting data.

Self-Care

For most of us, when we are in the middle of a big project, it can be challenging to remember the positive reasons we got into it in the first place. This can certainly be true of research work. Whether it is chatting to interested colleagues about your work or taking breaks at the right times, being able to step back from your work and think about the big picture is important. Such a removal can offer perspective for specific challenges you are facing; it can also sustain you by reconnecting with your intrinsic motivations or the successes of your work to-date. You can do this! And for the things you cannot do, support is never too far away.

When conducting any field work, be aware of your own personal safety. Do not arrange to meet persons unknown to you (research participants) unless in a public space. Let others know of your plans in advance and check in with them on completion of the data gathering exercise. Be wary of giving personal details to strangers, particularly your home address or personal mobile number. If you find the process of gathering data to be traumatic, for whatever reason, speak with your supervisor who can advise on the supports available in each college. Your own well-being is paramount.

Word count

For most students, their thesis may be the longest written assignment they have to complete during their studies. Adhering to word-count requires planning on your part. Consider how long each chapter of your thesis should be (discuss precise details with your supervisor). Think also about the iterative nature of writing a thesis – you will write, then review though reading, conduct fieldwork, etc. and then edit your writing. Rather than seeing the word-count as a target, consider it as the space you have to best represent your research work. Check to see if the reference list is included or excluded from the overall word limit.

Submission dates

Aim to have your work completed a few days before the final date for submission. This gives you a buffer for unexpected life-events which may impact upon your plans to submit on time e.g., your server fails, your computer crashes, you become ill etc. Work backwards from the submission date as you plan the timeline for the completion of your dissertation. You may find it helpful to agree local, regular submission dates with your supervisor. Remember, they will need time to read and review your written work and you, in turn, will need time to reflect upon what they advise and edit your manuscript accordingly.

Chapter Style

Ensure that, in most cases, each chapter has an explicit 'Introduction' and a 'Conclusion'. Usually these are the last sections of each chapter that you write. In other words, write the body of the chapter first and once completed, write your introduction and conclusion. Generally speaking, your introduction contains a broad indication of the purpose and scope of the chapter as well as a detailed map of what is included in the chapter – e.g., This chapter is divided into four sections. Section 1.1 examines..., this is followed by... However, your supervisor will discuss this with you as some disciplines may have different norms in terms of thesis structure. Keep your language formal. For most theses, it is advised that you avoid using 'I'. Instead, use the Passive Tense – e.g., It has been argued... Smith (1999) maintains... Research suggests... However, once again, there are important exceptions to this rule. Those who are engaged in action research or who are employing autobiographical methodologies such as autoethnography, for example, will have to use 'I' and detail their own personal experiences. This is both appropriate and valid. Your supervisor will advise on this before you embark upon writing your dissertation. Whatever your research paradigm, you must avoid using slang, contractions (haven't, can't, don't etc.), as well as language/terminology that is discriminatory or offensive to others. Use the spellcheck function in Word but be aware that some words may escape this protective functionality e.g., Principal vs. Principle.

As a general rule of thumb, keep your sentences relatively short. If they are longer than two lines, they may be too long. Each paragraph should contain one idea and no paragraph should be longer than approximately half a page. Be precise in your writing – for example, a sentence that begins with 'this shows' requires the reader to be really clear as to what the author meant by 'this'. Proofread each chapter and consider asking a friend or colleague to look over your work prior to submission. There should be a narrative thread throughout your dissertation i.e., one section should flow logically into the other. Use linking sentences between sections and chapters to point out what is coming next or to highlight how the section helps answer your research question. One way to improve the fluency of your writing is to avoid dividing your chapters into too many sections/subsections as this can serve to make your writing appear disjointed.

Be kind to your reader. It can be helpful to picture someone and write 'to them' (your principal or an education colleague would be good examples). Be mindful that the person you are writing to may not have read as widely as you have on the topic and that you should not make assumptions. The function of your manuscript is to convey the good work you have done, using language that is both straightforward and accessible. You want to bring the reader with you and convince them, through your writing, that what you have done is interesting and reliable.

Correlation vs. Causality

In your thesis, be careful what you suggest is the cause of a phenomenon or behaviour, remember that correlation does not necessarily imply causality. If we said that every person who has ever climbed Mount Everest drinks tea, this is correlation – the association between two variables (climbing Mount Everest and drinking tea). However, knowing/understanding this relationship between two variables does not prove that one causes the other. In this example, we cannot safely say that the reason that these people were able to climb Mount Everest was because they drank tea. This would imply causality – the relationship between a thing that happens/exists and the other thing that causes/produces it.

References and Citations

Keep your list of references up to date. Use software like EndNote, for instance, to help you in this endeavour. Save copies of the papers that you reference into individual folders on your computer. For example, ensure that the sources you cite in the first chapter are saved in a folder named 'Chapter 1 Papers'. As well as journal articles, draw upon policy documents and newspaper/magazine articles (try to focus on reputable publications rather than tabloids, unless there is a specific point you are highlighting). Ensure that all papers/articles, books etc. you have cited are included in your reference list. In most cases, the list of references should be alphabetised and not numbered, or bullet pointed. Again, check this with your supervisor to be certain that you are rigorously adhering to the citation style required by your institution or department. More details can be found in Chapters 3 and 9.

Plagiarism

If you claim the work of others as your own, or if you do not acknowledge others' works in your dissertation, you are in danger of undermining your academic credibility and, as a result, failing your dissertation. To plagiarise another person's work is a very serious offence and most institutions have a dedicated policy on how they deal with such infractions. Please read the relevant policy prior to undertaking your thesis.

Sharing your Work

Your research constitutes a unique piece of work that should be of special interest to you. Be sure to share your motivations, methodological approach and findings when you have completed your thesis. You might consider presenting your work at a conference or writing a research paper (perhaps with your thesis advisor) so that others working in education can learn from your research.

We hope that your first experience of conducting education research will be a positive experience for you: one that impacts the ways in which you think about education and one that empowers you to shape the future of education in your communities.

Best of Luck!
Declan and Shane

List of Contributors

Declan Fahie is a lecturer in sociology of education and Director of School Placement at the School of Education, University College Dublin. A qualified primary school teacher, Declan has published nationally and internationally on workplace bullying, toxic leadership in higher education, qualitative research methodologies and queer issues in education. Declan's previous edited collection (with Aideen Quilty and Renee de Palma Ungaro) *Queer Teaching, Teaching Queer* is available from Routledge. He is co-author (with Shane Bergin) of the children's book *Peigí's Adventures in Science*. Declan can be contacted at declan.fahie@ucd.ie

Shane Bergin is a physicist and an Assistant Professor in science education at the School of Education, University College Dublin. Shane is the director of the MSc Maths and Science Education where he works with people who wish to become science and maths teachers. Shane's research looks at public engagement with science as well as the impacts of informal learning. He can be contacted at shane.bergin@ucd.ie

Rachel Farrell is an Assistant Professor and Director of the Professional Master of Education (PME) programme at the School of Education, University College Dublin. A former Deputy Director of the Professional Development Service for Teachers (PDST), Rachel's research interests include initial teacher education, inclusion in education, and democratic pedagogical practices. She can be contacted at rachel.farrell@ucd.ie

Aisling Leavy is the Head of the Department of STEM Education at Mary Immaculate College of Education, Limerick. A former editor of the journal, *Irish Educational Studies* and current Associate Editor of Statistics Educational Research, Aisling's research interests include children's mathematical thinking, the development of statistical reasoning, Lesson Study, the mathematics preparation of pre-service teachers, STEM education and the development of conceptual understanding of mathematics in primary classrooms. She can be contacted at aisling.Leavy@mic.ul.ie

Rory McDaid is Director of Research and lecturer in sociology of education and research methods at Marino Institute of Education, Dublin. Rory is visiting Research Fellow at CAVE research group, School of Education, Trinity College, Dublin. His research interests include teacher diversity and 'educaring' for refugee and migrant children in Ireland. Rory is the coordinator of the Migrant Teacher Project at Marion Institute of Education. He can be contacted at rory.mcdaid@mie.ie

Aibhín Bray is an Assistant Professor in mathematics education at the School of Education, Trinity College Dublin. Aibhín has experience in the design and validation of research instruments as well as in large-scale (quantitative and qualitative) data collection and analysis. She is a former teacher of Mathematics and has worked with teachers at national and international levels through a variety of Irish and EU projects. She can be contacted on brayai@tcd.ie

Joanne Banks is a lecturer and researcher in inclusive education at the School of Education, Trinity College Dublin. Joanne's research interests are in the field of inclusive education and educational inequality. She has published widely on the social and academic experiences of students who experience barriers to learning in mainstream education. She is creator/presenter of the Inclusion Dialogue podcast series. She can be contacted on banksjo@tcd.ie

Ann Devitt is an Associate Professor of language education at the School of Education, Trinity College Dublin. Her research interests lie in the area of language teaching and learning, and technology enhanced learning. She is particularly interested in the use of computational, corpus, and network science methods to examine language data. She can be contacted on devittan@tcd.ie

Aoife Lynam is Director of Primary Education in the School of Education, Hibernia College, Dublin, Ireland. Aoife's research investigates issues relating to pupil well-being with particular focus on SPHE (social, personal and health education), bereavement, and separation and divorce. She can be contacted on alynam@hiberniacollege.net

Conor McGuckin is a chartered psychologist and Associate Professor of Education at Trinity College Dublin. His research interests are in the areas of psychology applied to educational policy and processes, educational psychology, bully/victim problems among children and adults, special educational needs, disability, intellectual disability, rare disease, and psychometrics. He can be contacted at conor.mcguckin@tcd.ie

Mary Kelly is Head of the School of Education at Hibernia College. Her research interests include literacy, early childhood education, educational leadership, and teacher education. Mary also serves on the Teaching Council. She can be contacted at mkelly@hiberniacollege.net

Audrey Bryan is an Associate Professor of Sociology in the School of Human Development, Dublin City University, where she teaches courses across the range of programme offerings on the Humanities (Human Development) and Education programmes. Her research interests lie in an exploration of the subjective experiences of those who are 'othered' or marginalised by inequitable and discriminatory educational structures, relations, and practices, and with the broad pedagogical and ethical question of what it means to educate for social and global justice. She can be contacted at audrey.bryan@dcu.ie

Tom O Donoghue is Professor of Education in the Graduate School of Education, the University of Western Australia. He is also an elected fellow of both the Academy of the Social Sciences in Australia and of the Royal Historical Society (UK). He specialises in the history of education in the English-speaking world, with particular reference to the history of teachers and the process of education in faith-based schools. He can be contacted at tom.odonoghue@uwa.edu.au

Judith Harford is Professor of Education and Deputy Head of the School of Education, University College Dublin. She has published internationally in the areas of history of women's education, gender and educational leadership, and teacher education policy and is the Ireland Canada University Foundation Flaherty Visiting Professor, 2017–18, a Fulbright Scholar in the Social Sciences, 2018–19, a Fellow of the Royal Historical Society (London), and a Visiting Fellow at the University of Cambridge 202021. She can be contacted on judith.harford @ucd.ie

Aine Mahon is Assistant Professor in the School of Education, University College Dublin, a position she has held since September 2015. She researches and teaches on the philosophy of education and the philosophy of literature. Áine is a founding member of Philosophy Ireland, a network of academics and teachers who have collaborated on the introduction of philosophy as a short course on the reformed Junior Cycle. She is also co-founder of the Irish Young Philosopher Awards (youngphilosopherawards.ucd.ie). She can be contacted at aine.mahon@ucd.ie

Emma Farrell is a Senior Interdisciplinary Researcher in the School of Education, University College Dublin. With expertise in qualitative research approaches, Emma's research has focused on understanding the lived experience of people with mental health difficulties; school-aged children, their parents, grandparents, teachers and principals; and people living with obesity. She can be contacted on emma.farrell@ucd.ie

Enda Donlon is an Associate Professor in the school of STEM Education, Innovation and Global Studies at the Institute of Education, Dublin City University, where he teaches on the use of ICT in teaching and learning. He is the Area of Professional Focus (APF) leader for Digital Learning on the Doctor of Education (EdD) Programme at DCU. Enda is a former president and vice-president of the Educational Studies Association of Ireland (ESAI) and served on the national executive of the Computers in Education Society of Ireland (CESI) for over ten years. He can be contacted on enda.donlon@dcu.ie

Clíona Murray is a lecturer on the Máistir Gairmiúil san Oideachas, where she teaches sociology of education, research methodologies, modern languages pedagogy and sociolinguistics. Her research interests span the sociology and philosophy of education and include teacher identity studies, inclusive teaching, education policy studies, and feminist theory. She can be contacted on cliona.murray@nuigalway.ie

Is léachtóir ar an MGO í Dr Clíona Murray agus is iad socheolaíocht an oideachais, modheolaíochtaí taighde, an tsochtheangeolaíocht agus oideolaíocht na nuatheangacha na hábhair teagaisc atá aici. Luíonn a réimsí taighde i socheolaíocht agus fealsúnacht an oideachais. Tá suim ar leith aici i dtaighde ar an oideachas ionchuimsitheach, ar fhéiniúlacht an mhúinteora agus ar bheartas oideachais, maraon le réimse teoirice an fheimineachais.

Is feidhmeannach ríomhaireachta é Niall Mac Uidhilin le hAcadamh na hOllscolaíochta Gaeilge, Scoil de chuid Coláiste na nDán, Ollscoil na hÉireann Gaillimh. Tá PhD san oideachas agus BSc. agus MSc. sa teicneolaíocht ag Niall. Tá taighde páirce déanta aige i mbunscoileanna na Gaeltachta leis an saibhriú teanga a chur chun cinn.

CHAPTER I

Where to Begin: Choosing and Refining Your Research Question

Declan Fahie, School of Education, University College Dublin,
Shane D. Bergin, School of Education, University College Dublin and
Rachel Farrell, School of Education, University College Dublin

1.0 Introduction

This book has been written for the novice researcher – i.e. a student who must complete a research module as part of their primary (undergraduate) or higher (postgraduate) degree. Focusing particularly on the field of education, it offers clear insights into the research process, the formation of sensible research questions, the application of appropriate methodologies to engage with those research questions, and on broader contexts around the role of research in education. Drawing on the considerable expertise and experience of national and international education experts, this book will help you to 'plot' a research course that satisfies your interests, while supporting the collection and analysis of high-quality data.

One of the first issues that confronts any researcher is selecting an appropriate, realistic research question. This can, quite understandably, prove challenging for any student of education. Choosing what to research is something that takes time and requires careful thought on your part (Newby, 2010; Cohen, Mannion, and Morrison, 2017). This chapter offers practical guidance for the novice researcher on how to choose a research question. It will outline what a research question is, how the research question shapes all aspects of your research project and, ultimately, informs the quality of the finished work. In particular, it will encourage you to read extensively around your topic to support your decision-making as a researcher as well as the many conversations you will have with your thesis advisor.

Often, much of the first meeting between a student and their thesis advisor is spent considering whether the student's initial plans may be overly ambitious and/or impractical given the timeframe or overall scope of the project in question. We hope that this chapter will support the student in managing and organising their research project so that the experience is enjoyable, challenging and academically robust. When reading our practical advice, be mindful that your programme will have specific, local, guidelines for your research project and you will need to be familiar with them to contextualise the advice we provide here.

1.1 What is Education Research and Why Do We Do It?

A research-informed approach to teaching and learning is core to our collective practice as educators. No doubt, you will have engaged extensively with education research throughout your studies and professional practice. Writing a thesis[1] invites you to be an education researcher, building upon your academic knowledge and professional experience. Through doing this work, you will better understand, and contribute towards, the process and practice of research in education. While each of you will have an academic supervisor(s)/advisor who will advise on and guide your work, it is important that this experience is student-led. Your thesis is an opportunity for you to delve deeper into an area of interest. Perhaps that will connect to research papers you have read, ideas you have encountered during lectures, or elements of your professional practice. It is hoped that this research experience will inform, empower, and inspire your engagement with research throughout your career in education. Before considering topics that you might like to research, we feel it important to briefly discuss what education research is for and how it works:

- While grounded in personal experiences, ideas, and motivations, research is methodical. It follows a series of conventions, or accepted rules, that increase the trustworthiness of its outcomes. It should be noted that a wide range of methods are open to the researcher and that each have their strengths and weaknesses. Many of these methods will be the subject of subsequent chapters.
- Education research can underpin the development of a deeper understanding of an issue (related to teaching or learning, for example). Acknowledging the limits of that understanding reinforces the credibility of the claims made.
- Developing research skills can support the researcher's professional agency (i.e. their ability to act) with regard to their area of expertise.
- Research is a communal or collegial enterprise. The practices and norms associated with it are 'held' by the community of researchers – for example; we cite the work of others; we peer-review one another's' findings; and we share our findings through published written work.

- Research can lead to collective expertise that may influence system-level change (e.g., curricular or policy development).

It is important at an individual, school, and system level that education research informs how we work. It can give us confidence in our practice as well as tools to identify ways to do better at every level. Having said that, many working in education often feel that research is something that is done 'to them' or that it is used to force change. In the book *What are Universities for?*, Collini (2012) reminds us that scholarship is a 'human activity' that cannot be separated from the persons doing it. It is essential, therefore, that, rather than just consuming research outcomes, those working in education should possess the research skills necessary to actively influence policy and practice. Research should enrich the conversation any community has on its values, practices and makeup, empowering individuals and communities to confidently articulate their knowledge in a research informed manner.

Choosing an area that interests you!

While your thesis is a graded piece of work that represents a sizable chunk of most education degrees, recognising that it is primarily a tool for your growth and education is important when thinking about what area your thesis should focus on. Extrinsic motivators such as your grade, trendy topics, or areas your supervisor might like, may seem attractive at the beginning. Such avenues can become tiresome as you struggle to sustain motivation. Choosing a topic that you are intrinsically motivated by is far more beneficial. It is our experience, however, that students can struggle to identify and clarify such personal motivators. Before your first meeting with your academic supervisor, you may wish to think about the questions posed in Table 1.1 and reflect on what areas you find interesting.

Table 1.1: Initial questions to consider

Question	Clarification
What aspects of your education studies have you found most enjoyable?	This could be the pastoral or relational aspect of education; It may be ideas you have come across during lectures; Perhaps your own education and your teacher identity; It could be related to your discipline and associated pedagogies etc.

What positive feedback have you received?	What have your lecturers, tutors, placement supervisions, teacher colleagues, etc. said you do well? Perhaps these comments were part of a formal assessment, a whole-school evaluation, or an informal conversation on your work. What have your pupils said to you about your teaching? What are you proud of? Perhaps reflective writing you have completed may help here. What strengths might your classmates/peers associate with you? What role do you feel you play in your class or staffroom?
What matters to you in education?	What type of teacher do you wish to be? What does effective teaching look like to you? What do your reflections say about your mindset, your disposition and your values? If you had a magic wand and could change an aspect of your practice or the wider education system, what would that change look like? What directions do you imagine your career might go in and how might that be influenced by your research focus?

It is not uncommon for students to feel overwhelmed by the freedom to choose an area of interest or the pressure to have a precise research question formulated for the first meeting with their academic adviser. When it comes to honing in from a broad area of interest (e.g., pedagogy, inclusion, informal learning, etc.), you might find it useful to keep a few options open before settling on one. For each, reflect on what attracts you to the area, read some academic papers to get a sense of the field (see Nassaji, 2019 and Seery, 2020, for example), and talk to others about your thinking. Subsequently, you may start to *drill down* to the specifics of your research project. At this point it's important to remember that the primary aim of the work is for your education and growth. You are not expected to invent a new education theory or discover something radical that will forever change education. Instead, the focus is typically local, or personal – How can 'X' work in my class? What is the state of 'Y' in my school? How does Ireland's way of doing 'Z' compare to other countries?

1.2 Reading into Your Project

Published work will help at every level of your research project. At the initial stages, reading will help you to choose areas of interest. The literature will also guide you to focus on a niche within your broader area of interest, create an interesting research question, choose an appropriate research methodology, and a assess mode(s) of analysis. Your findings will be positioned within the context of other published work and may suggest areas for future research. This multi-faceted engagement between your work and the work of others is part of what makes the process scholarly; it gives a basis for what you are doing while also serving to test it. Given the central role that literature plays in your work, it is important therefore to think about what you read and how you read it.

Published work can be divided into peer-reviewed and non-peer-reviewed work. Items that have been peer-reviewed have been audited/reviewed by experts in the field before they are published; the claims made within them are viewed as more trustworthy than those put forward in non-peer-reviewed sources. Typically, academic journals/papers and books that are written by scholars and student researchers are peer-reviewed. Publications like newspaper articles, websites, blogs and government policies tend not to be peer-reviewed. These items require more scholarly scepticism on your part. When reading you may wish to ask questions of them such as: is data provided to support claims? Do the authors appear to have an agenda? Was the piece subject to editorial oversight?

As novice education researchers, you should read work from a variety of sources to form a rounded view of issues. For example, peer-reviewed articles may tell you about the objective and effectiveness of a particular pedagogical approach. A government policy may talk about how such pedagogy informs a national curriculum. A newspaper article may tell you what opinions teachers or students have of the pedagogy in their schools. While each of these are informative, the education researcher will weigh-up each of them. That weight is typically linked to the process used to write the publication. A peer-reviewed journal must include data to support claims and will have been checked by experts; a government policy may have been informed by peer-reviewed work but typically is in-line with a political agenda; newspaper pieces tend to be a person's opinion and tend to be based on sources of varying reliability. As you read your way through your research project, you should make sure you are reading from a variety of sources and that you know where to look for them. Your supervisor and classmates may have suggested texts for you to start with.

Learning how to effectively read any publication is a key skill. While a 'how to read' section of this chapter may seem trivial, giving it some thought can have a transformative effect on your research project. Peer-reviewed publications tend to have abstracts – succinct summaries of the main findings and a little on their context. Given you cannot read every publication written on your area of interest, reading the abstracts of papers is an effective way to filter your literature search. It is also important that you give thought to where you are sourcing potential reading material. We would recommend asking your supervisor for some key reading to start you off. Ask them what online data bases they use. You might also take a trip to the college library and browse the relevant sections. At the early stages of your research, it might be helpful to read 'review articles' or books that are a summary of the main findings in an area. The big picture is helpful for a number of reasons. Firstly, it can give context and broaden your knowledge. Secondly, it can help you drill down to an aspect you are interested in. Finally, it will provide references to more specific papers on those aspects, helping you with the next level of reading.

When reading a peer-reviewed paper where original data is presented, there are a number of things on which you should concentrate. The primary focus is on the *claims* of the paper. That may be something like 'student-led activities in practical science classes have a positive effect on their science identity'. Once you have established the claim, you may wish to investigate what the authors mean by the terms used in their claim. Terms like 'student-led' or 'science identity' may be defined with reference to other publications. Remember that the field of education is a social discipline: terms like 'identity', 'engagement' or 'well-being' may not enjoy a universally accepted meaning. The next step in your reading is to examine how the paper supports the claims that are made. What methodologies does the researcher(s) employ? How might the choice of methodology affect the reliability of their claim? How is the data presented? How does the researcher draw meaning from the data? Thinking about these questions can help place the paper in context and, in turn, perhaps shape an aspect of your research project.

Non-peer-reviewed publications are also essential in shaping our view of issues within education. When reading non-peer-reviewed pieces, be mindful of the source, the degree to which claims are supported and the agenda that may be informing the piece. A good rule of thumb for assessing the trustworthiness of a claim is to look for a broad base of support within the peer-reviewed education literature. As you build your skill as a researcher, you will become more adept at spotting poorly supported claims – e.g., an opinion piece claiming 'eating green vegetables directly affects students' behaviour in class' that cites one researcher's work in the area should not receive the same weight as a state agency's policy that looks to reform aspects of the education system and is based on several published sources (noting that state agencies are influenced by political actors).

1.3 Arriving at a Research Question

Once you have read a few key texts from a variety of sources, you should begin to notice themes (or key ideas) they have in common. You will, perhaps, have developed a more sophisticated view of your broad area of interest and may, through conversations with your thesis supervisor, feel confident in drafting some research questions. You shouldn't feel alarmed if this takes you some time: arriving at the question(s) your research will consider is a gradual and informed process. When working with our own students, we have felt somewhat nervous about those who have a fully formed research question before they begin their thesis work. Such hesitation on our parts can be for several reasons. Firstly, the student feels they know the outcome of the work before they've done it and the research is just a formality. Secondly, the student's sense of what their research module is about is misinformed. Broad, perhaps unanswerable, questions are examples of this (e.g., 'Does active learning work?'); so too are methodologically driven theses (e.g., 'I've heard a lot about multi-variant analysis. Can I do something with that?'). Reading helps to address each of these issues. It ensures conversations between you and your advisor are informed and are connected to things you are interested in and can meaningfully engage with over the course of your research study.

Examples of creating a research-informed research question

The following research projects are based on former students of ours. They serve as exemplars, connecting the students' intrinsic motivations with courses of action that have been informed by a careful reading of the relevant literature.

> **Example 1**
> Áine, a Physics teacher, had an interest in drama. She frequently taught science lessons with drama-based pedagogies and wished to do research in this area. The particular lessons that Áine taught drew upon the work of one author in particular. Áine was quite confident in her ability to translate ideas from his work to her classroom practice. Conversations with Áine on the perceived benefits of teaching this way, touched on her disposition toward science education, the curriculum, and her classroom environment. Based on this, we arrived at the question 'how might teaching science through drama-based pedagogies affect students' understanding of scientific concepts?'. Given Áine's research was so directly connected to her teaching, we agreed an action research' methodology was prudent. Grounded in the relevant literature, Aine

focused on research-informed lesson designs and the selection of valid ways to reflect on their effects.

Example 2
Vincent, a Biology teacher, was interested in studying how homework was helping his students learn. He was concerned the types of homework he was assigning did not connect well to the learning outcomes of the classes and was keen to improve things. To inform our conversations, Vincent had read the relevant subject specification as well as some peer-reviewed articles. Vincent talked about how much he enjoyed student-led, active learning and how the homework he set contrasted with these pedagogies. The homework he set was, he felt, performative and more about repetition/recall, rather than learning. Connecting ideas from the subject specification and the academic papers, Vincent decided to create homework options for his students (based on Bloom's taxonomy) and to reflect on 'how students' engagement was affected by choice of homework offered to them'. Research informed the planning of the homework tasks, the nature of the reflection Vincent engaged in, and contextualising the outcomes.

Example 3
Emma, a primary school teacher, was interested in examining how school communities supported newly qualified teachers working within them. Her professional experiences led her to believe that some schools had developed very effective practices that others might benefit from. Keen to understand more about 'why certain approaches were effective in supporting newly qualified teachers', Emma interviewed several such teachers following a semi-structured/open format. To inform this, Emma read relevant government policies and peer-reviewed papers that discussed issues from an international perspective. A thematic analysis of the interviews yielded common themes that Emma discussed in the context of the published work she had read.

These are just a flavour of the research projects our students have engaged with (noting the students' names have been changed). We would recommend that you ask within your institution about work research students have undertaken previously. Reading through a few completed theses is a wonderful way to get a *feel* for the task ahead of you. As you read, bear in mind that you are setting out to do your own research – the aim is to learn about structure and writing, not to copy and paste a format from a successful former student. Many of the chapters that follow this one outline research methodologies and frameworks. The essence of your research work will be connecting your research question with an appropriate methodology in a way that is ethical and meaningful.

1.4 The Three Ps: Positionality, Power and Privilege

Having decided on your broad research question(s) you will, no doubt, be keen to embark on the practical aspects of your research. However, as you begin to explore the existing published scholarship in your area of interest and consider methodologies that you might employ to answer these questions, it is important to be mindful of Positionality, Power and Privilege (the three Ps) in education research. Reflecting on the Three Ps will help you refine and reframe your research question(s) by challenging you to think strategically and critically on how your own identity influences how you interpret/understand the world around you. This section will help with your thinking on these issues and, ultimately, prompt rich discussions with your thesis advisor.

How we see the world, how we interpret what is happening around us, how we decide on *cause* and *effect* are all mediated, or shaped, by structural factors like our gender, social class, age, culture, ethnicity etc. So, for example, a young, able-bodied athlete may view the importance of disabled access to buildings very differently than an elderly wheelchair user. Therefore, the analysis and interpretation of the data you gather (interview/focus group transcripts, survey results, documentation, archival material etc.) is always subjective i.e. determined by personal feelings, experiences, biases, histories and attitudes. It is really important that you acknowledge and address this issue of positionality in research. Positionality may be defined as that way that the researchers own identity influences, and potentially biases, the way they engage in, conceptualise, conduct, and write about research (Denzin and Lincoln, 2007). Recognising these formative structural factors and outlining them in your dissertation as potential impediments to absolute impartiality and objectivity, demonstrates your own commitment to robust and rigorous research standards. But the impact of positionality is not only relevant to data analysis, it is also an integral formative force in the selection and framing of your research question. The researcher's own identity, their experiences and view of the world, will impact upon *what* you want to investigate and *why* you think it is important. Since no human being is impervious to the influence of wider society, it is the responsibility of every researcher to reflect upon this as they consider the scope of their study as well as the question(s) they must ask in order to realise its aims and objectives.

As a novice researcher you may find it difficult to accept that you have the ability to exercise considerable power. Nonetheless, it is important to recognise that researchers exercise power in the manner in which they *shape* their research i.e. how they select the research question, how they choose their research methods, how the data is analysed and, ultimately, how the findings are presented. Decisions made by you, the researcher, on what to include or omit from your study will have a significant impact on the outcomes of the research and you have an ethical responsibility to (re)present your data and results authentically and honestly. Furthermore, some of your research participants, for example, may feel intimidated or overawed by the idea of a college/university researcher asking them questions. They may be fearful of giving 'incorrect' or, what they consider to be, 'stupid' answers and/or they may worry that you will use *'big words'* and, as a result, that they may struggle to understand you. So, despite your own feelings of insecurity and anxiety, a reflection on power, and how it is exercised, should inform the refining of your research question and your behaviour throughout the research process.

When thinking about the aims and objectives of your dissertation, consider the individuals or groups with whom you will be interacting. Are your interview participants children? Are members of your focus groups vulnerable? Is the topic you are researching sensitive or controversial? If the answer to any, or all, of these questions is 'Yes', then the Latin phrase *Primum, non nocere* (First do no harm) applies. In other words, there is a fundamental principle that your research, and the techniques of data gathering that you choose, should not in any way hurt or damage those who participate in the research. It is your responsibility to ensure that their safety and welfare is safeguarded. This demands a level of reflexivity on your part. Therefore, when thinking about your research questions it may be helpful to ask yourself the following questions

- Is this question fair?
- Will it upset anyone? What happens if it does?
- Will participants feel pressurised to answer this question?
- Are assurances of anonymity and confidentiality enough to safeguard the well-being of participants?
- Can I ask the question in a more non-threatening and inclusive way?
- Is my use of language appropriate and inclusive?

For vulnerable research participants, like some children and young people for example, the desire to *please* you, to give the 'right' answer, will not only skew your data, but may also encourage an engagement with the research that could potentially be harmful to their emotional and psychological well-being. Be guided by your own common sense as well as by the advice of your supervisor in this regard.

To undertake research is a privilege. With that privilege comes responsibilities. Responsibility to your research participants, to yourself, to your profession and to your institution. To be a good researcher, you must care about the well-being of those who take part in your research and care also that you represent your data/findings accurately and truthfully. To do this, ethical behaviour must inform the whole research process from its conception to conclusion.

1.5 Conclusion

As you begin to *play* with potential research questions that are associated with your area of interest, it is essential that you remind yourself that the education researcher who is aware of their positionality, power, and privilege is, in our view, one who is best placed to make meaningful contributions to knowledge.

It is inevitable that during your research, you will hit some bumps in the road. The clarity that comes with deciding upon a research question can quickly become lost as your project advances – e.g., trying to apply a research methodology and drawing meaning from the data you may collect. As those challenges present themselves, return to the reasons you choose your area of research interest and think about what inspired you to begin your work. When concluding your thesis, be sure to return to the beginning and give careful thought to how your work responds to the research question you posed. This *should* be your contribution to knowledge – i.e. what is understood, or known, at the end of the process, that may not have been known before. We hope it will be work that you can stand over and be proud of.

Suggested Readings

Bell, J., and Waters, S. (2018) *Ebook: Doing your research project: A guide for first-time researchers* (New York: McGraw-Hill Education (UK)).

Fahie, D. (2014) 'Doing sensitive research sensitively: Ethical and methodological issues in researching workplace bullying', in *International Journal of Qualitative Methods*, 13(1), pp 19–36.

Gray, D. E. (2021) *Doing research in the real world* (Thousand Oaks, California: SAGE).

Thomas, G. (2017) *How to do your research project: A guide for students* (Thousand Oaks, California: SAGE).

Zina, O. (2021) *The essential guide to doing your research project* (Thousand Oaks, California: SAGE).

References

Cohen, L., Mannion, L. and Morrison, K. (2017) *Research Methods in Education*, 8th edn (London: Routledge).

Collini, S. (2012) *What are universities for?* (London: Penguin Books).

Denzin, N. K. and Lincoln, Y. S. (2007) 'Introduction: The discipline and practice of qualitative research', in N. K. Denzin and Y. S. Lincoln (eds.), *The Sage handbook of qualitative research*, 3rd edn, (Thousand Oaks, California: SAGE) pp 1–43.

Johnson, R. B., and Christensen, L. (2019) *Educational research: Quantitative, qualitative, and mixed approaches*, (Thousand Oaks, California: SAGE).

Maynard, E., Barton, S., Rivett, K., Maynard, O., and Davies, W. (2021) 'Because "grown-ups don't always get it right": Allyship with children in research – from research question to authorship', in *Qualitative Research in Psychology*, 18(4), pp 518–536, https://doi.org/10.1080/14780887.2020.1794086

Nassaji, H. (2019) 'Good research questions', in *Language Teaching Research (LTR)*, 23(3), pp 283–6, https://doi.org/10.1177/1362168819845322

Newby, P. (2010) *Research methods for education* (Harlow, England: Pearson Education).

Punch, K. F., and Oancea, A. (2014) *Introduction to research methods in education*, (Thousand Oaks, California: SAGE).

Seery, M. K. (2020) 'A guide to research question writing for undergraduate chemistry education research students', in *Chemistry Education Research and Practice*, 21(4), pp 12–127, https://doi.org/10.1039/d0rp90010a

Tuckman, B. W., and Harper, B. E. (2012) *Conducting educational research* (Plymouth, United Kingdom: Rowman and Littlefield Publishers).

White, P. (2017) *Developing research questions* (Basingstoke, United Kingdom: Macmillan International Higher Education).

Notes

1. In this chapter, we use the terms 'thesis', 'dissertation' and 'research project' interchangeably. However, there may be different institutional expectations between, for example, 'thesis' and 'research project' in respect of word count, scope and structure and you should always check with your local adviser/supervisor.

CHAPTER 2

Ethical Research: The Foundation of Good Practice

*Aisling M. Leavy, Department of STEM Education,
Mary Immaculate College, Limerick*

> Ethical behaviour helps protect individuals, communities and environments and offers the potential to increase the sum of the good in the world. As social scientists trying to make the world a better place we should avoid (or at least minimise) doing long-term systemic harm to those individuals, communities and environments. (Israel, 2015, p. 2)

2.0 Introduction

All education research studies are different. They are driven by distinct research questions, incorporate various designs, engage a variety of participants and utilise an array of research methods. Whether your study involves inquiry in schools or other workplaces, engages with children or adults, utilises qualitative interviews, or requires the administration of surveys or collection of quantitative data; you, the researcher, are responsible for conducting ethical research throughout the study.

This chapter discusses some of the issues and dilemmas that occur when engaging in a research study. While there are several ethical issues common to most studies (informed consent is one example), the contextual nature of research and the ethical issues that may arise are often unique to your research situation. Careful planning before engaging in research will allow you to anticipate some of the ethical issues that may arise and let you plan in advance for them. However, it may not be possible to predict all ethical issues which may occur and you will rely on your own judgement and the guidance of others to direct your decision making. This chapter guides you in identifying the types of issues to monitor as you plan for and engage in your research study. Practical advice and guiding principles will support you in assessing vulnerability and risk across all stages of your research and guide you when incorporating practices to ensure that you meet the standards of ethical research.

As outlined in the chapters in this book, there are multiple different approaches to conducting education research. In seeking answers to research questions, researchers may carry out interviews or focus groups online, via phone or in person. Questions can also be posed via postal or online surveys. Insights can also be gained through observation of phenomena, self-study, ethnography, and a range of other qualitative approaches. Data can be gathered via artefacts such as images and video, newspapers, historical records, records of correspondence, student work, and reference to databases. Researchers also access and analyse secondary data collected by others. Some examples of such databases in Ireland are the census data of Ireland (http://www.census.nationalarchives.ie) and the *Growing Up in Ireland* national longitudinal study of children (https://www.growingup.ie). Once these data are collected and analysed, there are also a plethora of approaches that researchers can use to report their findings. Some examples include reporting descriptive and inferential statistics, infographics, narrative, and case study approaches, and using arts-based and visual methods. Across all of these modes of inquiry and reporting, some important ethical questions and considerations need to be considered.

Naming ourselves and others in the research

Researchers are very purposeful in choosing the labels to refer to themselves and those who provide them with their data. The term 'participant' has replaced the traditional use of the term research 'subject.' 'Participant' has roots in the social sciences and implies a more active and partnership role in the research study as compared to the more depersonalised and somewhat subservient connotations associated with the term 'subject'. The term 'subject' originated from medical research, suggests a unidirectional relationship and a passive role. In contrast, referring to 'participants' suggests valuing the person and their contribution to the research study alongside a view of them as an equal in the researcher-researched relationship. Similar consideration may also be given to the use of the terms 'respondent' and 'interviewee'. Less contentious, yet also worthy of consideration, is the choice of terminology for those who collect the data. The term 'researcher' has widespread use and appears less value-laden than the 'subject'/'participant' debate; however, there has been a move to link the researcher to their professional role through terms such as 'teacher-researcher' and 'practitioner-researcher' where they apply.

2.1 Ethical Frameworks and Approaches

Almost all research conducted by researchers in Europe and across much of the world is subject to ethical review by highly regulated ethics committees. The emergence and evolution of research ethics regulation is a disturbing narrative of change brought about in response to abuses in medical and social research in the last century. Both the Nuremberg Code (1947) (see Shuster, 1997) and the subsequent development of the World Health Organisation's Declaration of Helsinki (1964) were established as a result of abuses to people arising from medical experimentation conducted during the Second World War. Despite these highly influential ethical statements, further abuses, and ethical scandals in biomedical research (such as the Tuskegee syphilis study carried out on poor African Americans from 1932–1972) and social research (such as Milgrams (1963) obedience to authority experiments) continued throughout the twentieth century. Ireland has its own shameful history revealed most recently by the Commission of Investigation into Mother and Baby Homes (Government of Ireland, 2021), which found no evidence of consent being sought or received for the 13 vaccine trials carried out between 1922–1998 on children in these institutions. Subsequent ethical statements formed in response to breaches of ethical behaviour in medical and social research (see Israel, 2015 for a more detailed discussion) have laid the foundations for the establishment of university research ethics committees that screen research on human subjects.

Ethical behaviour in research is guided by ethical principles developed by the research community and communicated in professional ethical guidelines. A discussion of the ethical frameworks which provide the criteria underpinning ethical decision making and frameworks is beyond the scope of this chapter (see Israel (2015) for an overview). However, it may suffice to be aware of four common approaches: (1) consequentalist – ethical decisions should be made based on the consequences of the action and whether it has a good outcome for an individual or wider society; (2) principlist – non-consequentalist approaches based on the belief that ethical decisions should be motivated by what is morally correct regardless of the consequences; (3) critical approaches to ethics, for example, the ethics of care (see Gilligan, 1982) – ethical decisions are based on a notion of care and compassion towards research participants rather than using sets of rules and principles to guide decision making; and, (4) virtue ethics (see Macfarland, 2009) – ethical decisions are informed by the moral characteristics of the researcher such as respectfulness and reflexivity. The ethical guidelines and regulations drawn up by institutional ethics committees draw predominantly from these four approaches and provide guidance in managing standard ethical issues when preparing an application for research approval. These, alongside a researcher's own moral judgement about appropriate courses of action, may also serve to provide guidance in dealing with unexpected issues that may arise during a research study.

2.2 Guiding Principles for Ethical Research

Careful planning directed by three guiding principles, identified by Poth (2021), can support researchers in ensuring they are implementing good ethical practices. These guiding principles are derived from *The Belmont Report* which was written by the National Commission for the Protection of Human Subjects of Biomedical and Behavioral Research (1978). The remainder of this chapter is structured according to the three ethical principles (respect for persons, beneficence, and justice) and the associated three primary areas of application to address these principles (informed consent, assessment of risks and benefits, and selection of subjects). Two scenarios are presented that provide practical insights into strategies that can be used to ensure ethical practices.

Principle 1: Respect for persons

This principle focuses on the study of participants and the data collected from them. Identifying participants is one of the first steps in the implementation of a research study and ethical considerations come into play almost immediately. For example, decisions regarding how to contact participants have ethical implications. When contacted electronically (via email or online) or by letter, participants have the time to consider the research, their involvement and its consequences. In contrast, when approached in person, people may find it difficult to refuse to participate and have little time to reflect on the request. In these situations, while it is not the researcher's intention, participants may feel coerced into agreeing to be involved. Consequently, ethical procedures ensure that participants freely consent to participate in the study and are not coerced into being involved. When considering this principle, ask these questions:

- What practices can you implement to ensure that participation is voluntary?
- How are you documenting consent?

The practices invoked to address this principle are **informed voluntary consent,** which is discussed later in this chapter.

Principle 2: Concern for welfare

This principle concerns the protection of participants by maximising the benefits of the research and minimising harm that may be caused due to participating in the research. This principle relating to the welfare of participants and responsibility 'to do good' is referred to as 'beneficence' by the Belmont Report and in the ethics literature. Ask yourself these questions:

- What are the possible risks for those participating in the research study?
- How can you protect the privacy of research participants?

The practical response to this principle focuses on safeguarding the **privacy and confidentiality** of participants.

Principle 3: A focus on justice

This principle attends to the fair and equitable treatment of all participants in the research study. The Belmont Report suggests that the principle of justice can be understood as the notion that participants should be treated equally. Key ethical issues concern reducing sources of bias in three areas: the researchers, the participants, and the research design. Ask yourself these questions:

- When recruiting and sampling participants, how can you ensure equitable and fair practices?
- When reporting your data, how can you ensure equitable and fair treatment of participants?

Ethical practices underpinning this principle focus on the **selection of participants.**

2.3 Applying Practices to Support Ethical Research

When designing a research study, it is advisable to prepare in advance for ethical dilemmas. This preparation begins very early in the planning phases of the study. Research studies are labour intensive and require the time and effort of participants, research supervisors and ethics committee. Consequently, initial ethical questions should focus on whether the research study is justifiable and warranted and should focus on the research questions, purpose, and methods used. The research question needs scrutiny – has this question already been answered? Is it necessary to ask all these questions? What is the added value to the research community in answering the research question? When the questions have been finalised, similar scrutiny needs to be applied to ensure that the methods being used are adequate to answer the question being asked. Then, ask yourself: Do the methods adequately address the research question(s)? Are they efficient and necessary? What are the advantages and disadvantages associated with the chosen methods? Is the sample sufficiently diverse to gain insights into all aspects of the question(s) being asked?

Once the issues raised by the questions above have been considered, the researcher is ready to embark on the study's planning phase. The following three questions are useful to identify and highlight areas that require ethical oversight:

1. What are the critical ethical issues for this research study?
2. In what ways can you respond to these issues as they arise in the study?
3. Can you explain the research clearly enough so that potential participants can give informed consent or decline to consent?

The remainder of this chapter describes recommended procedures to guide the conduct of ethical research. As mentioned in the last section, these practices arise from principles and recommendations of the Belmont Report (National Commission for the Protection of Human Subjects of Biomedical and Behavioral Research, 1979). It is always important to consider situations where it may not be ethical to carry out research or where additional measures need to be implemented to ensure ethical practice. For these reasons, particular attention will also be focused on discussing appropriate norms and recommendations for working with children in the following section.

The rights of participants

One of the emphases of the Declaration of Helsinki (World Medical Association [WMA], 1964/2013) is on the rights of research participants. Among its clauses, it refers to the right to receive full information and to be asked for consent. When seeking and providing consent, participants also need to be aware of their rights. They are under no obligation to agree to participate. Once engaged in the study, they have no obligation to answer every question or engage in every study aspect if they do not want to. Thus, they have the right to 'voluntary' participation explained in the Nuremberg Code (1947) as:

> 'The voluntary consent of the human subject is absolutely essential. This means that the person involved should have legal capacity to give consent; should be situated as to be able to exercise free power of choice, without the intervention of any element of force, fraud, deceit, duress, over-reaching, or other ulterior form of constraint or coercion, and should have sufficient

> knowledge and comprehension of the elements of the subject matter involved as to enable him to make an understanding and enlightened decision'

It can be difficult to assess if participants are free of controlling influences. For example, young people may feel compelled to participate in research being carried out or approved by those in positions of power. Concerns have been raised about the use of inducements, such as payment and small gifts, and how these may be viewed as non-coercive manipulation which compromises the individual's autonomy (see Faden and Beauchamp, 1986).

Participants should be notified as soon as possible if the circumstances of the research change, particularly if these changes alter the nature or extent of involvement. This will necessitate modifying and renegotiating the informed consent process. Participants have the right to withdraw without penalty and know that their decision will not be at any cost to them. Researchers also need to be sensitive to situational cues that may suggest participants no longer want to participate but may have difficulty communicating the desire to withdraw (for example, in the case of children). Participants also have the right to seek more information about the study and ask questions about any aspect of the study.

Informed consent

When participants consent to engage in a study, they affirm that they both understand the purpose of the research study (What is the study about?) and the nature of their participation (What will they be asked to do if they agree to participate?). Furthermore, participants must be provided the option to indicate whether they want to participate or not.

When presenting information about the study, there are two primary considerations to take into account. The first factor relates to the comprehensiveness of the information (How much information should a researcher provide?). Making an informed decision requires that participants have a 'substantial understanding' (Faden and Beauchamp, 1986) of the study. This requires that they understand the purpose of the research, the methods being used, the risks involved, possible research outcomes, how long data will be retained for and how findings will be disseminated. While comprehensive information must be provided, the inclusion of a lot of detailed information may reduce the user-friendliness of the document and reduce the likelihood of participants reading the information and/or agreeing to participate in the research.

The second consideration regards how comprehendible the information is (Is it user-friendly?). It is the researcher's responsibility to ensure that the purposes and obligations of the research are communicated in ways that ensure participants understand; this often requires high levels of literacy. If participants are children, are not proficient in the language of communication (in this case English), or are not proficient readers, you may also need to provide a verbal explanation and access to a video link explaining your research. Written communication in plain language or translated language versions is also recommended. Other easy-to-implement considerations such as attention to the font style and size, and inclusion of graphics and pictures, enhance understanding. It is a complex balancing act to simplify the study details while at the same time ensuring that the information does not become distorted or oversimplified in doing so.

Working with children

Specific considerations come into play when carrying out research involving the participation of children. Children and young adults may not be in a position to fully comprehend the procedures and implications of the research. Researchers may have to negotiate consent with many parties such as the school board of management, classroom teachers, parents or guardians, and children for studies involving educational research in schools. Traditionally, there are many instances in research where adults have been used as proxies for children's consent. However, two articles of the United Nations Convention on the Rights of the Child (1989) provide clear guidance on the rights of the child:

- Article 3: the best interests of the child must be a primary consideration in all actions concerning children.
- Article 12: the child's views must be considered and taken into account in all matters affecting him or her.

These two articles have led to the increasingly mandated practice of ethics review boards that researchers seek consent from guardians before approaching children regarding participation in research. If consent is provided, researchers can then seek consent or assent from the children themselves. However, complex ethical and philosophical debate surrounds issues of 'consent' and 'assent' within the context of children. A comprehensive overview of this contentious landscape is provided by Alderson and Morrow (2020), wherein they provide a strong argument against using the terms 'assent' in relation to children. They also address other important questions, including: What is the law on consent? Who can give consent? What does it mean to gain children's 'assent'? How can we decide on a child's capacity or competence to consent?

Recording consent

The use of signed consent forms is the norm for recording consent in the social sciences. Except for participants with literacy or language and communication challenges where recorded verbal assent or alternative communication forms are advised, securing a signature on consent forms increases the likelihood of understanding the study purposes and procedures. However, there is an interesting discussion by Israel (2015) outlining some caution from the research community about the threat to anonymity posed by signing informed consent.

Practical Advice on INFORMED CONSENT

Ask the following questions **before** the research:

- Am I providing an accurate and truthful account of the purposes of the study?
- Is the description of the study purpose and involvement accessible to the participants?
  - Is the study described in non-technical terms and presented in comprehensible language?
  - If the participants are minors, or vulnerable adults, is the presentation of the study information organised in a way to ensure maximal understanding?
  - Is the informed consent documented in ways that are appropriate for the participants?
- Are potential participants informed of their rights?
  - Are they aware of their right to ask questions about the study? To withdraw without penalty? To access the study findings?

Ask yourself the following list of questions **during** the research:

- Am I monitoring whether participants maintain their willingness to participate?
- Where the research participants are minors or vulnerable adults, am I putting in place additional procedures and efforts to ensure they have the opportunity to withdraw?
- Are data being collected and stored in a way that maintains participant privacy and anonymity?

Confidentiality and anonymity

Closely linked with informed consent are anonymity and confidentiality. Confidentiality can have several meanings and may refer to identifiable information about individuals not being revealed, the identity of participants being protected, or some information not being used in the research. Israel (2015) describes the ethical foundations for confidentiality as arising from consequentialist arguments highlighting the outcomes of not having the practice of confidentiality in place (for example, a possible lack of openness from interviewees if they believe their identity will be revealed) and rights-based arguments emphasising the right to privacy. Certain situations exist, such as oral history and working with those in public office, where anonymity or confidentiality do not occur or are negotiated; however, these are very specific situations.

Anonymity is one of the processes used to ensure confidentiality and involves applying pseudonyms to participants, organisations and locations. Assigning pseudonyms in the early stages of research is a critical practice that protects against the accidental breaking of confidentiality. Anonymisation of visual data, such as photographs and film, can be more challenging and sometimes impossible; however, obscuring facial features and careful positioning of cameras can be arranged to protect the identity of individuals. If interviews are audio recorded, care should be taken not to refer to the participant by name, thereby reducing the risk of revealing the participant's identity. When the research study is completed, researchers need to consider the uses their data may be put to if it continues to be stored or archived. Does all the raw data need to be retained? Or are anonymised quotes and extracts sufficient? If the data are quantitative, consider whether it all needs to be retained. Is there superfluous information that might reveal participant or institutional identities?

Managing risk: Ensuring the safety and wellbeing of research participants

During the planning phases of the research, the researcher should assess the risks, harms, costs, and benefits of participation. In social research, participation should involve no more than minimal risk. The first step is to identify the information that needs to be collected and the associated risks. Assessments of risk needs to take into account the emotional, physical, and economic wellbeing of participants. For example, participants may experience emotional distress or anxiety when answering questions. Travelling to interviews may come at a financial cost and personal inconvenience. Participants may also have concerns regarding maintaining anonymity during the recording of data and the risk of revealing sensitive information.

Some simple procedures can be put in place to mitigate these risks. Emotional stress can be reduced by allowing participants to control the audio recorder and pause it when they wish, thus allowing them the time to reflect, take a break or make statements off the record. If interviews utilise video conferencing, participants should be encouraged to turn on their video camera only if they wish, thus preventing capturing their visual image. The opportunity to return to a question at any phase of an interview should also be provided. Additional measures may be required to maintain the wellbeing of children and vulnerable adults (see Example 1). An approach is to rehearse different ways for children to communicate they want to stop the interview, take a break, or say 'no' to answering a particular question.

Despite efforts to maintain anonymity, once findings are published, it may be difficult to maintain anonymity, particularly in the case of an author's institution. This alone places additional responsibility on the researcher to incorporate measures to mitigate against the identification of research participants. Some methodological approaches and data reporting techniques manage to facilitate the reporting of sensitive participant data and at the same time protect identity. One example is the creation of composite cases or 'storying,' which Israel (2015, p.111) describes as 'creating composite and fictional accounts that correspond to participants' narratives but avoid presenting specific events that might be identifiable'. A general rule of thumb is to collect only the data you need, limit the number of people who have access to the data, avoid recording identifying information and anonymise the data as soon as possible. Also, be clear about where the data will be stored and for how long, how the findings will be disseminated and ensure that participants are informed about the risks and benefits associated with the research.

Research studies depend on the openness and generosity of participants to share their time, experience, beliefs and practices. There may be some benefits for participants from engaging in the research. Participants may be interested in the study and researchers can support that interest by providing them with the background to the research and/or the motivation of the researcher for engaging in the research. Participants may also be interested in hearing about the scale of the research and similar research that has taken place in other institutions or countries. At the very least, researchers should acknowledge and communicate the critical role their participation plays in supporting the research.

> **Practical Advice on MANAGING RISK**
>
> Ask yourself the following list of questions:
>
> - What risks do you anticipate for your participants?
> - Are you collecting confidential or sensitive information?
>   - If so, what protections have you in place for your participants?
> - Are you collecting information that can reveal the identity of your participants?
>   - If so, what protections have you in place for your participants? How long will data be stored? What plans have you in place to protect the security of the data?

Selecting research participants

Exclusion criteria in social and medical studies, usually developed to protect individuals, have inadvertently resulted in unbalanced and often inaccurate views about important issues. For example, the exclusion of women and children from medical research (see Liu and Mager, 2016), and the consequent overrepresentation of men aged 16–60 years old in research trials, means we know little about the reactions of women and children to medicines. Criado Perez (2019) argues eloquently about how data bias, and the neglect of attention to collecting data from women, have ramifications for women across all aspects of society. Concerns about the risks of involving children in research have also led to the absence of their voice and perspectives on issues directly affecting them. While greater efforts have been made to incorporate children's voices, some voices are still excluded from research, particularly children with disabilities and those who speak little English. Consequently, greater effort needs to be invested into the equitable recruitment of participants.

When working with questionnaires, even the most experienced researchers can become overly focused on the response rate; of arguably greater importance is the need to ensure diversity in the recruitment of participants. When sampling or distributing questionnaires via the Internet, participants are automatically limited to those who have Internet access and are computer literate. Consequently, effort should be invested in gathering the perspectives and opinions of all people relevant to the issue under study. For example, if investigating the views on new road infrastructure bypassing a town, efforts need to be made to garner the opinions of all stakeholders – cyclists, town residents, retail owners, commuters, farmers and landowners. Similarly, when examining the educational outcomes for school children as a result of a new instructional intervention, children of all abilities should be included in the study to ensure that programme efficacy is assessed for all learners and not just those who might be expected to benefit from it.

Working with children

Recent perspectives on the sociology of childhood have focused on how to work meaningfully with children when selecting methodological approaches (See Chapter 6 for more detail on this topic). The use of traditional social science research methods has led to a resounding 'culture of silence' (Reason 1994, p. 328) from children due to methods that 'barely scrape the surface of what children are able to tell' (Hart, 1992, p. 14). Childhood researchers argue that listening to children's voices in participatory research is not enough. There is the need, Geertz (1998, p. 245) claims, to challenge the new 'text positivism' and 'dispersed authorship' that assumes research reporting what children say is an authentic (and hence unproblematic) representation of children's voices.

Recognition of the limitations of an over-dependence on language-oriented methods in research with children has led to a search for diverse, participatory, culturally appropriate and creative child-centred methods that empower children and give them voice within a research process. Arts-based research methods utilise a range of modes for expression that can uncover phenomenon not accessible through other, more traditional means. While such participatory methods favour visual techniques such as drawing and photography, other methods such as film, theatre, dance and new media are all being used to support the representation of experiences unconfined by language and literacy (White, Bushin, Méndez and NíLaoire, 2010). Furthermore, they support researchers in working collaboratively and non-exploitatively in ways that challenge asymmetrical power relations between the researcher and the child.

At this stage, you should have some insights into the challenges associated with educational research and some ways to respond ethically. The following two scenarios of research studies in an education setting illustrate approaches that might be taken to protect participants and incorporate ethical research practices into all stages of the research.

Example 1:
A teacher-researcher has received funding as part of her doctoral studies to support city schools in promoting walking, cycling and scooting as ways to get to school. As part of the first study phase, she wishes to conduct focus group interviews with primary children to gain insights

into the obstacles and enablers around these means of transport to school. One of the schools has large ethnic diversity and many families are newcomers to Ireland. The researcher is concerned about the most appropriate means to communicate the purpose of the study to parents and engage in ethical practices that promote children's engagement.

Action (focusing on parents – providing information about the research and an invitation to consent): The researcher first identifies the critical points of information that must be communicated to parents (research title, researcher's name, purpose and aim of the research, methods that will be used, benefits and risks, how to ask questions and seek further information about the study). These points of information are written in plain language, and research jargon and technical terms are avoided. The information is then presented on a pamphlet accompanied with images to support communicating meaning. Due to their expertise working and communicating with parents, the researcher asks three teachers to provide feedback on modifications and improvements to the pamphlet. A short one-minute video is produced to communicate the information presented on the pamphlet and support access to information for all parents. The pamphlet is printed and sent to homes. A digital version is distributed using the school digital platform with a clickable link that allows parents to check a yes/no box indicating their decision around consent.

Action (focusing on students – providing information about the research): A user-friendly student information pamphlet is designed. The information is written in large black print using short sentences, one idea per sentence, and plain everyday language. Information is supplemented by images that reveal aspects of the study (a map showing routes to school and images of children walking and cycling). A small photograph of the researcher is included. Speech bubbles are used to pose and respond to questions children may want to ask.

Action (focusing on students – explaining consent): The researcher explains in clear language that consent means saying 'yes' or 'no' to participate in the study. She also suggests that children may want to learn more about the research and encourages them to ask the researcher, the teacher, or chat with friends and family. It also explained that there is no rush in making a decision. The researcher is also eager to communicate that consent is not a one-off event and can be withdrawn. She explains that it is okay for children to change their minds at any time about taking part in the study. Pictures are used to describe the 'Stop-Go' system that will be in place (using a red card for stop and a green card for go) throughout the study.

Action (focusing on students – during the research): The researcher is concerned about ensuring children are comfortable in all phases of the research study. The 'Stop-Go' system is explained at the beginning of all interviews. Children are encouraged to use the cards if they wish to pause, take a break, not answer a question or end the interview. The researcher also develops and uses a series of protocols to support her in monitoring non-verbal cues indicating that a child may be communicating the withdrawal of consent to continue (e.g., body language indicating fatigue, distraction, boredom, or discomfort).

> Example 2:
> A researcher is conducting interviews with teachers regarding their experiences of effective practices for teaching reading. The researcher had piloted the questions with teachers and had not anticipated any risks associated with the questions. However, partway through an interview, one participant recounted her experiences as an 8–year old child and the distress she felt when she was placed in a reading group for struggling readers. The participant became distressed as she recalled her feelings of shame, humiliation, and frustration at the time.

Action: There are times when researchers ask about issues that may be sensitive; however, it is not easy to predict the experiences of participants and the feelings they may evoke. It is advisable to remind participants at the beginning of an interview that they can decline to answer a question. Providing a participant with a brief overview of the topics you will discuss or providing the interview questions ahead of time can also provide advance warning to participants of the interview schedule and topics for discussion.

2.4 Conclusion

As the methods education researchers use to collect and report data evolve, so do the ethical considerations that need to be taken into account. Ethnographic studies and naturalistic observations raise many ethical questions regarding informed consent, the nature of the interactions that may occur and require great cultural sensitivity. The rapid growth of digital technology, while opening up opportunities to access new research spaces, carries risks relating to privacy and consent, particularly concerning the digitisation, collection, storing and sharing of visual (and other) data. There are ethical questions about the privacy and ownership of data collected from online spaces, such as discussion boards and chatrooms, which users may consider private spaces but could be easily accessed by researchers. Data transported or stored on mobile devices risk being mislaid or lost, whereas data transmitted electronically are also subject to data breaches. Predicting these new ethical challenges and responding ethically to unexpected obstacles that may arise is not a trivial task. Institutional ethics protocols and ethics boards provide a range of guidelines and supports for researchers to ensure ethical research practices. Ultimately, it is the responsibility of the individual researcher to ensure adherence to ethical protocols and make sure that 'no harm is done'.

Recommended Readings

Alderson, P., and Morrow, V. (2020). *The Ethics of Research with Children and Young People: A Practical Handbook* (London: SAGE).
Oliver, P. (2010). *The Student's Guide to Research Ethics*, UK Higher Education OUP Humanities and Social Sciences Study Skills (Glasgow: McGraw-Hill).
Israel, M. and Hay, I. (2006). *Research Ethics for Social Scientists* (London: SAGE).
Israel, M. (2015). *Research Ethics and Integrity for Social Scientists*, 2nd edn (London: SAGE).

References
Criado Perez, C. (2019). *Invisible women: Exposing data bias in a world designed for men* (London: Penguin, Random House UK).
Geertz, C. (1988). *Works and Lives: The Anthropologist as Author* (California, USA: Stanford University Press).
Gilligan, C. (1982). *In a Different Voice: Psychological Theory and Women's Development* (Cambridge, MA: Harvard University Press).
Faden, R. R. and Beauchamp, T. L. *(1986). A history and theory of informed consent* (New York: Oxford University Press).
Government of Ireland (2021). *Final Report of the Commission of Investigation into Mother and Baby Homes.* https://www.gov.ie/en/publication/d4b3d-final-report-of-the-commission-of-investigation-into-mother-and-baby-homes/
Hart, R. A. (1992). *Children's Participation: From Tokenism to Citizenship.* Innocenti Essays No. 4 UNICEF. https://www.unicef-irc.org/publications/100-childrens-participation-from-tokenism-to-citizenship.html
Israel, M. and Hay, I. (2006). *Research Ethics for social Scientists* (London: SAGE).
Israel, M. (2015). *Research Ethics and Integrity for Social Scientists*, 2nd edn (London: SAGE).
Liu, K. A., and DiPietro Mager, N. A (2016). 'Women's involvement in clinical trials: historical perspective and future implications', in *Pharmacy Practice*, 14(1), p. 708.
Macfarland, B. (2009). *Researching with Integrity* (New York: Routledge).
National Commission for the Protection of Human Subjects of Biomedical and Behavioral Research, Department of Health, Education and Welfare (DHEW) (1978). *The Belmont Report* (PDF) (Washington, DC: United States Government Printing Office) https://videocast.nih.gov/pdf/ohrp_belmont_report.pdf
Poth, C. N. (2021). *Little Quick Fix: Research Methods* (London: SAGE).

Reason, P. (1994) 'Three Approaches to Participative Inquiry', in: Denzin, N. K. and Lincoln, Y. S. (eds) *Handbook of Qualitative Research* (Thousand Oaks, C.A: SAGE) pp 324–339.

Shuster, E. (1997). 'Fifty Years Later: The Significance of the Nuremberg Code', in *The New England Journal of Medicine*, 13, pp 1436–1440.

UN Convention on the Rights of the Child (UNCRC). (1989). *Convention on the Rights of the Child.* https://www.ohchr.org/en/professionalinterest/pages/crc.aspx

White, A., Bushin, N., Méndez, F. C., and NíLaoire, C. (2010). 'Using visual methodologies to explore contemporary Irish childhoods', in *Qualitative Research*, 10(2), pp 143–158, DOI: 10.1177/1468794109356735.

World Medical Association. (1964). Declaration of Helsinki.. https://www.wma.net/policies-post/wma-declaration-of-helsinki-ethical-principles-for-medical-research-involving-human-subjects/

CHAPTER 3

Doing a Literature Review

Rory Mc Daid, Marino Institute of Education, Dublin, Ireland

3.0 Introduction

A well-crafted, critical report on reviewed literature provides the foundation stone for a high-quality piece of educational research. Based on a comprehensive interrogation of the extant knowledge in the field under investigation, the review helps the novice, or inexperienced, education research student to establish their own theoretical position and to acquire a thorough understanding of the most important empirical knowledge across the phenomenon under investigation. Just as important to establishing what is known about the field of study, a literature review also identifies those areas that remain un- or under-investigated; it is this gap that the student seeks to fill through their research. Given the central position which this work occupies in student research projects, the process of reviewing literature and the product of that work, the 'literature review chapter' proves challenging for many students (Chen, Wang and Lee, 2016). This is unsurprising, given the complexity of the task-at-hand, what Kamler and Thomson (2014, p. 28) refer to as 'persuading an octopus into a glass'.

This chapter provides students who are engaging with education research for the first time with some basic supports to enable the construction of a high-quality literature review. The first section outlines the key contributions that a literature review provides to the entirety of the research project, paying particular attention to the importance of critical interrogation of the literature. The second section provides an exposition of the variety of most helpful strategies currently available to education students, including advice on the use of online databases. The final section addresses the composition of the report on the process, to be included in the completed dissertation. Samples of student's work, in various stages of development, will be used to communicate key ideas throughout the chapter.

3.1 Reviewing Literature and Literature Reviews: Process and Product

According to Ridley (2012), when thinking about the concept of 'literature reviews' it is most helpful to split this into two components, the *process* and the *product*. For Hart (2018, p. 11) an appreciation of the importance of this distinction encourages researchers to consider the review of related literature as 'more than a stage to be undertaken or a hurdle to get over.' The product is the easiest of these two components to understand. It is the chapter of a dissertation, most normally located after the introduction, where the student presents their evaluation and synthesis of the relevant literature in their field of study. It is also the chapter which is used to position the student's own research project within the broader field. For Creswell and Creswell (2017) this chapter also serves to provide a benchmark for comparing the results of a study with those of other important studies within the field. Hempel (2020, p. 3) describes how 'literature reviews summarise existing research to answer a review question, provide the context for new research, or identify important gaps in the existing body of literature.' A high-quality literature review takes the reader by the hand, leads them through the important empirical and, if relevant, theoretical contributions to the field of study. In so doing, it sets a scholarly context for the work and offers the reader a considered overview of the relevant national and international scholarship of the topic under investigation. Furthermore, it presents a critically informed argument while identifying any deficits or weaknesses in the extant literature. By the time the reader completes the chapter, they see why a student is asking the proposed research question(s) and seeking to answer it/them through the chosen methodology. The chapter works, therefore, as the 'driving force and jumping off point' (Ridley, 2012, p. 3) for a student's research investigation.

The processes involved in the production of this chapter are much more complicated. These involve the systematic selection of sources to be critically read and reviewed. The insights gained from this work must then be brought together to deliver a narrative which will provide an overview and examination of the specific field of research in question. The processes involved here are complex and require a significant investment of time so that the student can write with authority on the topic. At each point along the way, the student must make informed choices so that they can best inform their study. Choosing which literature to include and to omit, for example, can be a fraught exercise. An abundance of literature leaves the problem of which to omit, while a dearth of suitable literature in the field means a student has to push their search into wider, allied fields.

The student as a critical reader

Critical reading of this gathered literature is a necessity for the production of a high-quality literature review. Fairbairn and Fairbairn (2001) claim that 'along with listening and observation, reading is an important way in which we gain information about the world. It will underpin much of your academic work as a student ... and [it will] allow you to adopt a scholarly approach to your written work'. According to St Clair-Thompson, Graham and Marsham (2018), students who read more than their peers perform more strongly in assessments, participate more in class discussions and develop stronger reading comprehension and writing skills. Bharuthram (2012) argues that the level of reading required for students in higher education is 'much more demanding and sophisticated than in school' and maintains that students will be required to read across a broad range of different materials which 'requires sophisticated analytical and interpretative skills' (p. 210). Yet the prolonged, critical reading required for the production of a literature review chapter is scholarly activity that many students find difficult. Critical reading requires a deep and active engagement with each text (Sutherland and Incera, 2021) which moves beyond a superficial extraction of knowledge to critically appraising the trustworthiness and appropriateness of a text, and then moving to synthesising these observations. Ridley (2012) encourages students to try to answer a series of questions as they read the literature they have selected. These questions include: What is the author's central argument or main point? What conclusions does the author reach and what evidence does the author advance in support of those conclusions? What is the context in which the text was written? Does the cultural and historical context have an effect on the author's assumptions, the content and the way it has been presented? In answering these questions, students will develop a critical stance in relation to research studies rather than accepting content at face value. These critical thinking and reading skills are what are demanded of emerging educational researchers and will serve to strengthen the entirety of the research project.

3.2 Reviewing the Literature

This section explores some of the dilemmas which may arise when accessing and selecting the literature to include in the literature review. It focuses particularly on the use of online databases and reference management software as supports for students in these processes. The chapter then addresses the follow-on challenge of what to do with the literature once it has been chosen. This is explored across the summary, evaluation, and synthesis continuum.

Selecting the literature

At the beginning of a research process, many students experience a similar dilemma regarding where to start with an area or topic for investigation. The most helpful advice is to pick an area that they are passionate about and to read their way into it. This reading will help the student to refine a focussed and answerable research question, which will very often frame their study. The best way to generate a research question is to read, read and read some more. For those students who have entered a degree programme with a clearly defined idea for their research project, they need to become more focussed and refined in their reading. For others who are unsure of a topic of area, it can help to return to reading lists of modules that they have encountered on their programme. It might also be helpful for a student to arrange to meet their thesis advisor or to speak with a lecturer in a field that they may be interested in who may then point the student in the right direction with some initial readings. In some compressed, pressurised programmes, particularly at post-graduate level, students may need to begin to think about their research topic quite soon after beginning the programme. It is always helpful for students in these circumstances to look at the relevant programme handbook to examine what modules and content will be taught on the remainder of the programme. If some of these are of interest, the student might like to ask for copies of the core readings in advance of the module or to make contact with the module lecturer who should be very happy to share a reading list.

Once a student has secured a broad topic area, the next step is to begin to engage with the literature. Due to the vastness of potential literature, it is important to approach this process in a way that is systematic and planned. It is estimated that there are somewhere in the region of 28,000 peer-reviewed research journals globally. Many of these will have at least four issues per year (some, such as the *International Journal of Academic Research in Education and Review*, publish one issue per month!). This is also before we begin to consider other potential literature such as books, theses, conference papers and policy documents. It is generally recommended that reviews should not include social or other media contributions. While information from these sources may provide context, and this might be drawn upon in the introduction to a dissertation, normally, these should not be reviewed and presented as scholarly literature in the field. Students may also discover content on websites that may be of interest to their study. If these are official published reports or governmental position papers, they can be treated as literature for review. In the case of more commentary-based work, it is best to understand these in the same way as social or traditional media sources.

With this volume and diversity of possible sources of information, it is absolutely necessary for a student to systematically plan their way through this work. The process of refining searches so that they can fully engage with the most important contributions in their chosen field begins at this initial point. It is about refining searches so that the student can access that content which is most pertinent to their study. Students can access peer-reviewed academic journals through two routes: physical hard copies or a soft copy online. Physical hard copies are generally found within libraries while soft copies will either be accessed via the website of a particular journal or online databases such as ERIC, the British Education Index, Academic Search Complete or JSTOR. Note: College libraries offer excellent supports for the novice researcher and will have a 'bank' of online tutorials/resources available to help those engaging with research (and databases!) for the first time.

Students may be interested in a particular journal because it publishes key studies in their field. For example, if a student is conducting research in early childhood care and education, they should probably explore each issue of the *Journal of Early Childhood Research*. Depending on the field of study and the depth of material available, it will certainly be important to examine the most recent six to eight years, though students may have to examine older material in a field for which there are limited studies. Another reason that students might examine a specific journal is that, while it may not be a specialist journal in the field, it might be of geographic importance. *Irish Educational Studies*, for example, is the official journal of the Education Studies Association of Ireland (ESAI) and publishes multidisciplinary educational research on theory and practice from early childhood, primary and post-primary schooling through to higher education. Much of the work published in the journal is drawn from an Irish context and, as one of the very few such resources on the Irish social sciences landscape, it will be a vital read for anyone considering a study in the field of education in Ireland.

Online databases such as those mentioned above are refined versions of more generic internet search engines that, depending on access rights, will provide students with links to journal articles and other literature in their chosen field. These are generally password protected, linked to the student's higher education institute (HEI). Some HEI libraries have information on the most relevant databases for particular fields of study available on their website. This information can also be obtained from the library staff. Having decided on a database, it is helpful to set up a personal account on that database. In addition to keeping a record of all searches which a student can utilise in describing the process of reviewing literature in the methodology section of their dissertation, it is also possible to save selected articles in these accounts so that they are available when the student is ready to read them. One of the main benefits of online databases is that they allow users to search for content using terms and key words. Developing these terms takes time and attention. Students should first examine key words in journals that they have read on the topic. It is also helpful to reflect on synonyms for content that they are interested, for example, while a student might be interested in an area of 'special educational needs', they should also search for content related to 'additional educational needs'. Students might find it helpful to discuss some of these search terms with their thesis supervisor. If selected key words are not finding useful results, it will be necessary to try alternative key words. For example, Bell (2014) suggests using 'hurdles' instead of 'barriers (to learning)' and 'postgraduate' if a search for 'higher education' fails to unearth useful content. Depending on the type of study, students might want to refine their search to include only articles based on quantitative studies or peer-reviewed journal articles. Another search parameter that demands attention is the dates of publications of studies. There may be reasons as to why students would choose more recent studies or to extend their search into earlier material; this should be negotiated with the supervisor. While contemporary literature is important, and should form the majority of sources, students will more than likely also have to draw on seminal literature. Houser (2018, p.112) describes these as a 'classic work of research literature that is more than 5 years old and is marked by its uniqueness and contribution to professional knowledge.' Supervisors will often point their students in the direction of these key texts, though the student themselves may encounter a source that is continually referred to in their reading and it is worth expanding the literature to bring in more from that source.

Whether students search for articles within specific journals or follow the results of a search on a database, the next task is to decide which texts are worth investigating further or to ignore. Initial interactions will be via the author and title of the source. If these are of interest, examine the abstract of that article. This will very often provide enough information to rule an article in or out. Save a copy of the journal in a defined space from where you can retrieve it when you are ready to read it in proper detail. Again, the use of an account on the database is helpful here as you can save a version to that account for retrieval at a later stage. While it is understandably tempting to read an interesting article as soon as it is found, it is best to continue methodically through the search and engage with the reading once that search has been complete.

In addition to peer-reviewed journal articles, students should also examine available databases for books, book chapters and theses that might provide further literature for review. Many of these are now available in electronic format, which makes them very accessible. It is also worth devoting some time to examining the content of books on shelves in your library. Throughout the entirety of a research project, librarians are a source of terrific support to students. They are particularly helpful across all areas of accessing literature including locating copies of texts which are not available in their own library.

Working their way through the suggestions above, should provide students with access to an abundance of relevant literature, if such literature is available. Three further routes may also prove fruitful for this work. The first of these is to utilise the list of references at the end of a piece of work they are reading. If the article is relevant to your study and of high quality, then the sources employed within that article should be helpful. The second route is to follow the work of certain academics who write in the area. For example, if a student finds a particularly interesting and engaging piece of work, it is often the case that the author may have contributed other literature to the field. Students can probably access a list of the author's publications on their page on the website of their HEI, while some academics curate personal webpages and blogs. Through open access publishing, students may find links to freely available versions of their work. Finally, it is also important to remember to look up the publications of every author listed on a single publication. It will often be the case that academics work with each other on projects and the list of authors can vary on a publication, especially if the data upon which the publication is based are drawn from a substantial research project.

Reference management

At some point in their current or previous programme of study, students may already have developed skills in working with forms of reference management software. A number of such software packages are available, for example Mendeley, Zotero and EndNote. Some of these packages offer relatively basic citation tools, while others support more advanced work with sources, such as the direct importation of online sources from a number of databases. It is likely that most students will utilise two supports within the software: inserting references in the written text and the creation of a list of references.

Doing a Literature Review

Working with the literature

Once a student has selected a range of sources for review, the next part of the journey is for the student to make their own sense of the chosen literature. This will involve three basic packages of work: summarising, evaluating and synthesising. While these are presented in chronological order below, this is not generally the case as evaluation and synthesis often take place contemporaneously with summarising.

Summarising

Students will very often have summarised research articles in other modules on their current or previous programme. The process here is quite similar, though it will be more important to focus on the ways in which the article relates to the research project for which the article is being reviewed. This may mean, for example, that in addition to paying attention to the findings of the study, students pay particular attention to the research paradigm, the research sample/participants, and the methodology employed. It is at this point that students must engage in the critical reading discussed above. Students need to record notes on the basis of that reading. The sections provided in Table 3.1 below cover most of what is required for maintaining robust notes taken on a source. While this process may appear cumbersome initially, students very quickly see the benefit of this structured approach and find it a very helpful way of interrogating a piece of literature.

Table 3.1: Sample 'note taking' framework

Title and Source	
Author(s) and Date	
Research Question(s)	
Conceptual Framework	
Research Methodology, Sample & Instruments	
Findings and Analyses	
Recommendations	
Overall Observations	

These notes will very often provide the content for a summary of a source, which can then be included in the literature review chapter. Creswell and Creswell (2017, p. 42) provide a clear example of a summary of the major components of a qualitative study that one of them was involved with:

Creswell, Seagren, and Henry (1979) tested the Biglan model, a three-dimensional model clustering thirty-six academic areas in hard or soft, pure of applied, life or non-life areas, as a predictor of chairpersons' professional development needs. Eighty department chairpersons located in four state colleges and one university of a Midwestern state participated in the study. Results showed their professional development needs. Based on the findings, the authors recommended that those who develop in-service programs need to consider differences among disciplines when they plan for programs.

This summary utilises much of what might be included on the proposed record sheet above. Creswell and Creswell start with the author and the date and then provide a review of the central purpose of the study. They then provide a brief overview of the data generation methods, including a specific mention of the research participants (or sample). Following this, the authors state the major results of the study and conclude the piece by presenting the relevant recommendations of the study. In this case, they have presented the practical recommendations or implications of the study but it might also be helpful to identify the research recommendations made by the authors. This can help to build the case for a student's own research as attending to an observed gap in the literature. The notes taken should not simply reiterate the key points of the study but they also need to be evaluative.

Evaluation

One of the hallmarks of writing an authoritative review of literature for a research project is the ability of the author to evaluate the quality and trustworthiness of a source. Menter et al (2011) provide a helpful section for students on judging the quality of literature. The authors present three sets of criteria, each with their own specific purpose, which can be employed by a student to discern the quality of a source. The first focuses on the American Educational Research Association's (AERA) understanding of scientifically based research and outlines some of the key requirements against which a reader can judge a source. These range from requirements that the methods are appropriate to the questions posed, the data and analysis are adequate to support findings and that there is clear and detailed explications of procedures and results. The second set of criteria are drawn from the work of Furlong and Oancea (2006) and are more useful in assessing the quality of applied and practice-based research. These include explicitness in designing and reporting, adherence to ethical codes of practice and concern for enabling impact. This set may be particularly helpful for emerging practitioner researchers in education. The third set of criteria are specifically for assessing the methodological quality of sources and are based on the work of Fink (2010). These include asking the following questions: Is the study's research design both robust and appropriate? Are the data sources reliable and are the results meaningful in practical and statistical terms?

Depending on the nature of the study, you should give careful attention to methods such as those listed above that help you discern the quality of a piece of academic literature. Your capacity to conduct such an evaluation makes an important contribution to the overall quality of your literature review. See, for example, in the selection below taken from Elizabeth Matthew's doctoral thesis (2011) which examined the mainstreaming of deaf education in Ireland. This is an excellent example of how to evaluate the trustworthiness of a source (Hung and Paul, 2006), while making judicious use of the data contained within the study:

> Hung and Paul (2006) reveal more positive findings from their research with 241 hearing students in settings along with D/HH peers with 75% of students [having] positive attitudes towards their deaf peers. Unfortunately, we are given little information regarding the type of inclusion programmes being implemented in the two schools from which the sample was drawn. Neither do we know the level of deafness of the students with whom they were integrated. Furthermore, there may be issues surrounding the reliability of the data since it may be unlikely for students to express negative opinions towards their peers in a survey specifically designed to examine their attitudes towards that group (Inclusion of Deaf or Hard-of-Hearing Students Inventory). Nonetheless, the fact that only 25% of students displayed negative attitudes towards D/HH peers, with only 1.2% of those being strong negative attitudes point at the least to neutral if not slightly positive outcome for inclusion in the schools involved.

Synthesis

Constructing the literature review chapter of a thesis can be quite a challenge for students. It is difficult to synthesise all of the summaries and evaluations you have created for each article/book/etc., to create a coherent narrative. Hempel (2020, p.18) describes the process of synthesis as a student's 'unique contribution'. This is the point where the student paints the picture of the field as they deem it relevant to their study. Making the jump from evaluation to synthesis can sometimes prove difficult. Where this has not taken place, students will often present an evaluation, or worse, a summary of a piece of research in a kind of 'he said, she said, they said' way. This is often accompanied by large tracts of quotations which appear to the reader as filling up space. Hempel (2020) provides helpful guidance on the ways in which students can best synthesise their reading of the literature. Depending on the nature of the study being undertaken, these can range from a summary of findings that are structured by elements such as outcome measures of individual studies to a thematic 'compare and contrast approach'. This is the approach probably most suited for studies being undertaken by emerging educational researchers. In the extract below you will note how Matthews (2011) synthesises her reading of the literature on the history of deaf education in Ireland and establishes gaps in the literature:

> While research exists in Ireland into the history of deaf education (Griffey, 1994; Crean, 1997; Pollard, 2006), as well as a number of reports into education in schools for the deaf (O'Mahoney, E., 2009; Ryan, P., 2006; Swan, E., 1994), contemporary research on education as a whole is limited to commissioned reports (Conroy, P., 2006) including one extensive but unpublished work by Leeson (2007) on behalf of the National Council for Special Education. As a result, there is a particular dearth of research into the mainstreaming phenomenon which only became active in legislation in 1998 (Education Act) and with more force in 2004 (Education for Persons with Special Educational Needs Act).

In addition to determining recurrent patterns across studies, it is also vital that students make visible those areas of conflicting evidence and take a position in relation to these debates. It is very rare in social science research that there will be absolute consensus regarding a topic. Your close reading of the literature will unearth these tensions, even in areas which may, on the surface, appear to be fairly uncontentious. My own doctoral work, which examined the language learning experiences of a selection of minority language pupils in Irish primary schools, led me to interrogate much of the literature on immigrant related bilingual education. In that reading, I rejected work by Imhoff (1990) which dismissed all but very limited tolerance of the use of children's first languages in helping to develop proficiency in English, preferring instead a time-on-task argument that the more time children spend learning English, the greater the outcomes are in relation to English proficiency. In rejecting that position, I identified that I agreed with other key scholars in the field:

The 'time-on-task' argument has been overwhelmingly discredited by the findings of Thomas and Collier (1997) and Ramirez (1992) as outlined above, both of which identified that time spent learning a child's first language had the effect of promoting proficiency in the majority language. Cummins argues further: [i]n virtually every bilingual program that has ever been evaluated, whether intended for linguistic majority or minority students, spending instructional time teaching through the minority language entails no academic costs for students' academic development in the majority language. (2001a, pp 175–6).

3.3 Drafting the Chapter

While it is often towards the end of the entire research process that students (and their supervisors) become happy with the structure of their review of literature, deciding on an appropriate structure will certainly help in constructing a high-quality chapter. It is important that students begin to construct this chapter early on in the process of reviewing. It is not uncommon for those initial drafts to bear very little resemblance to the final version of the chapter which will be submitted for examination; however, writing helps to clarify thinking and by making attempts at structure students realise what will not work and why, and as a result, they are closer to the final version.

The concept of a 'golden thread' running through a high-quality piece of research work, is a well-discussed concept in the field of dissertation writing. James and Slater (2014) describe the many components that must come together in the generation of this concept. For the purposes of this chapter, it is their advice that every section of the dissertation relates to the research and that the dissertation is eminently readable, which are most applicable. Knowing this at the outset of a research project is very important and students and their supervisors need to pay attention to it the whole way through the work. If I may play with the metaphor, however, it is very difficult, if not impossible to push a piece of string into a nice straight line from its point of origin. A straight, taut string is only achieved by pulling on both ends, from the beginning (Introduction Chapter) to the end (Conclusion Chapter). This is absolutely the case in the production of a dissertation and indeed in the construction of that smaller element of the dissertation, the review of literature chapter.

As students work their way through the creation of this chapter, the use of headings and signposts are important elements in making the dissertation text and argument accessible to the reader. Headings provide organisational scaffolding for the review of literature chapter. In addition to this, however, as Kamler and Thomson (2014) point out, headings must carry part of the argument so that it ought to be possible for a reader to ascertain some sense of the flow and major points of the argument by reading the headings. Headings should be available to read in the Table of Contents section at the front of a dissertation and can make a very good, or not so good, first impression. The sample below (Figure 3.1) is from a dissertation (Sala Rothen, 2018) supervised by this author that investigated teacher diversity in Ireland. From reading the headings and subheadings, it is possible to obtain a clear picture of the elements of the reviewed literature and, just as importantly, an insight into the argument being made by the student.

Chapter Two: Literature Review	7
Changed Demographics in Schools of Ireland	7
Experiences of Minority Ethnic Children in Irish Schools	9
Preparing Teachers to Teach in Diverse Settings	12
The Importance of Teacher Diversity	16
Diversity of the Irish Teaching Workforce	20
Ethnicity.	20
Gender.	21
Social class.	23
Religion.	23
The Problematics of Diversifying the Teaching Workforce	24

Figure 3.1: Table of Contents from Sala Rothen (2018)

One of the key skills of writing the literature review chapter is the ability to paraphrase content from your source studies. The ability to paraphrase adds a sophistication to the text of this chapter, though this does come with a risk of plagiarism, if undertaken without due care and diligence. As students work their way through the writing of this chapter, it is important to properly acknowledge sources. It is always a good idea to become familiar with the relevant HEI referencing and presentation requirements. Given that a research project is usually undertaken towards the end of the programme, most likely in the penultimate or final year, then the relevant guidelines should have been employed in the preparation of assessments in previous years. Nevertheless, it is always worth refreshing knowledge on these areas.

3.4 Conclusion

Educational research projects should build on existing knowledge and not simply reinvent the wheel (Denscombe, 2017, p. 360). The construction and presentation of a high-quality review of literature chapter provides the evidence that the author has engaged critically with the extant literature. On the basis of this evidence, the reader is convinced that the author is sufficiently prepared to pursue answers to their research question(s) and to interrogate those answers through the empirical and conceptual bases of the field within which the study is being undertaken. This chapter has sought to provide emerging educational researchers with a rationale for the depth of work that is required to properly engage with research literature. In focussing on both the *process* and *product,* the chapter has highlighted key challenges and provided some supportive strategies for students as they engage with this component of their overall research project.

Recommended Readings

Hart, C. (2018) *Doing a literature review: Releasing the research imagination*, 2nd edn (London: SAGE).
Ridley, D. (2012) *The literature review: A step-by-step guide for students*, 2nd edn (London: SAGE).
Kamler, B. and Thomson, P. (2014) *Helping doctoral students write: Pedagogies for supervision*, 2nd edn (London: Routledge).
Denscombe, M. (2017) *The Good Research Guide: For small-scale social research projects*, 6th edn (Berkshire: McGraw-Hill).

References

Bell, J. (2014) *Doing your research project: A guide for first-time researchers in education, health and social science* (Berkshire: McGraw-Hill).
Bharuthram, S. (2012) 'Making the case for teaching of reading across the curriculum in higher education', in *South African Journal of Education*, 32(2), pp 205–214.
Chen, D-T.V., Wang, Y-M. and Lee, W. C. (2016) 'Challenges confronting beginning researchers in conducting literature reviews', in *Studies in Continuing Education*, 38(1), pp 47–60.
Creswell, J. W. and Creswell, J. D. (2017) *Research design: Qualitative, Quantitative, and Mixed Methods Approaches*, 5th edn (London: SAGE).
Denscombe, M. (2017) *The Good Research Guide: For small-scale social research projects*, 6th edn (Berkshire: McGraw-Hill).
Fairbairn, G. and Fairbairn, S. (2001) *Reading at university: A guide for students* (Berkshire: McGraw-Hill).
Hart, C. (2018) *Doing a literature review: Releasing the research imagination*, 2nd edn (London: SAGE).
Hempel, S. (2020) *Conducting your literature review* (Washington: American Psychological Association).
Houser, J. (2018) *Nursing research: Reading, using and creating evidence*, 4th edn (Burlington, MA: Jones and Bartlett).
James, E. A. and Slater, T. (2014) *Writing your doctoral dissertation or thesis faster: A proven map to success* (London: SAGEDOI: https://dx.doi.org/10.4135/9781506374727
Kamler, B. and Thomson, P. (2014) *Helping doctoral students write: Pedagogies for supervision*, 2nd edn (London: Routledge).
Mathews, E. S. (2011) 'Mainstreaming of deaf education in the Republic of Ireland: Language, power, resistance' [Unpublished doctoral thesis] (Maynooth University).
Menter, I., Elliot, E., Hulme, M., Lewin, J. and Lowden, K. (2011) *A guide to practitioner research in education* (London: SAGE).
Mc Daid, R. (2009) 'Tears, teachers, tension and transformation?: Minority language children reflect on the recognition of their first languages in Irish primary schools' [Unpublished doctoral thesis] (Dublin City University).

Ridley, D. (2012) *The literature review: A step-by-step guide for students*, 2nd edn (London: SAGE).

Sala Rothen, M. F. (2018) 'Investigating teacher diversity in Ireland' [Unpublished masters thesis] (Marino Institute of Education).

St Clair-Thompson, H., Graham A. and Marsham, S. (2018) 'Exploring the reading practices of undergraduate students', in *Education Inquiry* 9(3), pp 284–298.

Sutherland, A. and Incera, S. (2021) 'Critical reading: What do faculty think students should do?' in *Journal of College Reading and Learning*, 51(4), pp 267–290.

Chapter 4

Quantitative Research Methods

*Aibhín Bray, School of Education, Trinity College Dublin,
Joanne Banks, School of Education, Trinity College Dublin and
Ann Devitt, School of Education, Trinity College Dublin*

4.0 Introduction

When approaching a research project, the first question to ask yourself is 'what do I want to find out?' or, more formally, 'what is my research question?'. Once you have this clear in your head, you can begin to look at the range of available ways to try to answer your question. The approach you use to collect data in your thesis will depend on the question you are asking. If, for example, you are looking to respond to issues that are quite well defined, you may choose to use methods that rely on quantifiable data (e.g. does the amount of time spent on homework affect the student's grade). For concepts that are more subjective (e.g. how does a child's sense of belonging affect their views of education), more qualitative forms of data are appropriate. This chapter focuses on research methods for quantitative data when they are appropriate and how to use them.

Quantitative research is the process of collecting and analysing quantifiable data, which is often numerical. Distinct from qualitative research (see Chapter 5), which might be generated through interviews, focus groups, or observations for example, quantitative research involves mathematically-based methods or statistics to understand data in numerical form. Quantitative data are often collected using instruments such as surveys, polls, or performance tests. Some argue that quantitative analysis tends to be more objective than qualitative and, depending on the size of your sample, is more likely to be generalisable, however, others strongly contest this claim (Morgan, 2016).

If you are reading this chapter, it probably means you think you have research questions that can be addressed through the analysis of quantitative data alone, or that require a mixed-methods approach using a combination of quantitative and qualitative methods. The aim of this chapter is to provide a basic introduction to quantitative methods. We focus, in particular, on what you need to consider when undertaking small-scale quantitative research as a novice researcher writing a thesis or dissertation. We begin by providing a high-level overview of the value of quantitative methods in education research. We outline the different types of education data available both in Ireland and internationally. The chapter then provides a practical step-by-step 'how-to' guide for students to undertake a small-scale quantitative study with a particular emphasis on survey research.

4.1 Why Use a Quantitative Approach in Your Research Project? (and the Types of Data You Can Use)

Quantitative approaches are often adopted in education research as they can provide a broader picture of a phenomenon compared with qualitative approaches. Although claims for objectivity are contested, the collection of quantitative data tends to allow for larger numbers of perspectives to be included in the research than would be possible through qualitative research alone. While this may be more likely to lead to statistically robust and generalisable conclusions, it is important to remember that whenever you analyse data, you are making assumptions and subjective decisions about what tools and tests to use, and what the results mean (Bray, 2020; Morgan, 2016)

In an educational context, the researcher can collect their own data, known as primary data, or use data that has been collected already (secondary data). Primary analysis of quantitative data can be particularly useful for exploring the impact of an intervention, measuring change over time, comparing groups, and providing insights into the interactions between the individual and the setting. This means, for example, you can examine the experience of students and teachers within the broader setting of a class or school, and even compare these experiences across different school contexts. Alternatively, you may wish to use existing data to carry out secondary analysis or simply as a reference for data that you are collecting as part of your research study. The analysis of existing data that has already been collected can be a very fruitful methodology for novice education researchers. There are numerous sources of rich data at both national and international levels. At an international level, large-scale education research tends to be based on quantitative data. Perhaps the most commonly cited data source is the OECD's *Programme for International Student Assessment* (PISA) study, which compares the reading, mathematics, and science results of students from over 90 countries around the world (OECD, 2019a). Data on teachers and school principals are also gathered by the OECD and published as part of the *Teaching and Learning International Survey* (TALIS) (OECD, 2019b). This survey collects data on a range of teacher-related issues including instructional practices, school leadership, professional practices, and teacher education (OECD, 2019b).

In Ireland, there is a number of large-scale education data sources available that have been collected by government departments to inform policy decision-making. These can be used for secondary analysis or to provide important context to a small-scale education research project. Some sources include:

- Census data: national data from the Census of Population (CSO, 2016) which collects individual level information from households (including education) every five years.
- Administrative data: another key data source which can be used is administrative or government data collected by, for example, the Department of Education. (DES, 2021) The Education Statistics (2021) webpage publishes reports on schools, pupils and teacher numbers, provides access to the Education Statistics Database (DES, 2021), and school enrolments, student retention. This web page also provides access to relevant international statistical reports by the OECD (described above).
- Cohort data: this differs from the above as it involves a longitudinal aspect, where data are collected from groups of respondents with a shared characteristic (such as year of birth, year of graduation) over time. In the mid-2000s, the *Post-Primary Longitudinal Study* (PPLS) provided the first mixed-methods longitudinal analysis of young people as they moved through the second level education system (Smyth et al., 2004, Smyth et al., 2011, Smyth et al., 2005). Over the past decade, the *Growing Up in Ireland* (GUI) study has transformed our ability to examine the education of children and young people with detailed information on their school, home, and community (Smyth, 2015, Smyth, 2016, Smyth, 2017, GUI, 2019, GUI, 2016, GUI, 2012, GUI, 2009, McCoy et al., 2012). More recently, the *Children's School Lives* (CSL) study has begun to provide in-depth insights into the school experiences of children in primary school (Devine et al., 2020, Symonds et al., 2020).

These data sources can and should be used to provide important contextual information for education research projects. In addition, many of the datasets are available through the Irish Social Science Data Archive (ISSDA) if you wish to undertake secondary data analysis.

4.2 Practical Advice for Using Quantitative Research Methods

This section explores each of the different phases of the quantitative research process with specific reference to education research. The individual steps in the process are broken down into two main categories: the planning phase, including instrument design and sampling strategies; and the execution stage with a focus on data collection, data cleaning, analysis, and write-up.

Planning your study

If you are reading this chapter, you may have already begun the process of developing your research question(s) or a hypothesis you would like to test. The main goal of this phase is to decide what kinds of data you need in order to address your research question. It is highly recommended that you consult the literature in the topic or area you are studying to provide context, and to see if there are similar studies or if there is a gap in the literature. Your research advisor may be able to offer assistance here, depending on their own research expertise. In particular, your advisor can help identify any existing data sources you could use as secondary data or whether you need to generate your own data yourself.

If you are generating your own data, you will need to think about the kinds of instruments available to you such as surveys, tests, observations, logs and more. When considering the design of an instrument to generate quantitative data, the rule of thumb is to use existing, validated instruments whenever possible, rather than creating your own (Field, 2009). One of the reasons for this is that the use of pre-validated, well-established scales or tests allows you to talk about concepts that are understood in a particular way. Examples include well-being, engagement, self-efficacy – that is, things that cannot be measured using a single, standalone question. Familiarity with the field of research should help you to identify appropriate instruments that you can incorporate wholesale or adapt for your own research.

While the literature contains many validated tools that you might use to generate data, it is often necessary to develop at least some components of the tool yourself. As many people use surveys in their research, we will focus on survey design to demonstrate how you might do this.

Surveys: Design and Implementation

Quantitative data can be generated or collected from a range of sources, for example existing secondary data sets (as set out above), test results, user logs, attendance records, computational text analysis and many other data sources. This section addresses one of the most common methods for generating quantitative data – the survey. Survey design should be a somewhat iterative process. It is advisable to develop a draft, which can be piloted and revised based on feedback. Surveys in education research generally seek different types of information about people including their attitudes, opinions, beliefs, behaviours, attributes (demographic characteristics) or preferences. The way your survey is structured, and how the questions are posed, can directly impact on survey completion rates and response rates overall. It is worth considering the overall length of the survey and how much time it will take respondents to complete it.

Providing clear information and instruction to respondents is very important. On the first page of any survey, you should briefly introduce yourself, give a short description of the purpose of the research, how the data collected will be stored and used, and a statement of assurance around confidentiality and anonymity (if relevant). This is also an opportunity for you to give respondents information on how long the survey should take to complete and any other relevant instructions specific to your survey.

Surveys should be created so that they are easy to understand and answer, whilst providing you with the desired data for analysis. In designing your survey, thought should be given to the ordering of questions with more sensitive questions to the end of the survey in order to limit potential emotional influence on other responses (Geisen, 2018). How you frame your questions is also important, particularly the use of non-leading questions to maximise objectivity (Aarons, 2020). Some simple considerations to avoid poorly constructed questions are presented in Table 4.1.

Table 4.1: What to avoid in survey questions, source: Salkind and Frey (2021)

Lengthy wording	Lengthy question	Lack of specificity
Lack of frame of reference	Vague language	Double negatives
Double-barrelled questions	Using jargon and initials	Leading questions
Cultural differences in meaning		

The types of survey questions

There are two broad types of questions in any survey: closed- and open-ended. Closed questions yield quantitative data and open-ended questions provide qualitative results. Closed questions can range from binary or dichotomous questions which have two possible responses (e.g., yes/no; true/false), to multiple-choice questions, based on levels of measurement.

In order to illustrate some of the most common question types, examples have been taken from the Growing Up in Ireland survey (GUI, 2008).

Multiple choice questions are probably the most popular form of survey question as they allow respondents to select options from a pre-defined list of choices. They can consist of multiple options, where respondents are asked to provide a single answer:

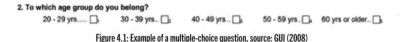

Figure 4.1: Example of a multiple-choice question, source: GUI (2008)

Checkbox responses can also be used where respondents may need to give more than one answer to a multiple-choice question. Such questions provide flexibility to choose more than one option, so that respondents can select multiple answers from a predetermined list.

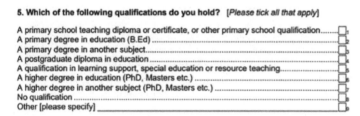

Figure 4.2: Example of a multiple-choice checkbox question, source: GUI (2008)

One limitation of multiple-choice questions can be that responses are restricted to a pre-determined list of options, which may not suit all applicants and can result in biased results. It may be helpful to offer an 'Other' category so that respondents have the option to input an answer that has not been listed.

Interval, or ratio, questions present a linear set of options that increase or decrease in intensity or strength. Rating scales can be used to generate a value (or rating) to quantify intangible or abstract concepts. These kinds of closed questions provide response options in the form of a range of choices from a theme that can include respondents level of satisfaction, or the extent to which they agree or disagree with a statement.

Figure 4.3: Example of a rating-scale question, source: GUI (2008)

Quantitative Research Methods

Widely used in the social sciences, Likert-type scales are a particular type of rating scale that enable you to collect data on respondents' opinions by providing a set of responses that include a neutral point or opinion in the middle and opposite positions or views at either end. A five-point Likert-type scale could, for example, consist of five levels of satisfaction with a topic where respondents are asked to select one.

F5. Thinking about your final year in school in general, how satisfied are you with the programme you took (for example, the regular Leaving Cert, LCA, LCVP)?

Very Satisfied ☐₁   Satisfied ☐₂   Neither satisfied or Dissatisfied ☐₃   Dissatisfied ☐₄   Very Dissatisfied ☐₅

Figure 4.4: Example of a Likert-type scale question, source: GUI (2008)

Matrix surveys can be used if you wish to ask a number of Likert or rating scale questions in a block. They are frequently used in survey scales, where a number of questions that relate to a given topic are grouped together. However, it is important to use them carefully as too many questions in a single block can be confusing for respondents and negatively impact the response levels for these questions.

48. In general terms (a) how *stressed* do you feel by your job and (b) how *satisfied* do you feel with your job?

	Very	Fairly	Not Very	Not At All
a. How **stressed** do you feel by your job	☐₁	☐₂	☐₃	☐₄
b. How **satisfied** do you feel with your job	☐₁	☐₂	☐₃	☐₄

Figure 4.5: Example of a matrix question, source: GUI (2008)

Open-ended questions are used to gather respondents' opinions, additional perspectives, or any other information that you have not captured in the survey. With no pre-defined answers provided, open-ended questions often allow for more in-depth perspectives or insights into a particular topic. Examples include asking respondents to list items or expand on an issue raised not easily captured using closed questions.

F38. Looking back, do you have any regrets about your subject choice for the Leaving Cert?

Yes ☐₁   No ☐₂

F39. If yes, which subject and why?

_____

Figure 4.6: Example of an open-ended question, source: GUI (2008)

Whichever questions you decide to use in your survey it is really important that respondents are provided with clear instructions about what they need to do. Depending on the response scales, these might consist of:

- Please select the extent to which you agree or disagree with the statements below (Likert-type scale questions)
- Please select one answer (multiple-choice questions, with only one answer)
- Please check boxes for all answers that apply (you may select more than one answer)

Piloting your survey

Prior to sending out your survey, there are a number of checks and administrative tasks that need to be undertaken. It is recommended that you validate your survey with a number of experts in the research area you are examining and in survey design more generally; this is known as face validation. At this point, it is important to carry out a pilot of the survey with a small number of respondents from your target group. A checklist of considerations is provided in Table 4.2.

Table 4.2: Survey design: a checklist

1	Use face validation with a group of experts
2	Pilot the questionnaire with target group
3	Develop a cover letter (introduce the study; deadline for return; guarantees for data anonymity)
4	Decide on your survey mode (face-to-face, postal or online survey)
5	Develop a follow-up letter for non-respondents
6	Develop a strategy to maximise 'buy-in'

Identifying population and sample

Sampling is the selection of a subset of individuals from within a larger population. When it is not feasible to collect data from an entire population of interest, a subset – or sample – is drawn from the full group for analysis. In order to use this sample to estimate the characteristics of the whole population, the sampling process should aim to be representative. There are a number of different methodologies that can be used to select the sample from the larger population. These can be broadly categorised as probabilistic methods (simple random, systematic, stratified or clustered sampling), and non-probabilistic methods (convenience, voluntary response, purposive or snowball sampling).

As probabilistic methods are more likely to produce results that are representative of the whole population, large-scale education research, studies tend to use these more systematic approaches. For example, stratified sampling, where the population is first divided into subgroups that share a similar characteristic, has been used in the Growing Up In Ireland study (2010). However, despite being less likely to produce a representative sample due to the higher risk of volunteer bias (those who agree to take part may be different from those who choose not to), for smaller scale, educational research, non-probabilistic methods are generally seen as more practical. Some of the main sampling strategies are outlined below:

Probability sampling

1. Simple random sampling: In this case each participant is chosen entirely by chance and each member of the population has an equal probability of being selected.
2. Systematic sampling: In order to ensure an adequate sample size, individuals are selected at regular intervals from the population.
3. Stratified sampling: The population is first divided into subgroups (or strata) who share a similar characteristic such as gender, age, socio-economic status, etc.
4. Clustered sampling: The population is divided into subgroups (or clusters), each with similar characteristics to the whole population. These clusters are used as the sampling unit, rather than individuals and are randomly selected to be included in the study.

Non-probability sampling

1. Convenience sampling: Convenience sampling is perhaps the easiest method of sampling, because participants are selected based on availability and willingness to take part.
2. Voluntary response sampling: Instead of the researcher choosing participants and directly contacting them, people volunteer themselves (e.g., by responding to a public online survey).
3. Purposive Sampling: Also known as judgement, selective, or subjective, sampling, this technique relies on the judgement of the researcher when selecting potential participants. Researchers may attempt to intentionally choose a more representative sample by approaching individuals with certain characteristics.
4. Snowball sampling: This method has been commonly used when investigating hard-to-reach groups and is becoming increasingly popular through social media platforms such as Twitter. Existing subjects are asked to nominate further subjects known to them

(or to retweet/share), so the sample increases in size like a rolling snowball.

Every method of sampling has limitations. Among other things, sampling frame, sample size and sampling bias should be considered.

Collecting your data

While it is possible to collect survey data using pen and paper or face-to-face methods, online data collection is becoming the prevalent format due to reasons such as practicality, accessibility, reach, and ease of use. There is a wide variety of online platforms that can be used for data collection, some of which are freely available such as Google Forms and Microsoft Forms. Other platforms that require a fee may be available through your institution. Remember to check that the platform meets the data protection requirements in your jurisdiction.

A good survey platform allows you to customise each question and easily create multiple choice questions and rating/Likert scales. Most of these platforms also facilitate high-level, descriptive analysis of the data. Data can also be directly exported into a format such as a spreadsheet for preparation and analysis. Before you begin to prepare your data for analysis, it is important to be able to distinguish between different kinds of data types, and how they might be used. The next section explores this in some detail.

Understanding your data: variables

Before deciding what to do with your data, it is important to understand what kinds of data you have. This section explores how to talk about, classify and work with different kinds of quantitative data. In quantitative research, a variable is defined as an attribute or characteristic that can be used to describe your respondents and the situations you are studying (in education research these are students/teachers/principals/etc. and schools, towns, countries, etc). It is called a variable because the value may vary between respondents in a population and may change in value over time or in response to other variables. In a survey, for example, each question can be considered a variable, and the participant's response to a question is a specific value for that variable. For test results, the test score can be considered a variable and each participant's individual result are the specific values for that variable.

It is important to be able to recognise which types of variables you are working with in order to choose appropriate statistical tests and

Quantitative Research Methods

to subsequently interpret the results of your research. Variables can be numeric, or categorical. Within each of these, there are a number of subtypes (see Figure 4.7 below).

Numeric variables take numeric values that describe a measurable quantity. They answer questions like: how many?; how much?; how high?; how long?. Numeric variables can be:

- Discrete: Counts of individual items or values such as the number of schools in a given county, the number of students in a class, etc. each of which is measured in whole numbers/integers.
- Continuous: If a variable can take any value between its minimum and maximum value, it is known as a continuous variable. Examples of this are distance, volume, or age.

Categorical variables represent groupings. They are sometimes recorded as numbers, but these values represent categories rather than quantities.

- Binary: Yes/no outcomes.
- Nominal: Groups with no rank or order within them, such as names of school, form name etc.
- Ordinal: Categories that are ranked in a specific order, e.g., grade bands in an exam, Likert-type rating scales in a survey.

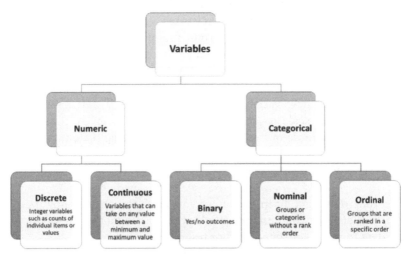

Figure 4.7: Variable types

At times, variables can be considered as more than one type. For example, Likert-type items of five points or more (e.g., strongly disagree to strongly agree) are ordinal, however, they can often be used as continuous for the purpose of statistical analysis (Norman, 2010, Sullivan and Artino Jr, 2013). In addition, Likert scales, consisting of sums or averages across many Likert items, will result in a rating that is in effect continuous and can be treated as such in your statistical tests.

Analysing your quantitative data

Before you begin to analyse the data, it is important to clean the data first, which involves fixing or removing duplicate data, data that has been incorrectly formatted or entered, or incomplete data in your dataset. This is often a good time to remove any respondents who have not given consent to their data being used for analysis. If your data isn't correct, then your output and analysis will be unreliable (although it may look correct!). There are a number of steps you should follow when preparing your data for analysis:

- Remove any duplicate responses.
- Review for outliers (unusual responses).
- Give your variables meaningful labels for ease of analysis (e.g., replace 'Q1a' with 'gender').
- Missing data: if a respondent has not completed a question, leaving a gap in your data, there are various ways of dealing with this. Some advocate replacing a missing score with a mean, median or modal value. Alternatively, you can remove some of the responses and meaningfully run your analysis on the remining data. How you deal with missing data is something that should be given some consideration at this stage and should be noted in your write-up.
- Creating new variables can be important if you have used a validated scale to collect data relating to a given construct. A good example of this is the Warwick wellbeing scale that consists of seven items that need to be summed in order to generate an overall wellbeing score.[1]

Once your data have been prepared, you need to consider how best to describe them and what tests you might want to conduct if you want to use your data to make generalisations or test a hypothesis.

Descriptive statistics are used to quantitatively summarise or describe the characteristics of your dataset. There are three main types of descriptive statistics: frequencies, which provide a count of the number of times each variable occurs; measures of central tendency such as mean (often referred to as average), median and mode; and measures of variability or spread, which describe the dispersion of the data within the dataset. The most common measures of variability are standard deviation and range.

When reporting descriptive statistics, it is important to note the sample size, denoted by 'n'. Frequency data should be summarised in the text using appropriate measures such as percentages, proportions, or ratios. For example: in a study of post-primary teachers (n=503), 68% identified as female, 31% as male, and 1% of respondents preferred not to say.

When describing central tendency, it is important to identify the particular measure of central tendency being used, along with a measure of variability. For example: the mean weight of a first-year student's schoolbag (n=350) is 5kg + 1.6kg. In this case, the mean weight is 5kg, with a standard deviation of 1.6kg.

Data visualisation using statistical graphs can be very helpful for illustrating the shape or distribution of a sample or a population. Using graphical representations of the data can be more effective, and more easily understood, than simply presenting numerical data. Some common types of graphs that can be used to present descriptive data include bar charts (simple or stacked), histograms, frequency polygons, and pie charts.

Research studies and experiments are often designed with the goal of describing the nature of the relationship between variables. In order to do this, it is essential to decide what effects you are interested in (e.g., students' grades in an exam) and what might influence these. It is important to remember however, that quantitative analysis can be very subjective; it is not always clear which variables might be causing the effects you are interested in. Sometimes all we can say is that there is an association or relationship between variables, without being able to identify the directionality of that relationship. This is known as correlation analysis.

For more experimental study designs, it is important to be able to distinguish between dependent and independent variables.

- Independent variables (also known as predictor or explanatory variables) are (generally) not changed by other variables you are trying to measure. For example, someone's age could be an independent variable. Factors such as how much the person likes school, or how much they use social media are not going to alter a person's age, but their age might have an impact on the other variables.
- Dependent variables (also known as outcome or response variables) are those that depend on other factors. For example, a test score could depend on several variables such as amount of time spent studying, how much you like the subject, etc.

There are cases in which one variable clearly precedes the other (for example, schools designated as disadvantaged (DEIS) leads to government funding, rather than the other way around). In these cases, you may call the preceding variable (i.e., DEIS status) the independent/predictor/explanatory variable and the following variable (i.e., the government funding) the dependent/outcome/response variable.

There are two main reasons why you might want to conduct statistical tests:

1. To determine whether there is a statistically significant relationship between two variables. This type of test is applicable when the predictor variable is numerical.
2. To determine whether there is a statistically significant difference between two or more groups in a sample. This type of test is applicable when the predictor variable is categorical. This kind of test can be used to test for significant differences in a single group before and after an intervention (using a pre-test post-test design), or to identify differences between groups.

Statistical tests begin with a prediction that there is no relationship or no difference between groups – this is known as the null hypothesis. This is usually contrary to your initial hypothesis, known as the alternate hypothesis, which predicts that a relationship between variables or a difference between the groups does exist. The statistical test is used to determine whether the null hypothesis can be refuted, giving weight to your claim.

Once you have collected your data, you may have been able to identify some dependent and independent variables, either through logical reasoning or review of relevant literature. If this is the case, Figure 4.8 below provides a simple decision tree to help you to determine what statistical test might be appropriate for your data and your research question. Two examples are provided to illustrate how to use the decision tree.

Example 1: Relationship between variables

Sample research question: 'Is there a relationship between the amount of time a student spends studying, and their test results?'

In this example, both the independent variable (amount of time) and the dependent variable (test results) are numerical. In order to determine whether or not there is a relationship between the two variables, without inferring anything about the direction of the relationship, we would simply use correlation analysis. If we wish to explore the relationship between the amount of time spent studying and the cumulative result (one outcome variable) then we would use a simple regression. If we wanted to explore the relationship between the time spent studying and the exam results across various subjects (more than one outcome variable), then we would use a multiple regression design.

Example 2: Differences between groups

Differences between groups can relate to changes over time, where the first group is the sample at time one and the second is the sample at time two, or it can refer to different groups of participants. You might want to explore differences in outcomes based on gender for example, or differences between a treatment and control group for a given intervention.

Sample research question: 'Did the class using iPads perform better in their English exam than the one without?'

In this example, the predictor variable is categorical, and the outcome variable is numerical. As there are only two groups, an independent samples t-test is the appropriate statistical test to identify whether there is a statistically significant difference in mean values between the experimental group (iPads) and the control group.

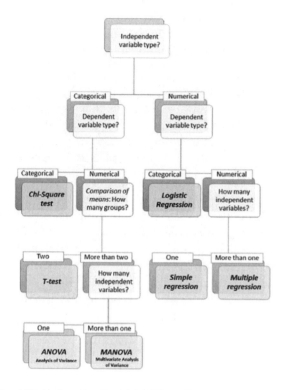

Figure 4.8: Decision tree to determine what statistical tests might be appropriate for your data

Interpreting your results

When you run a statistical test, a number (the test statistic) is calculated that describes how much the relationship between variables in your test differs from the null hypothesis. The test will also calculate a probability value (the p-value) that describes the probability that your results could have occurred by chance. A smaller p-value means that there is stronger evidence in favour of the alternative hypothesis. A p-value of less than 0.05 () is frequently considered an acceptable indicator of a statistically significant relationship or outcome.

As you move forward and become increasingly confident in your statistical analysis, there are many other aspects of testing that can and should be considered. Certain tests are only appropriate when your data adheres to given assumptions, such as a normal distribution. Some terms that you might like to explore are parametric/non-parametric, normality, linearity, skewness and kurtosis. Only use tests that you fully understand from a mathematical point-of-view, and that match the characteristics of your data. Your thesis advisor will, no doubt, be in a position to advise you here.

4.3 Conclusion

This chapter has set out some of the 'what', 'why' and 'how' of quantitative research methods, focusing in particular on what to consider if you want to take a survey approach for a small-scale education research project, as would be typical for most novice education researchers. Quantitative methods are a deep and rich field of their own or can be combined with qualitative research in a mixed-methods study. As an education researcher, you can use different data sources for contextualisation of your study or to carry out secondary analysis. For those wishing to carry out their own empirical research, the chapter offers an introductory 'toe in the water'. It provides a step-by-step guide for the novice quantitative researcher, guiding the reader from research hypotheses and instrument design to analysis and interpretation of results.

It is important to remember, however, that although quantitative methods may offer relatively objective processes for working with data, every decision you make through your research project is subjective and can have profound implications on the outcomes of your study. Who do I include? What do I ask? How do I ask it? What variables do I examine? What tests do I run? How should I interpret the results? – Each choice can have far-reaching consequences for your findings. This should also be taken into consideration when reading other studies where quantitative research has been undertaken; the responsibility is on you – the reader – to understand that choices have been made before accepting the results of someone else's statistical analysis.

Recommended readings

Bueno de Mesquita, E., and Fowler, A. (2021). *Thinking clearly with data: A guide to quantitative reasoning and analysis* (Princeton and Oxford: Princeton University Press).

Kerry, M. J., and Huber, M. (2018). 'Quantitative methods in interprofessional education research: Some critical reflections and ideas to improving rigor' in *Journal of Interprofessional Care, 32*(3), pp 254–6, https://doi.org/10.1080/1356 1820.2018.1426267

Lemercier, C., Zalc, C., and Goldhammer, A. (2019). *Quantitative methods in the humanities: An introduction* (Charlottesville, VA: University of Virginia Press).

Mertens, D. M. (2020). *Research and evaluation in education and psychology: Integrating diversity with quantitative, qualitative, and mixed methods*, 5th edn (London: SAGE).

References

Aarons, H. (2020). *A practical introduction to survey design: A beginners guide* (Melbourne: SAGE).

Ainsworth, Q. (2021). 'How to write a survey introduction (plus examples)', *JotForm Surveys*, https://www.jotform.com/blog/survey-introduction/

Bray, D. (2020). 'Quantitative analysis is as subjective as qualitative analysis', *Sonalake Blog*, https://sonalake.com/latest/quantitative-analysis-is-as-subjective-as-qualitative-analysis/

CSO (2016). Census of Population 2016 – Profile 10 Education, Skills and the Irish Language, Dublin: Central Statistics Office, https://www.cso.ie/en/releasesandpublications/ep/p-cp10esil/p10esil/le/

DES 2021. Statistics, Dublin: Department of Education and Skills, https://www.education.ie/en/statistics/

Devine, D., Symonds, J., Sloan, S., Cahoon, A., Crean, M., Farrell, E., Davies, A., Blue, T. and Hogan, J. (2020). *Children's School Lives: An Introduction, Report No.1* (Dublin, University College Dublin).

Education Statistics. (2021). https://www.gov.ie/en/publication/055810-education-statistics/?referrer=http://www.education.ie/en/statistics/#

DES. (2021). https://www.gov.ie/en/organisation/department-of-education/?referrer=http://www.education.ie/en/Publications/Statistics/Education-Statistics-Database/

Field, A. (2009). *Discovering statistics using SPSS* (London: SAGE).

Geisen, E. (2018). 'XM Blog: How to Ask Sensitive Survey Questions', *Qualtrix XM*, https://www.qualtrics.com/blog/how-to-get-the-truth-when-asking-survey-questions-about-sensitive-topics/

GUI 2008. 'Teacher-on-self questionnaire', *Dublin: Growing Up in Ireland – the national longitudinal study*, https://www.growingup.ie/pubs/9-Year-Cohort-Teacher-on-Self-Questionnaire.pdf

GUI 2009. 'Growing Up in Ireland Key Findings 9 Year Olds No. 3 The Education of 9 Year Olds', *Dublin, Growing Up in Ireland*.

GUI 2010. 'Sample Design and Response in Wave 1 of the Nine-Year Cohort of Growing Up in Ireland', *Dublin, Growing Up in Ireland*.

GUI 2012. 'Growing Up in Ireland Key Findings: 13 Year Olds School Experiences Among 13 Year Olds', *Dublin, Growing Up in Ireland*.

GUI 2016. 'Growing Up in Ireland Key Findings: Child Cohort at 17/18 Years No. 1 Education and Early Work Experiences', *Dublin, Growing Up in Ireland*.

GUI 2018. 'Young Adult Main Questionnaire – 20-year-olds', *Dublin: Growing Up in Ireland*, https://www.growingup.ie/pubs/Cohort-98-at-20Yrs_Young-Adult-Main-Questionnaire.pdf

GUI 2019. 'Growing Up in Ireland Key Findings: Cohort '98 at 20 Years Old in 2018/2019 No. 4 Education, Training and Employment', *Dublin, Growing Up in Ireland*.

Mccoy, S., Quail, A., and Smyth, E. (2012). 'Growing Up in Ireland Influences on Nine Year Olds' Learning: Home, School and Community' *Dublin, Growing Up in Ireland*.

Morgan, D. L. (2016). 'Living Within Blurry Boundaries: The Value of Distinguishing Between Qualitative and Quantitative Research', in *Journal of Mixed Methods Research*, *12*(3), pp 268–279, https://doi.org/10.1177/1558689816686433

Norman, G. (2010). 'Likert scales, levels of measurement and the "laws" of statistics', in *Advances in health sciences education,* 15(5), pp 625–632.

OECD (2019a). *PISA 2018 Results What Students Know and Can Do Volume* (Paris: OECD Publishing).

OECD (2019b). *TALIS 2018 Results (Volume I) Teachers and School Leaders as Lifelong Learners* (Paris, OECD Publishing).

Salkind, N., J. and Frey, B. B. (2021). *Statistics for People Who (Think They) Hate Statistics* (Kansas: SAGE).

Smyth, E. (2015). *Wellbeing and School Experiences among 9 and 13-Year Olds: Insights from the Growing Up in Ireland Study* (Dublin, ESRI and NCCA).

Smyth, E. (2016). 'Social relationships and the transition to secondary education', *The Economic and Social Review,* 47(4), pp 451–476.

Smyth, E. (2017). *Off to a Good Start? Primary School Experiences and the Transition to Second-Level Education,* (Dublin, Growing Up in Ireland).

Smyth, E., Banks, J., and Calvert, E. (2011). *From Leaving Certificate to Leaving School A Longitudinal Study of Sixth Year Students* (Dublin, Liffey Press).

Smyth, E., Byrne, D., and Hannan, C. (2005). *The Transition Year Programme: An Assessment* (Dublin, ESRI).

Smyth, E., Darmody, M., and Mccoy, S. (2004). *Moving Up. The Experiences of First-Year Students in Post-Primary Education* (Dublin, Liffey Press).

Sullivan, G. M., and Artino Jr, A. R. (2013). 'Analyzing and interpreting data from Likert-type scales', *Journal of graduate medical education,* 5(4), p. 541.

Symonds, J. E., Devine, D., Sloan, S., Crean, M., Moore, B., Martinez Sainz, G., Farrell, E., Davies, A., Farrell, J. and Blue, T. (2020). *Experiences of Remote Teaching and Learning in Ireland During the Covid-19 Pandemic (March – May 2020)* (Dublin, University College Dublin).

Further useful resources that provide more depth to the ideas explored in this chapter are identified in the Resources section below. It is now up to you to begin your quantitative analysis journey.

Resources

Survey Design:
https://help.surveymonkey.com/articles/en_US/kb/How-to-create-a-survey

Data Visualisation:
https://statanalytica.com/blog/statistics-graphs/

Missing data:
https://towardsdatascience.com/handling-missing-data-for-a-beginner-6d6f5ea53436 https://www.mastersindatascience.org/learning/how-to-deal-with-missing-data

Statistical tests:
https://stats.idre.ucla.edu/other/mult-pkg/whatstat/
https://www.scribbr.com/statistics/statistical-tests/

Notes

1. https://www2.uwe.ac.uk/services/Marketing/students/pdf/Wellbeing-resources/well-being-scale-wemwbs.pdf.

CHAPTER 5

Using Qualitative Research Methods in Education Research

Aoife M. Lynam, School of Education, Hibernia College; Conor Mc Guckin, School of Education, Trinity College Dublin and Mary Kelly, School of Education, Hibernia College

5.0 Introduction

The aim of this chapter is to gently introduce you, the novice researcher, to the world of qualitative research. Our goal is to provide you with an understanding of what is known as the qualitative paradigm and ensure that you have a clear roadmap when beginning your research project. Qualitative research allows you to become an explorer and gain an insight into the lived experiences of people in order to examine their perspectives, values, and interpretations of everyday life; this is a wonderful privilege. Qualitative research methodologies can complement – and in some ways go beyond – the quantitative approach to data collection, by delving deeper into the experiences of being human. Qualitative research facilitates the development of a nuanced understanding of issues in education related to behaviours, attitudes, experiences, habits, and opinions in order to come to a better understanding of the world in which we live (McLeod, 2001).

In a pragmatic and evidence-informed approach, this chapter offers a practical guide for education students and novice researchers who seek to use qualitative approaches (methods) to gain a rich and deep understanding of the human experience of education – whether at policy level, from a practice perspective, or to help facilitate a deeper understanding of experiences and motivations. The chapter identifies and demystifies some of the different forms of qualitative research methods (e.g., interviewing, focus groups, and case studies), thus ensuring that even the most inexperienced researcher can engage with qualitative methodologies with confidence and certainty. This chapter presents you with clear and easily understood explanations associated with the qualitative methodologies showcased (e.g., paradigms, phenomenology, interpretivism, methodology, method). The benefits which underpin them, as well as the rich opportunities for qualitative methodologies in educational research will be examined – all with a view to informing the selection of an appropriate research method to best answer your research question(s). The overarching goal of the chapter is to bring qualitative research methodologies to life and to showcase their value in educational enquiry.

5.1 Definitions and Description

The most basic definition of qualitative research is that it is a methodological approach which uses words as data. Qualitative data is collected and analysed in a variety of ways (Braun and Clarke, 2013). It examines the ways in which people make sense of their own real-life experiences by drawing on their thoughts, perspectives, and opinions as articulated through their own words (Cropley, 2019). The goal of qualitative research is to gain insights into constructions of reality and to tease out the nature of the world as it is experienced, structured, and interpreted by people in the course of everyday lives (Cropley, 2019). Qualitative research methodologies in education allow the researcher to capture the real-life world experiences involved in every aspect of schools/schooling and, indeed, the broader education landscape.

Qualitative research sits in the world view of 'interpretivism' or the 'interpretivist' research paradigm. This means that, as researchers, you need to interpret the lived experiences of people. Interpretivism indicates that the social world cannot be studied in the same way that the natural world is studied. It emanates from different Western sources and academic disciplines such as philosophy, social science, and anthropology. Whilst the natural sciences deal with matter which has no consciousness, the social world does have meanings for social actors, and thus, these meanings need to be revealed and explored. Qualitative research is concerned with understanding the social world or phenomena in which we live and why things are the way that they are. Qualitative research seeks to ask 'why' and 'how' questions such as: (i) Why do people behave the way that they do?, (ii) Why do people form particular opinions, attitudes, and practices?, (iii) How are people affected by events?, and (iv) How and why have cultures and/or practices developed?

Philosophical underpinnings of qualitative research

This section details the philosophical or theoretical assumptions which underpin qualitative research. Writing on the subjective nature of human understanding of the social world, Goffman (1974) presented the idea of frames and framing which, he argues, '…are the principles of organisation that govern social events and the actors' subjective involvement in them' (p.10). Participant subjectivism would suggest that meaning is imposed on the object by the subject, and thus, the object does not contribute meaning. Qualitative research can acknowledge that there are multiple interpretations of, and perspectives on, situations and events. It suggests that 'reality' and, indeed, 'truth' is complex and multi-layered, and that it is necessary to (re)examine and (re)interrogate situations/experiences through participants' eyes (Cohen et al., 2007). However, it is important to note that the interpretive approach in research is not without criticism. Cohen et al. (2007) summarise some of the major criticisms, including the potential for subjective reports to be incomplete or misleading, and the potential to impose artificial boundaries on subjects' behaviours. However, there are ways to reduce these concerns by, for example, using a combination of quantitative and qualitative data (i.e., mixed methods research). This type of research can provide a level of triangulation, where both types of data can offer validity over the other (Denzin, 1978).

Qualitative research approaches

There are many different approaches to undertaking qualitative research. These varying approaches imply different 'world views' and will influence the approach that you take. There are also many different types of qualitative research, which include, for example, conversation analysis, discourse analysis, interpretative phenomenological analysis, ethnography, grounded theory, content analysis, narrative analysis, thematic analysis, and many more. It can be challenging to try to understand the different forms of qualitative research as they can appear to overlap and intertwine. Furthermore, terminology in relation to thematic analysis and content analysis can sometimes be used inaccurately which can lead to further confusion. The list presented below is not an exhaustive list of qualitative approaches, but it does highlight the popular methods for educational researchers, both novice and experienced.

- Conversation analysis explores conversation and speech through, for example, interview data. This approach explores how social interactions are structurally organised. This approach includes detailed analysis of recordings, examining things like turn-taking, lengths of pauses, inflections, hesitations, '...ums', '...ers' and laughter.
- Discourse analysis is concerned with the study of language and how language is used. Data can include both talk and text such as, for example, transcripts of recorded speech but also

texts such as newspapers, and policy documents. This type of research is concerned with how discourses (written or spoken communications) are organised to present a particular world view. Researchers search for patterns in words and text to examine how they are used. From an educational perspective, discourse analysis can help educators to understand historical, social, and political factors as well as teaching and learning processes.

- Interpretative phenomenological analysis (IPA) is a phenomenological approach that seeks to make sense of, and understand, participant experiences. This approach is popular in psychology, nursing, and education. It is an interpretive approach that enables the researcher to interpret meanings in data through emerging themes and connections in order to understand people's attitudes, understanding of events, and personal experiences. Interviews, observation, and focus groups are common methods of this approach.
    o The term Ethnography essentially means a 'portrait of a people' and it is a methodology for the descriptive study of peoples and cultures. Ethnographic studies entail extensive fieldwork by the researcher. Data collection techniques include both formal and informal interviewing, often interviewing individuals on several occasions, and participant or non-participant observation. Ethnography is extremely time-consuming because it involves the researcher spending long periods of time in the field. In educational settings, this might look like a case study approach that includes investigating an approach, programme, or behaviour that is happening in a particular school.
    o Grounded theory (e.g., comparative approach) involves collecting and analysing data about a phenomenon and developing a new theory that can describe and predict future behaviours and experiences. This phenomenological approach attempts to understand how participants make sense of their experiences and does not assume that the data collected refers to a verifiable reality – or is common to most people. The data that emerges is used to develop new theories. An example of grounded theory can be seen in the work of Kübler-Ross (1969), whose work with terminally ill patients produced a theory of grief that explained the different stages that patients with a terminal illness might experience when they receive a diagnosis (e.g., denial, anger, bargaining, depression, and acceptance). Interviews and observation are qualitative methods that can be used for this approach.

- Content analysis involves researchers counting the frequency of a word, phrase, or theme. It can be used, for example, to explore how an issue might be represented in the print media (e.g., equity in teacher pay). A researcher might compare different newspapers to see how many photographs and pictures are used in the story (e.g., size, colour or black and white, position on page, image analysis). The text can be analysed to ascertain differences in word use (e.g., emotive, number of words per sentence or paragraph, page location in the newspaper), meaning being conveyed (e.g., them versus us), and the use of language as 'power'. This is why the term can sometimes refer to a quantitative approach too. Many researchers use this approach to capture both qualitative and quantitative data, but either can be used legitimately on its own. Data analysis usually involves a computer (e.g., NVivo, SPSS). This approach is particularly helpful when analysing documents such as newspapers and written responses to open-ended questions.
- Narrative analysis involves people's narratives or stories about themselves or a particular experience or event. This approach focuses on the story and how it unfolds. As a result, this approach usually includes a small sample size as it can be time consuming.

5.2 Review of Literature

It is important to see these approaches in action in order to fully understand how they work. Drawing on relevant scholarship in the area, the following section gives practical examples of important research that demonstrates the appropriateness, flexibility, and efficacy of qualitative research methods.

Example of a case study design

Durmus and Ergen (2021) took a phenomenological case study approach to explore primary school teachers' experience regarding the inclusion of students in the context of teaching mathematics. The participants of the study were selected using purposive sampling and consisted of primary school teachers (N = 21) who used inclusion approaches with their students. The data was collected by a semi-structured interview form that was developed by the researchers. The content analysis method was used for data analysis. Findings indicated that participants needed help in preparing Individual Education Plans (IEPs). It was concluded that inadequacy of time was the most common problem they encountered in the process of learning-teaching and assessment for the mathematics class.

Example of an interview approach

Nazi and Hameed (2019) examined and reflected upon the voices of out-of-school children in order to understand the implications for educational policy. Children (N = 216) who never attended any school were interviewed in a semi-structured interview approach. The interview schedule was based on the literature review for assessing the feelings and attitudes of out-of-school children. The interviews were video recorded. For analysis purposes, the interviews were transcribed and thematically coded. Software was used for analysis; NVivo 11 plus was used for the discussions and SPSS captured the quantitative demographic variables. The interview schedules were then prepared for thematic analysis through a process of transcription which was followed by transliteration (Regmi et al., 2010). This approach involved rephrasing and changing or harmonising the meanings of words in one language with the meanings of words of another. The findings from this study indicated that there were cultural, demographic, psychological, and socioeconomic factors that provided barriers to school attendance. Furthermore, poor design and implementation of education policies were also found to limit literacy. Overall, the findings of the study revealed that factors affecting school attendance included paternal unemployment, low income and financial problems, large family size, low parental motivation, fear of sexual harassment, and domestic conflicts.

Example of focus group research

Kilic and Sancar-Tokmak (2017) examined digital story-based problem-solving applications with pre-service primary teachers in order to understand their experiences and plan for future integration plans. A mixed methodological approach was used with one aspect including focus groups. A total of 7–10 participants were interviewed through four focus groups. Participants were selected according to their problem-solving performance and willingness to participate. The focus groups allowed for in-depth data to be elicited about the pre-service primary school teachers' experiences using digital story-based problem-solving applications. The focus groups lasted between 30–35 minutes per group and were video recorded. The focus group interviews were transcribed and coded independently using the Miles and Huberman (1994) three-phase classification system: (i) data reduction; (ii) data display; (iii) conclusion drawing/verification. For phase one (data reduction) the recordings were transcribed, the transcripts were read, and the data was selected and coded according to the theoretical framework and patterns that emerged. During phase two (data display) a table was created to present verbal information obtained from participants. In the final phase (conclusion drawing and verification) themes were interpreted and compared, and participant opinions were examined. To ensure reliability, the focus group interviews were analysed by the researchers independently, and inter-coder reliability was found to be .86 (i.e., a high level of independent agreement in how the coders analysed and reported on the material analysed). The researchers discussed the differences in categories and reached consensus on a final theme list.

5.4 Practical Advice

The data collected by qualitative researchers in order to gain an understanding of participants' experiences is often, though not always, gained through a narrative approach to explore how people understand and process their world. Qualitative data can be collected through speaking, writing, diaries, artwork, audio or digital recordings, or observation.

What qualitative method should I choose?

This section details the most common qualitative data collection tools and will focus on the most common approaches chosen by student researchers, namely, case-study design, interviews, focus groups, and observation.

Case-study design

A case study research design is an approach in which the researcher explores a real-life, contemporary bounded system (a case) or multiple bounded systems (cases) over time, through detailed, in-depth data collection involving multiple sources of information (Creswell, 2013). Yin (2014) argues that a case study is the optimal approach for research that exhibits three particular characteristics. Firstly, it is aimed at answering how and why questions, secondly, it relates to contemporary events and thirdly, the researcher has little or no control over participants' behaviour. A criticism of case study design is often the difficulty in generalising from a small number of cases studies to the population as a whole. However, a reader may often recognise aspects of their own experience in a case and can intuitively generalise from the case to their own practice.

In designing a case you really should consider if your research questions are being informed by your literature review. Some case studies have one or two main research questions that are generally 'how?' or 'why?' questions.

The case study design needs to be clear about what the study is actually about. Remember research questions are broad – you can focus on more specific questions in your interview focus group. Sample size in case-study is another important consideration and they are generally small, which is common in most qualitative research. The next step is to consider the data you are going to collect. There are multiple ways to collect data; interviews, documentation, focus groups, questionnaires, etc. Remember that if you use a survey instrument to collect data, it must be valid (i.e., measuring the concept that it is supposed to measure and not anything else) and reliable (i.e., able to precisely measure the concept each and every time). Other considerations will apply to interviews and focus groups. As a researcher you must make yourself aware of all the accepted protocols around your chosen instrument.

The next consideration must be given to your analysis techniques. Data analysis requires several phases. Perhaps the most important is to read your data over and over again and make yourself familiar with it. Patterns or themes or categories will begin to emerge which you can then begin to analyse or code. There are many examples of coding techniques, and you should choose whichever one suits your data best.

The final step will involve decisions around how you wish to report your findings. Remember you are trying to communicate to the reader the 'how' and the 'what' you have discovered in a particular field of knowledge. You want them to understand the richness of the data you have collected and provide a rich description of your findings.

Interviews

In case study research, interviews can be an essential source of evidence. In research, an interview is essentially a conversation between people in which one person has the role of researcher. There are various interview types used in qualitative research: (i) structured, (ii) semi-structured, and (iii) unstructured. The essential differences between these are based on where the control of the interview lies. Structured interviews are focused and are guided by specific interview questions (Bryman, 2004). Similarly, aligned questions are asked of all participants in the research. Semi-structured interviews are not as rigid, and these allow the interviewer to deviate or expand on questions in response to what the interviewee says. This can allow for deeper probing into particular areas as the interview develops and as the interviewee engages with the interview. Unstructured interviews refer to an interview concept without any set format, the interviewer can modify questions to suit the experiences being discussed by the interviewee.

It is generally advisable to start with designing an interview guide which lists the topics that will be explored in the course of the interview, along with probing questions which may be used to elicit further details from the interview participants. The development of an interview guide allows for easier manageability of the data collection process. Each interview schedule should commence by sharing with the interviewee an understanding of the context of the research. In semi-structured interviews, for example, the schedule acts as a guide rather than a rigid set of questions to be followed. For some questions, alternative questions and prompts can be put in place to allow flexibility.

If your experience of interviewing is limited, then it is always good to have a trial run with a critical friend. You may discover that you have too many questions or that they are not easily understood. It also gives you an opportunity to ensure your technology is working – there would be nothing worse than conducting an interview only to later find out that none of it was actually recorded, or that the interviewee was not audible!

Preparing interview participants in advance is also important as it ensures that both the pragmatic and ethical dimensions of the interview are considered. Participants should be informed of the following in the interview invitation: (i) the purpose of the study, (ii) the main topic areas of the interview, and (iii) practical aspects of the interview process, including the estimated duration of the interview.

It is generally advisable to send invitations prior to the event and send a reminder email or follow up with a phone-call. You should practise the introduction without referring to your notes and try to remember topics or questions without referring to the topic guide. Thank the participants for agreeing to participate in the research and reiterate the purpose of the research. It is important then to provide a relaxing and safe space for your participants to feel comfortable with both you and the questions. Agree with the participant which method you are going to use to record the interview at the beginning, ensure that you have informed consent and remind the participant that they can stop the recording or withdraw from the interview at any time. Once interviews are complete, you will need to transcribe them verbatim, and ensuring the anonymity of the participant. See Chapter 2 for a more detailed guide on interviewing.

Focus-group interviews

Focus-group interviews originated in marketing research and have been widely adapted in social science and qualitative research (Marshall and Rossman, 2016). They are often used to supplement other research methods. Focus groups are generally comprised of individuals with similar characteristics or shared experiences who sit down with a facilitator or moderator to discuss a topic. The key aspect of focus groups is the interactions between participants as a way of collecting qualitative data that would not emerge using other methods.

The process of planning for a focus group begins with preparing a list of questions or topics to be discussed, all aimed at addressing the research question. Once this has been done, consideration should be given to recruiting participants and this will depend on the main aim of the group. The focus group is generally characterised by homogeneity, but you should allow sufficient variation among participants to allow for contrasting opinions. Researchers often use different methods to recruit suitable participants, including recruitment questionnaires, asking people directly, or sampling. Purposive sampling is widely recommended since focus group discussion relies on the ability and capacity of participants to provide relevant information. Another important consideration is the number of respondents to be invited for discussion. It is widely accepted that between six and eight participants are sufficient. Select dates, times, and places that are convenient for the participants. It is important again, just as with interviewing, that you conduct a 'pilot' focus group before beginning your research and remember to ask for feedback from your participants on how it went and what might improve it.

Once the participants have been chosen, the facilitator needs to create a relaxed and comfortable environment, particularly if people do not already know each other. Merton et al. (1956) developed criteria for the effective focus group interview that include:

1. Range: It should cover a maximum range of relevant topics. A successful focus group interview would cover the range of topics that the researcher has deemed important in addition to topics that the respondents also raise.
2. Specificity: It should provide data that is as specific as possible. Focus group discussions have to be directed towards detailed accounts of the participants' experiences.
3. Depth: It should foster interaction that explores the participants' opinions in-depth through the level of involvement in the entire group.
4. Personal context: Attempts should be made to find out why people see things in a particular way.

The main methods of data collection during a focus group discussion include audio and tape recording, note-taking, and participant observation. Advances in information and communication technologies offer new opportunities for interviewing research participants. Video conferencing, for example, has become an increasingly used communication and education modality for hosting focus groups. The key advantages of digital technologies for researchers include convenience and cost-effectiveness of online methods compared to in-person focus groups, particularly when conducting research with participants over a large geographical spread. Similarly, for research participants, online methods may be more attractive than in-person interviews due to factors including convenience, efficiency, cost-effectiveness, and flexibility. The Zoom platform, for example, provides a data collection mode for qualitative research that is in real time and is safe and confidential.

Despite the advantages of this form of data collection, qualitative researchers have discussed a number of ethical, practical, and interactional issues associated with the use of video-conferencing technologies. Typical issues associated can include, for example, dropped calls, pauses, poor audio or video quality, or the inability to read non-verbal cues as a result of inconsistent or delayed connectivity. So, choose wisely when deciding how you will conduct your focus groups.

Observation

While there are other qualitative methods that can be chosen, the final qualitative technique explored in this chapter is observation, which does not require direct interaction with participants. This type of technique is often chosen when data cannot be collected through other means or when other methods such as interviews or focus groups would be of limited value and challenging to validate. At times, observation can be a valid way of assessing whether people behave in the ways that they say they do. On other occasions, the environment will be observed, not people. Your research may be centred on a particular environment – perhaps a school in an urban or rural area, a particular geographical location, or perhaps you are looking at a specialised educational facility such as an after-school or childcare facility.

Observation data can be collected through written description, video recording, or artefacts. Observations of people, a situation, or environment can be documented with written notes or visuals. Similar limitations to note-taking during the interview process are present as there is a risk that some observations could be missed due to note-taking. Thus, video recording provides a hands-free option for the researcher. The video recorder could be placed in a fixed area rather than carried around by the researcher to limit participant reactions to the camera. However, this limits observations and could impact on findings. Artefacts can also be included as data and could include objects that tell us about a phenomenon being studied. Examples would be resources used by teachers, equipment, or artwork in a particular school.

Whichever method you choose, remember the steps in your research: (i) select the right method; (ii) select an appropriate sample; (iii) establish the reliability and validity of a chosen method; (iv) collect data in an ethical manner; and (v) analyse and write up your research findings.

Sampling: How do I choose my participants?

Qualitative research employs sampling procedures that correspond to the philosophy of this type of research. In qualitative research, smaller samples are used but deeper information is elicited. Researchers need to find people to answer our questions: key informants, respondents, research participants, participants, or interviewees. Participants are chosen for their suitability; because the number of respondents is small, you have to make a choice about who to include. There are different types of sampling that you can choose from when selecting your research participants. **Purposive sampling** as we referred to previously, involves finding a sample for the purpose of the research. Whereas **convenience sampling** involves drawing a sample that is convenient, such as when exploring research on pedagogy, through interviewing the teachers in a school. **Snowball sampling** is where the interviewee introduces the researcher to another interviewee, for example, the teacher may have fellow teacher colleagues or friends that they will put you in contact with. **Targeted sampling** is when you identify a particular group of respondents, perhaps science teachers or principal teachers.

Common ethical concerns and how to address them

You will have read about the foundations of good practice and ethics in Chapter Two and this section reinforces how qualitative research ethical approaches must be strictly adhered to. When conducting qualitative research, you need to ask yourself the following questions:

(1) Do the participants really understand what they are agreeing to become involved in?
(2) Am I exploiting people with my questions?
(3) What good is anonymity if people recognise themselves and others in a case study?
(4) Who owns the data?
(5) Who owns the report?

(6) What if I believe that somebody is at risk of harm?

The following section outlines common ethical concerns in qualitative research and how to address them.

1. Informed consent: In qualitative research, a consent form is required. The form needs to contain information about your study – in common, everyday language that is accessible to the participant.
2. Right to withdraw: Researchers should recognise the right of all participants to withdraw from the research for any or no reason, and at any time, and participants should be informed of this right (BERA, 2018). Participants should know who to contact to do this.
3. Openness and transparency: Researchers should aim to be open and honest with participants and other stakeholders, avoiding non-disclosure unless their research design specifically requires it in order to ensure that the appropriate data are collected, or that the welfare of the researchers is not put in jeopardy (BERA, 2018).
4. Confidentiality and anonymity: It is important to be aware of the difference between confidentiality and anonymity; and to address both in your research where possible. Confidentiality is subject to requirements of legislation, including the General Data Protection Regulation. Researchers should maintain complete confidentiality regarding any information about participants acquired during the research process, and if published, will not be identifiable as theirs. If confidentiality or anonymity cannot be guaranteed, the participant must be warned of this.
5. Recording: Verbal data should be recorded when informed consent is provided for this. The tapes or electronic records should be identified by code numbers and kept in a password protected folder (if electronic). If permission to record is refused, permission can be sought to take written notes, and these can be shown to the participant who can agree, or disallow, their use. If disallowed, the interviewee has the option to retain the notes.
6. Debriefing participants: Participants should receive the information and contact details of the research student and their research supervisor and know how to make ask questions about the research or how to get a copy of the final dissertation. Otherwise, how will the researcher know about the potential adverse consequences of participation?

7. Participant safety: If questions are of a sensitive nature or are about mental or physical health issues, all participants need an information leaflet to give correct information and details of who to contact for further information or support.
8. Researcher safety: Student researchers need to consider their own emotional well-being in the case of studies of particularly sensitive subjects (e.g., mental health). Students collecting data in the field or in public need to consider their physical safety.
9. Storage: The storage and disposal of participant information and data need addressed to ensure you follow data protection regulations and your own institution regulations.
10. Incentives: Researchers' use of incentives to encourage participation should be commensurate with good sense, such that the level of incentive does not impinge on the free decision to participate (BERA, 2018).

See Chapter 2 for a more detailed guide on ethics.

Qualitative data analysis

In qualitative research we are interested in discovering the lived experiences of participants and we can choose from various techniques when it comes to analysis. The different methods chosen (e.g., interviews, case study, focus group, observation) will require different types of analysis. When transcribing your data, it should be verbatim with all identifying information removed from transcripts (e.g., where the interviewee talks about a school the name can be substituted in the transcript by a phrase such as 'school name').

Most of the options for analysis of qualitative data include categorisation of verbal or behavioural data in order to classify and summarise what has been found. There are often two stages of analysis: the basic (or manifest) level and the interpretive (or latent). The basic level of analysis is generally a descriptive account that explores what was said, documented or observed. There will be nothing assumed or interpreted which is why the first level of analysis is known as a basic (or manifest) level of analysis as it is purely descriptive. The second stage of analysis is the interpretive (or latent) level of analysis. This is generally considered to be a higher level of analysis where you are concerned with what the participant meant by their response or behaviour, and you begin to explore what was inferred or implied by the words or actions.

Become a reflexive researcher

Researcher reflexivity, which involves an interrogation of the researcher's position within the research is paramount in qualitative research. It involves laying bare any underlying beliefs and biases that may impact the research. Being explicit about such things enables the reader to see how the researcher may have made their particular interpretations and the assumptions that are underlying those interpretations. The researcher needs to be able to show convincingly how they got there, and how they built confidence that this was the best account possible.

Consideration of the role of the researcher is a key component of any research. Maintaining a reflexive diary contributes to an audit trail of the data collection and analysis process. This approach allows the researcher to become aware and conscious of the risks involved and to provide a forum to analyse thoughts and concerns about the process. Reflexivity requires the researcher and the reader to be aware that it is impossible to remain outside of the subject matter when conducting qualitative research and that the construction of meaning from data is influenced by the researcher's involvement.

It is, therefore, important that you interrogate your own position in relation to the research and your relationship with the participants. You need to recognise that you have your own perspectives on research and need to be mindful that these beliefs will have an impact on the type of questions posed. You must take steps to ensure that you do not let these perspectives colour your interpretations of the participants' views. You need to ensure that the voices that emerge from the research are the participant's own and are not distorted by your perspectives.

Reliability, validity and generalisability

How can we be sure that research reflects 'the truth'? Arguably, the goal of scientific enquiry or investigation is objective knowledge that is free of bias or prejudice. Heidegger's (1971) conceptualisation of 'truth' is appropriate for qualitative research. The aim of qualitative research is to uncover a new world or to open up a new horizon and bring about a new way of seeing and thinking. The value of qualitative research is not merely to reproduce the outside world, it is to destabilise existing perspectives and facilitate new kinds of thinking and seeing. The issue of objectivity and the role of values and ideology in conducting research is an area that is much discussed and debated. Researchers who argue that objectivity is possible claim that by using rigorous methods and measurements and ensuring open debate on topics, the objectivity of research can be protected.

The term validity is used in quantitative research to refer to the ability of the research instrument to accurately measure the proposed concept. Validity considers whether the design of research to provide credible conclusions, and whether the evidence which the research offers can bear the weight of the interpretation that is put on it. A simple example is that of a weighing-scales. If you step on the weighing-scales and it reads your weight, can you say that the result is a valid reflection of your weight? If the weighing-scales are working properly, the answer is yes, we can conclude that it is a valid reading of your weight. It is important to remember that some small-scale projects may not enable a determination about the validity of an instrument.

Reliability refers to the extent to which a method of data collection is consistent and repeatable and is not distorted by the researcher. For example, in order to find out if a weighing-scales is reliable, the study would need to be able to be replicated in a different setting to ensure it would give the same results. If a person stepped on it at one point in the day and it weighed ten stone, and one hour later it weighed the same person as five stone, and one hour later it weighed the person as being 15 stone, then we would determine that the weighing-scales are unreliable.

Generalisability refers to the claim that the findings from a survey are generalisable to a whole population. For example, if you surveyed 100 teachers in Ireland, can you say that the results are generalisable to all teachers in Ireland? The answer is no. The data from surveys is only generalisable to the whole population when large samples are used, otherwise, we say that research is descriptive. The findings from the data in the survey of 100 teachers would only describe the 100 teachers; therefore, it is important not to make claims about small research projects.

Validity, reliability, and generalisability are essential to quantitative research in order to ensure that the data generated is sound, replicable, and accurate. An example of this in practice is seen every year in the academic achievement of pupils in schools. This is measured by standardised tests (e.g., Sigma-T, Micra-T, Drumcondra Tests); experts in the fields of education and research design these tests and, therefore, the tests used need to be objective, valid, and reliable.

5.5 Conclusion

In qualitative research the data elicited is more subjective. The advantages of qualitative research are that it acknowledges that social research can never be value free and that there are no predetermined answers. It can provide valid, robust findings in a respectful environment where the respondent is the expert. It also considers outliers and exceptional cases to gain a complete understanding of a particular issue as it generates findings and ideas. The disadvantages include a slow process that include individual interviews and transcription. Furthermore, due to the smaller numbers in qualitative research, it is harder to generalise. This approach can be interpretive, and, therefore, subject to researcher bias as it relies on language and discourse. Critics of this methodology state that it is holistic and explanatory rather than reductionist and predictive.

Qualitative research is about exploring and understanding meanings, perceptions, processes and providing 'thick' descriptions in which the data findings are expressed in words rather than numbers. Qualitative methodology is suitable for the novice researcher who is aiming to provide in-depth insights and understanding of real-world issues. A key aspect of qualitative research is that reality is a phenomenon constructed by the participating individuals. It is important to remember that qualitative research is not in any way less than quantitative research and should be viewed as a different approach with a different objective. Qualitative research often provides a richness in data that is not easily achieved with quantitative methods and, for even the most inexperienced education researcher, can elicit rich data which will prove fruitful for analysis and discussion sections of any research project or thesis.

Recommended Readings

Bell, J. (2014). *Doing your research project: a guide for first time researchers in education, health and social science,* 5th edn (Maidenhead: Open University Press).
Cohen L., Manion L., and Morrison K. (2011). *Research methods in education,* 7th edn (USA: Routledge).
Marshall, C., and Rossman, G. (2006). *Designing qualitative research* (London: SAGE).
Silverman, D. (2005). *Doing qualitative research: a practical handbook* (London: SAGE).

References

BERA (2018). *Ethical Guidelines for Education Research,* 4th edn, https://www.bera.ac.uk/publication/ethical-guidelines-for-educational-research-2018
Braun, V., and Clarke, V. (2013). *Successful Qualitative Research: A Practical Guide for Researchers* (UK: SAGE).
Cohen, L., Manion, L., and Morrison, K. (2007). *Research methods in education* (New York: Routledge).
Cropley, A. J. (2019). *Qualitative research methods: A practice-oriented introduction for students of psychology and education,* doi: 10.13140/RG.2.1.3095.6888
Creswell, J. W. (2013). *Qualitative Inquiry & Research Design: Choosing among Five Approaches,* 3rd edn (California: SAGE).

Durmus, M.E., and Ergen, Y. (2021). 'Experience of Primary School Teachers with Inclusion Students in the Context of Teaching Mathematics: A Case Study', in *International Journal of Progressive Education*, 17(1), pp 172–195.

Goffman, E. (1974). *Frame analysis* (Boston: Northeastern University Press).

Heidegger, M. (1971). *Poetry, Language, Thought* (New York: Harper and Row).

Kilic, Ç., and Sancar-Tokmak, H. (2017). 'Digital Story-Based Problem-Solving Applications: Preservice Primary Teachers' Experiences and Future Integration Plans', in *Australian Journal of Teacher Education*, 42(12) pp 21–41, http://dx.doi.org/10.14221/ajte.2017v42n12.2

Marshall, C., and Rossman, G. (2016). *Designing Qualitative Research*, 6th edn (California: SAGE).

Merton, R. K., Fiske, M., and Kendall, L. (1956). *The Focussed Interview* (New York: The Free Press).

McLeod, J. (2001). *Qualitative research in counselling and psychotherapy* (London: SAGE Publications).

Nazi, F. and Hameed, A. (2019). 'Reflection of Voices of Out of School Children: Implications for Education Policy', in *Journal of Research and Reflections in Education*, 13(2), pp 320–338.

Yin, R. K. (2014). *Case study research, design and methods*, 5th edn (California: SAGE).

CHAPTER 6

Researching Children and Other 'Vulnerable' Groups

Audrey Bryan, Dublin City University Institute of Education, Dublin, Ireland

6.0 Introduction

Teachers already ideally possess many of the skills that are required to conduct high quality research with children, such as the ability to establish rapport and relate well to children; helping them to focus; actively listening to what they have to say, and eliciting meaningful responses from them. Engaging with children in a research capacity, however, involves a very specific set of additional considerations, practices, skills, techniques, modes of relating and inquiry. Conducting research with children and other 'vulnerable' groups can also pose unique challenges for the 'teacher as researcher', which can arise long before the fieldwork or data collection process begins. This chapter presents an overview of some of the main methodological approaches used to elicit the views and perspectives of children. It focuses on key issues that educational researchers, particularly novice ones, need to be aware of when researching children and other vulnerable groups. It begins by addressing the research implications of key insights derived from the 'new social studies of childhood' literature before highlighting some of the practical considerations and challenges that researching children and other vulnerable groups entails. It considers these issues with particular reference to children's classification as a dependent, protected class of people who often occupy multiple categories of vulnerability simultaneously (e.g., children with a disability; children who identify as LGBTQI+).

6.1 The New Social Studies of Childhood

The 1990s witnessed the emergence of a new paradigm in childhood studies in response to the criticism that earlier research had constructed children in deficit terms, stemming from their portrayal as 'adults-in-the-making,' rather than as a social category in their own right (Skattlebol, Redmond and Zizzo, 2017). This 'new social studies of childhood' paradigm called into question earlier formulations of childhood studies that defined children as incompetent, passive recipients of socialisation. Instead, it highlighted the need for more nuanced conceptions of childhood that recognise children as competent social actors and as active meaning makers who are deserving of scholarly attention in their own right (Leonard, 2016; Thorne, 2009). A number of key developments helped to bring about this paradigm shift, most notably the United Nations' Convention on the Rights of the Child (UNCRC), adopted by the UN General Assembly in 1989, which identifies children as rights-holders and stresses the importance of taking children's views into account in all matters affecting them (Article 12). In an Irish context, for example, this right has been translated into Irish law through Article 42A of the Irish Constitution and is reflected in the development of various strategies and policy frameworks to enhance children's participation. While barriers to meaningful and effective implementation of these rights persist, the importance of eliciting children's perspectives and ensuring their participation in decision-making is now widely acknowledged (Cuevas-Parra, 2020). Devising and implementing research methodologies that provide opportunities for children's voices to be heard and that maximise their active involvement or participation has become a priority within contemporary childhood research. The next section provides a brief overview of some of the major approaches and methods used to ensure children's meaningful participation and self-expression and may be useful in informing conversations between the student researcher and their thesis advisor.

6.2 Methodological Approaches

As outlined above, the emergence of a new paradigm in childhood studies had major implications for how research with children is conducted, leading to a repositioning of children in terms of how knowledge about their lives is produced (Leonard 2016; Mason and Watson, 2014). Among the basic principles of the new childhood studies is that research methods must provide opportunities for children's voices to be heard, although what this looks like in practice and how this is to be realised remain highly contested (Hammersley, 2017). Research methods in childhood studies are predominantly qualitative and are chosen to reflect 'a view of children as competent interpreters of the social world' (James, 2001, p. 246). Some of the most widely used methods, outlined in more detail below, include ethnography, open-ended interviewing, and approaches involving the use, creation and analysis of drawings, photographs etc. (Allerton, 2016; Hammersley, 2017).

Ethnography

Ethnography is a qualitative research method or process in which a researcher (or 'ethnographer') studies a particular set of social actors with the aim of better understanding them (Allen, 2017). The word 'ethnography' is derived from the Greek words, *ethnos* (people or culture) and *graphei* (to write) (Corsaro, 2003). Historically, ethnographers spent long periods (sometimes years) immersed in a particular cultural group, living amongst the community, learning the local language, forming close relationships with certain group members, and taking part in various activities and events in order to generate rich, 'thick' data and to develop a deeper understanding of patterns and systems of everyday life (Geertz, 1973).

While traditionally associated with the study of 'exotic cultures,' ethnographic methods have been more recently employed to study the social world that children inhabit, and reveal the complexities of childhood cultures (Corsaro, 2003). Ethnographic methods are believed to be particularly suited to studying children's everyday lives, particularly where the aim of the investigation is to conduct research with, rather than on, children (Corsaro, 2003; James and Prout, 1990). Ethnography has also proven to be an effective means of accessing the meanings of non-verbal research participants and of providing insights into the lives and identities of children with disabilities (Davis, Watson and Cuningham Burley, 2017).

Ethnographers actively participate in group/community activities as 'participant observers' – a method which allows them to gain an insider perspective and to gather empirical insights into social practices which might otherwise be hidden from public view (Parker Jenkins, 2018). Written ethnographic accounts (also known as 'ethnography') are typically based on data generated from participant observation, in-depth as well as informal interviews with group members, and an analysis of documents, artefacts etc.

Within education studies, some of the most widely cited ethnographies of children's social worlds include *Gender Play: Girls and Boys in School* by Barrie Thorne (1993), *Home Advantage: Social Class and Parental Intervention in Elementary Education* by Annette Lareau (2000) and *Unequal Childhoods: Class, Race and Family Life,* also by Annette Lareau (2011). Whereas *Home Advantage* and *Gender Play* were conducted in schools – observing children as they went about their daily lives in classrooms and in the playground – *Unequal Childhoods* involved a relatively untapped ethnographic approach comprising 'intensive family observations' of parents and their nine and ten-year-old children to examine the effects of class-based parenting strategies and approaches on children's educational experiences and outcomes (Lareau and Rao, 2020). The researchers spent time with families in their homes over a number of weeks, as well as accompanying them on shopping trips, doctors' visits and to family gatherings, enabling them to garner insights about the interactional processes that make up family life. The larger research project also involved in-depth interviews with families, although as Lareau (2011, p. 346) admits, she 'gave up on interviewing children when normally chatty children fell silent in front of a tape recorder'. Within the context of ethnography, interviews provide an opportunity to further interrogate situations and events that the participant-observer has encountered, or to develop a deeper understanding of the meaning participants ascribe to these various occurrences. As Lareau and Rao (2020, p. 42) explain:

> Interviews are much richer if one can use them to explore things that one has observed and vice versa. Intensive observations can reveal insights about interactional processes that make up family life. These processes cannot be fully captured through other means such as survey methods, time-diary data, or even in-depth interviews. For us, the details from observations were not just rich in themselves but were integral to producing analytically nuanced concepts and arguments – which is the goal of much qualitative research.

6.3 Challenges Associated with Researching Children

As highly experienced researchers' candid accounts of their own research reveal (e.g., Lareau, 2000; Lareau, 2011; Thorne, 1993), even the most celebrated of ethnographies are fraught with difficulty, particularly when children are the focus of inquiry. Part of the difficulty stems from the delicate balancing act that being a participant and an observer entails, especially when the research setting has very clearly defined hierarchies or expectations for how adults and children should behave (Harvey and Lareau, 2020; Lignier, 2008). Whereas observing children might seem like a relatively straightforward activity, participating in children's activities and peer-groups as an adult researcher can be extremely challenging (Allerton, 2016).

One methodological stance that seeks to address this challenge is the 'least-adult' role – a fully immersive approach to research which seeks to ensure the researcher's active involvement in children's worlds by suspending all adult-like characteristics except physical size; refusing to perform adult tasks that children may demand of them (e.g., tying their shoe laces; pushing them on a swing or holding them); and essentially acting as little like an adult as possible (Mandell, 1988). In many instances, however, assuming the least-adult role simply isn't attainable, desirable or convincing to children (Atkinson 2019; Epstein, 2008; Thorne, 1993). As Epstein (2008:31) remarks:

> In one sense, the adoption of the 'least adult role' is an attempt to reduce power differential with the children, but at the same time, it reinforces that very differential by imposing on them a 'least adult' construction when they might prefer to position the researcher in a more familiar adult position. And, clearly the power differential does not go away and the children will not be convinced – however much the researcher tries to perform the 'least adult role' – that he or she is not an adult!

This is especially the case in schools, where the structures of schooling can militate against researchers entering into a child's role or adopting a child's perspective on things and where age-based segregation is key to how schools are organised (Epstein, 2008; Harvey and Lareau, 2020). Thorne (1993), for example, discusses the tensions and challenges that emerged as she tried to assume the 'least adult' role in a school setting where adult authority and power dynamics were deeply entrenched. Harvey and Lareau (2020) have likened the need to comply with adult norms and responsibilities, on the one hand, while simultaneously building rapport with children, on the other, to 'walking a tightrope' (Harvey and Lareau, 2020, p. 26). The inescapability of certain undeniable differences between adults and (particularly young) children, therefore – not least in terms of their socially subordinate status relative to adults – makes certain ethnographic positions such as the 'least-adult' role untenable. As Thorne remarks, despite her best efforts, the 'very act of documenting children's autonomy…undermined it, for my gaze remained, at its core and in its ultimate knowing purpose, that of a more powerful adult' (1993, p. 27). As Harvey and Lareau (2020) elaborate, power differentials between adult researchers and child participants are inevitable, such that imitating children's experiences and ways of being as an active participant in their world side-lines this power differential and risks making others – such as teachers, parents etc. – angry. From their perspective, 'rather than seeking identification (i.e., the adult *is* a child), aiming for rapport between adult researchers and children, from a liminal position, is a more realistic goal' (Harvey and Lareau, 2020, p. 18; emphasis in original).

One of the approaches adopted by Harvey in his ethnography of nine to eleven-year-old children attending both an elite private school and a predominantly working-class school was to 'distinguish himself from actual teachers and other authority figures in various ways, such as not leading lessons, not telling students off, and sometimes joining in with children's games at recess when invited' (Harvey and Lareau, 2020, p. 27). The liminal position that Harvey occupied meant that he was treated like an older brother by many of the children, which presented both opportunities and challenges (Harvey and Lareau, 2020).

Whereas some researchers have gone to great lengths to highlight the challenges associated with researching children, others are of the view that researchers should make every effort to maximise children's active participation or to ensure that research is child-focused. Some have gone so far as to suggest that childhood research should be conceived, directed and executed by children themselves (see Hammersley (2017) and Kim (2017) for critiques of participatory/'child-led' forms of research). Thomas (2017, p. 161) documents a wide range of work and a variety of different approaches that fall under the category of 'child-led' research, including research that conceives of 'children as research assistants,' 'children as research partners' and 'children as research leaders.' These participatory modes of inquiry are often viewed as a more ethically responsive approach to researching children and are also seen as performing an important political function by demonstrating children's competence to make important decisions (Hammersley, 2017). As Thomas (2021) points out, proponents of child-led research are far from uncritical in their advocacy of this approach, often asking soul-searching questions about children's capacity to lead and undertake research or the purpose and the benefits of child-led research. While the question of whether children can, or indeed should lead research is far from settled, there has been a gradual shift in emphasis towards conducting research '*with*, rather than *on*, children, in a desire to position children as social actors who are subjects, rather than objects of enquiry' (Christensen and James, 2017, p. 1; emphasis in *original*). Notwithstanding the challenges outlined above, conducting research with children can be both rewarding and impactful. With the support of a supervisor/advisor, undertaking such research can provide the novice researcher (particularly those with an interest/expertise in education) with a rich corpus of data, which has the potential to enhance children's educational experiences and their lives more generally.

6.4 Participatory Visual Methods

Although ethnography has many advantages over other research methods used to research children's lives, researchers often supplement participant observation with additional techniques or incorporate more visual or arts-based elements into their ethnographic work (Allerton, 2016). Specific methodological approaches that are often regarded as 'child-friendly' include: focus groups where children share their perspectives in friendship groups; drama and role-play; reflective diary entries; drawing; photography; time-use charts; worksheets and mapping. Others have argued that there is nothing inherently child friendly about any of these techniques as children's attachment to any given methodological approach is likely to depend on their own skills, talents or 'intelligences' in the chosen methodological domain (Allerton, 2016).

One of the most widely used 'child-friendly' methods involves 'photovoice,' – also known as participatory visual methods, image-based research or visual ethnography. One of the most compelling visual ethnographies is Wendy Luttrell's *Children Framing Childhoods* study – a longitudinal project comprising a sample of 34 working-class immigrant boys and girls who used cameras to document their lives and their schooling at different time points in their lives (at ages ten, 12, 16 and 18) (Luttrell, 2010; 2020). Luttrell's innovative 'collaborative seeing' methodology – which helped to challenge deficit perceptions of inner-city schooling – formed part of a larger ethnographic exploration of how children living in urban, low-income, immigrant communities in the North-eastern US navigate linguistic, cultural, race/ethnic and economic differences, family-school relationships, and self and identity changes over time. The study combined traditional ethnographic methods with a multi-layered, reflexive approach involving photovoice strategies as well as photo elicitation interviews to enable the children to instruct the research as to their photos' meanings. The analysis of the children's photo albums combined visual and narrative analysis to understand their self, identity, and social consciousness. Luttrell explains her rationale for devising a collaborative visual methodological approach as follows:

> I turned to photography for two reasons: first, because it is an especially useful metaphor for thinking about how we read our social worlds, construct ourselves in relation to others, and express matters of the heart; and second, because it is a means to both rouse and reframe conversations (a) among the children themselves; (b) between the children and participating adults (researchers, teachers, parents); and (c) among viewers/ readers (specifically educators) about children's own understandings and experiences of childhood (Luttrell, 2010, p. 225).

One of the most noteworthy aspects of the *Children Framing Childhoods* study is the extent to which it challenges the notion that capturing children's voices is an uncomplicated task or indeed that children speak in unison. Rather, the research revealed that social categories such as gender, race, ethnicity, class, and immigrant status shape the photographs that children choose to take to represent their lives, and indeed what they say about these pictures. Furthermore, it revealed that what children say about those images varies considerably according to who is listening. In other words, what they might reveal to a researcher may differ from what they tell friends or teachers. Ultimately, the research generated an extensive audio-visual archive comprising over 2000 photographs; 65 hours of video- and audio-taped individual and small group interviews of the 36 participants talking about their images; and 18 video diaries produced by a subset of participants from ages 16 to 18. Luttrell (2021) has developed a website featuring a number of the photographs that the child participant-researchers took, as well as digital resources to encourage different ways of engaging with their images. The website also contains a number of videos which 'intentionally blur borders between research and art; analysis and evocation; looking and feeling; ethics and aesthetics; seeing and knowing' (Luttrell, 2021, no page).

Having outlined some of the key issues and methodological approaches that are widely used when researching children, the concluding section of this paper offers some practical considerations that the novice researcher should discuss with their thesis supervisor when researching children and other vulnerable groups' lives.

6.5 Practical Challenges and Considerations

All research involving 'human subjects' requires adherence to certain ethical principles, including a commitment to the well-being, protection, and safety of participants; a duty to respect the rights and wishes of participants; a responsibility to conduct high-quality scientific research; and a commitment to disseminate and communicate findings to stakeholders. The need to ensure child protection while complying with ethical, social, and legal standards in relation to children means that childhood researchers need to be particularly diligent and tread very carefully at all times (Harvey and Lareau, 2020). In most instances of research with children and other vulnerable groups, formal access to institutions and additional formal approvals are required. In the case of school-based research, for example, researchers typically need to obtain the permission of the school or schools' Board(s) of Management in addition to approval from their university Research Ethical Committee (REC) or Intuitional Review Board (IRB). Securing ethical approval from academic institutions can be protracted and, in some cases, impossible. Depending on the research project in question, it simply may not be feasible to conduct research with children due to the length of time that it can take to secure research ethical approval. Even when ethical approval is granted, significant limits can be imposed on the scope of the research, including who can take part. As securing institutional access and approval can be a protracted process, Harvey and

Lareau (2020) recommend commencing the access negotiation process at least six months prior to the proposed commencement of the research.

Because children are automatically classified as vulnerable from a research ethics point of view because of their age, there are ongoing practical considerations as well as additional procedural obligations that must be met when designing and carrying out research with 'minors.'[1] At a very minimum, all documentation pertaining to children's agreement (assent) to participate in research must be age and/or cognitively appropriate. In other words, all relevant information should be presented in a straightforward manner with due regard for the profile of the participants, their familiarity with the field of study involved, and their level of comprehension. For very young children, this means communicating various aspects of the process (such as the right to withdraw; the right to confidentiality etc.) visually.

Childhood researchers have to navigate the process of securing both the agreement (or assent) of child/vulnerable participants as well as parental consent while simultaneously respecting the view that children and young people are competent social actors (Cuevas-Parra 2020). In some instances, the parental consent stipulation means that children may have to disclose certain private aspects of their identity, experiences, or behaviour to their parents that they otherwise would not wish them to know about, in order to participate in the research. For example, in the case of LGBTQI+ people under the age of 18 who wish to take part in research about their experiences as a young LGBTQI+ person, only those who are already 'out' to their parents/guardians – or who choose to come out to them in order to participate – can be included in the sample (unless a waiver is granted). Depending on the focus of the research, a range of additional protective measures or protocols may have to be put in place (see for example Mayock, Bryan, Carr and Kitching (2009) for a detailed account of the procedures for protecting research *Supporting LGBT Lives Study*).

Researchers also need to be mindful that depending on a particular child or vulnerable person's individual circumstances or identity, certain research methods or activities may not be appropriate where that specific child is concerned. Lareau and Rao (2020) discuss the example of an ethnographic study involving researchers accompanying children to routine doctors' appointments. Whereas research activities of this nature may not ordinarily pose ethical challenges, for some children, such as those who identify as transgender, these interactions may be particularly sensitive due to the 'social policing' that surrounds even the most mundane interactions and practices of gender non-conforming children.

Moreover, whereas guaranteeing participant confidentiality is a criterion of 'human subjects' research, there are limitations to this guarantee where research with children is concerned, such as if a child discloses abuse or harm to a researcher, the researcher has a legal obligation to report the alleged incident. These child protection issues and legal limitations to confidentiality must be clearly explained to child participants as well as their parents/guardians as part of the informed consent process. Harvey and Lareau (2020) argue that research with children involves a constant 'double act' of having to simultaneously manage institutional procedures and obligations to children as well as their gatekeepers (such as parents, teachers, institutions). As these authors put it: 'This can cause difficulties when the actions, intentions, or needs of either party conflict or heavily outweigh the other, leaving the researcher trapped in the middle' (p. 31).

6.6 Conclusion

Childhood is an elastic term, encapsulating everything from a very young and totally dependent infant to a physically mature and highly competent, almost adult teenager. As Allerton (2016) observes, there is an ever-expanding multiplicity of labels that we attach to different stages of childhood, including infants, toddlers, young children, tweens, preteens, teenagers, youths etc., which underscores the diversity of childhoods. While dichotomous understandings of passive, vulnerable, dependent and incompetent children versus autonomous, agentic, competent adults feature prominently in the social imaginary, children's lived realities are infinitely more diverse, multi-faceted, complex and paradoxical. One of the major contributions of the new social studies of childhood is the idea that childhood is socially constructed, which illuminates historical, cross-cultural, and intra-cultural variations in how childhood is understood and how child-rearing and child-care are practised in different regions of the globe. This position challenges us to think beyond the notion that childhood is a universal, biological life-stage and encourages us to consider instead the differences among children rather than how their experiences are the same, and how what it means to be a child is determined by the broader social context within which children are embedded. The value of looking at childhoods from this perspective is that it can help us to develop a more reflexive stance towards the conduct of research with children and allows us to better appreciate the multiplicity of childhoods that exist. For example, as Allerton (2016, n.p.) reminds us:

> When it comes to conducting ethnographic research with children, cross-cultural differences in such varying distinctions can be important. A fifteen-year-old girl who according to one context might be considered a 'vulnerable' teenage research participant may, in another context, be about to embark on marriage and motherhood. A twelve-year-old who would be considered too

young to babysit in the UK might elsewhere be the primary carer for various younger siblings whilst her parents work the fields.

Commentaries such as these highlight the need for a highly nuanced engagement with children's lives and experiences when designing child-focused research, as well as the need to attend to the paradoxical qualities of their lives, such that they may require protection in one context or moment and rights of self-determination in another (Allerton, 2016).

As Harvey and Lareau (2020) remark, some of the most useful accounts of research are those which seek to dispel the idea that the 'right' method, framework or approach will automatically result in an uncomplicated and empowering research experience. The inescapability of certain undeniable differences between adults and (particularly young) children, therefore – not least in terms of their socially subordinate status relative to adults – makes certain ethnographic positions, as well as research ideals vis-à-vis children's participation or even direction of the research, untenable. Contemporary research with children – irrespective of what methodological approach is used to garner their perspectives or how involved they are in leading or conducting the research themselves – is incredibly labour-intensive and challenging, not least because of the tightrope that researchers (be they novice or experienced) have to walk as they attempt to comply with adult norms and responsibilities, while building rapport with children, combined with the constant double of having to simultaneously manage institutional procedures and obligations to children and their gatekeepers. Having an awareness of these difficulties and complexities from the outset is essential if researchers are to design and implement research with children and other vulnerable groups effectively.

Recommended Readings

Lareau, A. (2021). *Listening to People: A Practical Guide to Interviewing, Participant Observation, Data Analysis, and Writing It All Up* (University of Chicago Press).
Luttrell, W. (2021) Careful seeing: a visual research project with children, Cad. CEDES, 41(113), https://doi.org/10.1590/CC231883_PT
Alderson, P., and Morrow, V. (2020) *The Ethics of Research with Children and Young People: A Practical Handbook* (New York: SAGE).
Liebenberg, L. (2018). 'Thinking Critically About Photovoice: Achieving Empowerment and Social Change', in *International Journal of Qualitative Methods*, 17, pp 1–9.

References

Allen, M. (2017). *The SAGE Encyclopaedia of Communication Research Methods* (New York: SAGE).

Allerton, C. (ed) (2016). *Children: Ethnographic Encounters* (New York: Routledge).

Atkinson, C. (2019) 'Ethical complexities in participatory childhood research: Rethinking the "least adult role."', in *Childhood*, 26(2), pp 186–201.

Bryan, A. (2019) 'A Sociological Critique of Youth Strategies and Educational Policies that Address LGBTQ Youth Issues', *International Journal of Bullying Prevention*, 1, pp 255–268, https://doi.org/10.1007/s42380-019-00047-1

Christensen, P., and James, A. (eds) (2017). *Research with Children: Perspectives and Practices*, 3rd edn (Abingdon: Routledge).

Corsaro, W. A. (2003). *We're Friends, Right? Inside Kids' Culture* (Washington, D.C.: Joseph Henry Press).

Cuevas-Parra, P. (2020). 'Co-researching with children in the time of COVID-19: shifting the narrative on methodologies to generate knowledge', in *International Journal of Qualitative Methods*, 19, pp 1–12.

Davis, J., Watson, N., and Cuningham Burley, S. (2017). 'Disabled children, ethnography and unspoken understandings', in Christensen, P., and James, A. (eds.) *Research with Children Perspectives and Practices* (Routledge: Abingdon), doi:10.4324/9781315657349

Epstein, D. (1998). '"Are you a girl or are you a teacher?" The "least adult" role in research about gender and sexuality in a primary school', in G. Walford (ed.) *Doing Research about Education*, pp 27–41, (Abingdon: Taylor & Francis).

Geertz, C. (1973). *Thick Description: Toward an Interpretive Theory of Culture* (New York: Basic Books).

Hammersley, M. (2017). 'Childhood Studies: A sustainable paradigm?', in *Childhood*, 24(1) pp 113–127, DOI: https://doi.org/10.1177/0907568216631399

Harvey, P., and Lareau, A. (2020). 'Studying Children using Ethnography: Heightened Challenges and Balancing Acts', in *Bulletin de M'ethodologie Sociologique*, 146, pp 16–36.

James, A. (2001). 'Ethnography in the Study of Children and Childhood', in: Atkinson P., Coffey A., Delamont S., Lofland J., and Lofland L. (eds) *Handbook of Ethnography*, (London: SAGE), pp 246–257.

James, A., and Prout, A. (1990). *Constructing and Reconstructing Childhood: Contemporary Issues in the Sociological Study of Childhood* (New York: Routledge).

Kim C.Y. (2017). 'Participation or pedagogy? Ambiguities and tensions surrounding the facilitation of children as researchers', in *Childhood*, 24(1), pp 84–98.

Lareau A. (2011). *Unequal Childhoods: Class, Race, and Family Life*, 2nd edn (Berkeley: University of California Press).

Lareau, A. (2000). *Home Advantage: Social Class and Parental Intervention in Elementary Education* (New York: Roman & Littlefield).

Lareau, A., and Rao, A. H. (2020). 'Intensive Family Observations: A Methodological Guide', *Sociological Methods & Research*, pp 1–54, https://doi.org/10.1177/0049124120914949

Leonard, M. (2016). *The Sociology of Children, Childhood and Generation* (London: SAGE).

Lignier W. (2008) 'La barriere de l'age. Conditions de l'observation participante avec des enfants', in *Geneses*, 73(4), pp 20–36.

Luttrell, W. (2021). *Children Framing Childhoods*, http://www.childrenframingchildhoods.com/

Luttrell, W. (2020). *Children Framing Childhoods: Working Class Kids Visions of Care* (Bristol: Bristol University Press).

Luttrell, W. (2010). '"A camera is a big responsibility": a lens for analysing children's visual voices', in *Visual Studies*, 25(3), pp 224–237, http://dx.doi.org/10.1080/1472586X.2010.523274

Mandell, N. (1988). 'The least-adult role in studying children', in *Journal of Contemporary Ethnography*, 16(4), pp 433–466.

Mason J., and Watson E. (2014). 'Researching Children: Research on, with, and by Children', in Ben-Arieh A., Casas F., Frønes I., Korbin J. (eds) *Handbook of Child Well-Being*, pp 2757–2796 (Springer, Dordrecht), https://doi.org/10.1007/978-90-481-9063-8_109

Mayock P., Bryan A., Carr, N., and Kitching, K. (2009). *Supporting LGBT Lives: A Study of the Mental Health and Well-being of Lesbian, Gay, Bisexual and Transgender People*, Dublin: Gay and Lesbian Equality Network (GLEN) and BeLonG To Youth Service.

Parker-Jenkins, M. (2018). 'Problematising ethnography and case study: reflections on using ethnographic techniques and researcher positioning', in *Ethnography and Education*, 13(1), pp 18–33, DOI: 10.1080/17457823.2016.1253028

Skattlebol, J., Redmond G., and Zizzo G. (2017). 'Expanding Children's Agency: Cases of Young People Experiencing Economic Adversity', *Children and Society*, 31(4), pp 315–329.

Thomas, N. (2021) 'Child-led research, children's rights and childhood studies: A defence', *Childhood*, , 28(2), pp 186–188.

Thomas, N. (2017) 'Turning the tables: Children as researchers', in: Christensen, P., James, A. (eds) *Research With Children: Perspectives and Practices*, 3rd edn (Abingdon: Routledge).

Thomas, N. (2015) 'Children and young people's participation in research', in: Gal T., and Faedi Duramy B. (eds*) International Perspectives and Empirical Findings on Child Participation: From Social Exclusion to Child-Inclusive Policies* (New York: Oxford University Press), pp 89–110.

Thorne, B. (2009). '"Childhood": Changing and Dissonant Meanings', in *International Journal of Learning and Media*, 1(1), pp 19–27.

Thorne, B. (1993). *Gender play: Girls and boys in school* (New Brunswick, NJ: Rutgers University Press).

Notes

1. These additional considerations also apply to other 'vulnerable' groups in society (e.g., prisoners; those with a disability; people who identify as transgender or intersex). Moreover, some children are deemed additionally vulnerable by virtue of other aspects of their social identity or experience, for example, if they have a disability; if they identify as LGBTQI+; if they have undergone traumatic or adverse emotional events, etc. However, many of those classified as vulnerable from a legal/ethical perspective (by virtue of their age, identity, status etc.) may not necessarily perceive themselves as such. The positioning of children as universally vulnerable can obscure meaningful engagement with the diversity and complexities of children's lived realities, and the extent to which these experiences are mediated by inter-alia, family and personal circumstances, dis/ability status, sex, race, ethnicity, social class, etc. (Bryan, 2019).

CHAPTER 7

Historical Research in Education

Tom O'Donoghue, Graduate School of Education, The University of Western Australia and Judith Harford, School of Education, University College Dublin, Ireland

7.0 Introduction

A contested field, the history of education is fundamental to our understanding of broader issues in history, education and society. Connecting the past with the present enables us to fully engage with issues and debates in history, education, the social sciences and beyond, understanding consensus and conflict, continuity and change across time and space. This chapter offers the novice researcher an overview of historical research in education and provides a guide for those who may wish to employ this methodology. Drawing on our own experience, we offer several practical examples of historical methodologies and conclude the chapter by highlighting some areas that may be particularly relevant for those who are coming to this area of inquiry for the first time.

7.1 Definitions and Descriptions

It is helpful to distinguish between historians who engage in research in the history of education to produce knowledge that is of interest 'for its own sake' and those who do so in order to illuminate contemporary issues in education by tracing their historical antecedents. While this distinction is often fluid and sometimes contested, it is instructive in interrogating and problematising the field of history of education. Of course, many scholars straddle both fields, with the caveat that those of the first type are usually located within schools of history and those of the second are usually located within schools of education. Educationists thus engage in research in the history of education for a range of interconnected reasons, which include the following:

- Educators who know the history of their field of interest are well placed to understand the present and to address the future.

- Knowledge of the historical, cultural, social, and economic conditions surrounding an event generates a deeper understanding of the significance of the event.
- Identifying and repairing the absences or silences in the historical record allows us to give voice to those who have been marginalised.
- Understanding the distinct historical and cultural identities of different, often under-represented groups of people enables us to conduct ethical research in such settings.

Historical sources are central to the work of historians and historians of education. These may range across such a diverse depository of material such as oral literature, songs, folklore, proverbs, dances, myths, rituals, artefacts, and documents. The purpose should be to spread the net as widely as possible. There are two dimensions to that exercise. The first is to help to maximise one's understandings of developments that have taken place. Social scientists often refer to those as 'outsider' or 'etic' understandings, a term derived from the word 'phonetic'. They are generated by the researcher where it is considered that several sources seem to have structural properties in common that were not necessarily identified by the key actors at the time. The second dimension to the exercise is to help one maximise the opportunities for developing understandings of how people, during the specific period under investigation, constructed the reality they experienced. In other words, the aim is to investigate how the beliefs, assumptions, actions, events, meanings, and ideas of people in the past have influenced and shaped the present. Social scientists often refer to the understanding generated from adopting such a focus as an insider or 'emic' one, a term derived from the term 'phonemic'. Essentially, the task is to try to uncover the concepts that were used by individuals that represented their 'definitions of situations', and their ways of thinking about people and objects.

Historically, those involved in preparing individuals to become teachers and preparing practising teachers and other educationists for higher degree study and research exposed their students to courses containing elements of history of education alongside courses in the psychology of education, sociology of education and philosophy of education, often referred to as the foundation disciplines. In relation to the history of education, their concern originally was with the history of education thought and thinkers in education, the history of education systems, and the history of education policy. For a long time that was undertaken to move teaching from being a craft to being a profession with academic foundations. While there is still considerable merit in this approach to the teaching of the history of education, the field is now widely recognised as being more complex, diverse, and evolving.

7.2 Strategies for Engaging in Historical Research

Historians are typically prompted to engage in an original research project after reading and considering some aspect of the work of other historians. Often this emanates from a belief that there is a deficit in the existing corpus of knowledge on a topic or issue that warrants an investigation to open up the field. Alternatively, the motivation to research an issue stems from the position that the existing corpus of research on a topic requires expansion, revision or even correction. Conversations between the research student and their advisor are essential to exploring these prompts.

For the novice researcher who wishes to engage with historical research in education, the first step should be to have a clear idea of what one is studying, and central to this is to gain a comprehensive, rigorous understanding of the context within which the topic or issue sits. This includes gaining an understanding of the shortfalls or deficits in the existing canon of research on the issue. Reading the works of other scholars that are related or tangential to the issue or topic of interest may also provide valuable tools of investigation. Such works will be important especially for identifying key sources for additional reading.

Much of the material referred to above constitutes what are termed secondary sources by historians. They can include, but are not restricted to, the following:

- Books
- Encyclopaedias
- Dictionaries including biographical dictionaries
- Analyses and interpretation of data
- Journal articles
- Documentaries (which often include photos or video portions that can be considered primary sources)
- Reviews and essays
- Periodicals

Such sources are deemed to be one step removed from primary sources. They provide second-hand information and commentary from other researchers as a result of one describing, interpreting, and synthesizing primary sources. At the same time, the arguments that run through many secondary source accounts are usually heavily supported by reference to primary sources, often in the form of quotations from documents, along with photos, maps, and plans, typically embedded within layers of interpretation and analysis.

Primary sources are first-hand accounts generated by people who had a direct connection with an issue, a topic, or an event. They provide raw information and first-hand evidence. They can include, but are not restricted to:

- Texts of laws
- Texts of treaties
- Court records
- Government documents
- Birth, death, and marriage records
- Wills
- Newspaper reports
- Accounts in magazines
- Recordings of speeches
- Diaries
- Letters
- Transcripts and recordings of interviews conducted at the time under investigation
- Other audio material, including music recordings
- Census data
- Survey data
- Various bodies of statistics
- Visual data, including photographs and video material
- Artwork
- Maps, charts, diagrams, and plans
- Artefacts
- Buildings and other architectural features
- Performance material, including plays
- Other literary material

Scholars typically employ both primary and secondary sources, the blending of which allows for a more sophisticated, substantial argument or analysis. In addition, while primary sources are more authentic and thus more credible as evidence, the inclusion of secondary sources in an exposition can help to show how one's work, while original, also relates to existing research, as well as one's familiarity with the existing canon of scholarship.

It is important to never lose sight of the fact, however, that sources only become historical evidence when they are interpreted by the historian to make sense of the past. In other words, the answers that sources provide depend very much on the sorts of questions historians are asking regarding what it is they want to know. Accordingly, it makes little sense to ask if something constitutes 'good historical evidence', without knowing what evidence it is supposed to provide.

The division between a primary source and a secondary source, of course, is not always clear cut. For those conducting research in the field of the history of science education, for example, the likelihood is that they will locate chemistry textbooks written during the period under review. At the time these textbooks were written, they were secondary sources as they described and interpreted the state of the field but did not advance it or make an original contribution to it in any way. For the contemporary historian, however, they constitute primary sources since when compared with other textbooks used before and afterwards, they allow one to identify patterns of change in the science curriculum as well as how the subject was taught over time. The manner in which textbooks were laid out, the page size, the font sizes, the inclusion or not of visual material, and the posing or not of comprehension and enrichment questions within chapters, at the end of chapters, or in both locations, can also provide important information regarding what and how students were expected to learn during the period in question.

Finally, all sources, both primary and secondary, need to be assessed for their authenticity and credibility, the former being the quality of their authenticity and the latter relating to their apparent veracity. These matters can be addressed by posing the following questions of each source:

1. What is its physical nature – for example, is it an actual document or one that has been transcribed?
2. What is the nature of its material – for example, is it on official notepaper or is it a scribbled note?
3. Why and when was it created?
4. Under what conditions was it created?
5. Has it been edited?
6. How and why did it survive?
7. Was it later published and why?
8. What was the author's position and is it explicit or implicit, or are there features of both within it?
9. For whom was it intended?
10. How does the author convey his or her message? Are there any metaphors, symbols, or silences?
11. Does it contain any relevant information about the author?
12. How could he or she know the details such as names, dates and times outlined?

13. If it relates to an event, was he or she present?
14. Is the information in the source based on personal experience or reports written by others?

Regarding the credibility of the source, one should ask oneself:

1. Is it prescriptive, telling you what the author thought should happen?
2. Is it descriptive, telling you what author thought did happen?
3. Does it describe ideology?
4. Does it describe behaviour?
5. Does it convey the views of elites and if so from whose perspective?
6. Does it convey the actions of elites and if so from whose perspective?
7. Does it convey the views of 'ordinary people' and if so from whose perspective?
8. Does it convey the actions of 'ordinary people' and if so from whose perspective?
9. What benefits are to be gained from using this source?
10. What questions can this source not answer?
11. What limitations might be imposed by the use of this type of source?

Finally, those interested in the history of education in Ireland are particularly fortunate to have access to Susan Parkes' (2010) *A Guide to Sources for the History of Irish Education, 1780–1922*. This work outlines the key issues of education policy during the period under review and evaluates the wealth of official reports available to the historian of Irish education, both in British Parliamentary Papers and in such archival repositories as the National Archives of Ireland and the National Library of Ireland. It offers guidance on the use of these sources, particularly for local education studies. Equally fruitful is the three-volume collection of extracts from Irish documents on education from earliest times to the 1990s, co-edited by Áine Hyland and Kenneth Milne (1987, 1992, 1995). Most helpful also are the online databases produced by the Department of History at the University of Limerick that can be located by searching for 'Glucksman Library guide supporting the Department of History in the Faculty of Arts, Humanities and Social Sciences' and selecting the 'journals and databases' tab.

7.3 The Matter of Engaging in Oral History or Life History

Engagement in oral history research in relation to education has become very popular in recent years. It involves interviewing people in order to gain information about the past. Researchers are often led to such activity after identifying absences in the existing corpus of primary sources. It is also a contentious field. On the history of schooling, some, for example, have advocated conducting large-scale oral history projects in which we might hear over and over fundamentally common rhythms of the experience of schooling, of expectation, and of orientation. We hold, however, that the results of such projects could not be offered as 'true' representations of how a situation was. Rather, they yield generalizations regarding how selected groups of people remembered their experiences of schooling.

The point being made here is that those who engage in oral history depend on participants' memories. On that, the issue is that when adults reflect on their own schooling, for example, what is yielded are memories of what they believe they experienced at the time rather than accounts of what they did experience. Furthermore, even those memories can change over time.

In a similar vein, Abrams (2014, p. 95) notes that 'remembering is typically conducted using a memory frame that we might describe as a locus or field which makes remembering possible.' This can mean that some of our memories of specific schooling events, for example, are constructed when we compare and contrast them with other experiences that often come later. Related to this is the notion that how participants construct their memories of schooling can reveal issues that, while striking for them at the time of interview, could only have become clear after leaving school.

Notwithstanding the problems noted above, it is a valuable practice that the novice researcher may wish to engage with for several reasons. Here we offer three:

- Historians of education are increasingly turning their attention to trying to reconstruct how various groups experienced their education in the past. To follow the path they have opened up, necessitates the location of relevant documentary sources for analysis. The problem is that the identification of sources in the first instance is dependent on knowing what questions to ask, what issues to explore, and then where to look. Questions regarding participants' experiences of schooling in the past can often suggest themselves on reading newly constructure life-story accounts.
- Narratives based on oral testimony about the past are useful since their content can prompt us to generate unanticipated research questions and issues for further exploration in the traditional manner of the historian.
- Studies of memories can serve to remind us that while, as researchers, our target may be to try to understand individuals'

experiences of education at the time that they occurred, those experiences may have carried little import for them at that time. In other words, while education is our area of interest, we should not assume it was something to which individuals in the past, including students, attributed great importance.

It is important to note that the research approach referred to above is in the life history tradition rather than that of traditional history.

A life history is 'the history of an individual's life given by the person living it and solicited by the researcher'. It makes extensive use of the in-depth interview in order to encourage participants to reveal, in their own words, their perspectives on their lives, experiences, and situations. Accounts that emerge from the adoption of this approach are mediated by the researcher's interaction with the person during the telling of the story. Thus, one overcomes, to some extent, the problem inherent in traditional autobiography that what we read is what the author wishes us to know.

On this, it is apposite to recall a distinction drawn between the complete, or comprehensive, life story, and the topical life story. The complete or comprehensive life story is concerned with all aspects of the individual's life from birth and is usually a long and complex account of the overall flow of life of an individual. In contrast, when constructing a topical life story one focuses on soliciting from the person in question details on only one phase, aspect or issue in his or her life. Those interested in the history of education should be encouraged to construct the memories of education of various groups in order to generate topical life stories that could provide the basis for generating whole new research agendas in the field to be pursued using the research approaches of the historian.

7.4 Using Models from Other Disciplines

As experienced or novice researchers, we all belong to a broader academic community whose members study society from the position of the idiographic discipline of history rather than that of the nomothetic social sciences. In other words, we are interested more in description and instances than in the theoretical and the general. At the same time, we recognise that more than description is required of the historian. Accordingly, we locate many of our own expositions within various contexts, ranging from the local to the international, in order to assist the reader in appreciating not only what living in the period may have been like, but also why matters developed in particular ways.

Beginning or inexperienced researchers could commence a research project by addressing the 'whats', the 'wheres', the 'whos' and the 'whys' of their topics. In relation to studies in the history of education, one would also benefit from considering such questions in relation to what various social historians have for some time considered to be the most important category types in society. Those are class, regionality/locality, ethnicity, gender, sexual identity, and religion.

Historians can enrich their work by drawing on theoretical models from the social sciences and other disciplines. Having said that, we caution against the tendency of some to adopt a theoretical position from the outset with a view to marshalling as much historical data as possible in order to illustrate or prove the theory or theories in question. This stance provides a safeguard against deliberately seeking out only what one expects to find. What is important is that one should be open to hearing the unexpected and to discovering the unanticipated.

Theories and theoretical models can, nevertheless, be helpful in enhancing understanding of the past. Historians of education, for example, can learn from the insights developed in social scientific theory, while at the same time being critical and sceptical of the theories themselves, as opposed to applying them uncritically and indiscriminatingly. To adopt this perspective would be to follow the advice of those who propose that social theory can be brought into historical analyses through a transactional relationship. In other words, as one proceeds to generate a historical narrative and to construct various generalisations based on patterns detected in sources, one may find certain pre-existing frameworks helpful for organising one's exposition, while being mindful of their limitations. Sometimes what that framework may be can suggest itself from one's prior reading. Equally, it may be suggested by a colleague or tutor. In other cases, yet again, one may embark on a reading programme to see what might be available for consideration. We now provide examples we found helpful in our own work.

Example One:
In our book *Secondary School Education in Ireland: History, Memories and Life Stories, 1922–1967*, we drew on certain human science concepts. They included those that guided revisionist historians of education in the USA in the 1960s and 1970s, inspired to highlight inequality and discrimination in schooling historically. Influenced also by the sociological notion of 'ideal types', we set out to produce an account that would be helpful for engagement in comparative study by virtue of being a synthesis of a great many diffuse phenomena arranged into a unified analytical construct. On that, we recognised that there were teachers, students and others who engaged in actions that departed

from the general pattern we foreground. Accordingly, we invited readers to be open to the possibility that the efficacy of our interpretations lies not only in their capacity to describe what were regular patterns of actions and interactions, but also in their potential to prompt one to ask questions regarding what may have been unusual, exceptional, and even deviant.

Example Two:
In 2020 we embarked on a research project aimed at investigating a strike initiated by female students in a religious-run teacher training college in Ireland in the 1970s (Harford and O'Donoghue, 2020a; O'Donoghue and Harford, 2020). What was particularly remarkable about that strike was that the women activists were protesting at a time when Irish society was at its most conservative, when Church control was at its zenith, and when women's rights were most restricted. Yet, they were not rising up against the male dominant hegemony. Rather, they were rising up against the female religious managers of the college. The sources we identified and analysed brought us to that conclusion. However, we also sought to try to communicate the central ideas in a manner designed to hold the attention of the reader throughout. To that end we found it helpful to draw upon cultural historical activity theory as a framework for identifying and illuminating the specific elements of the strike by the female students in relation to broad sweeps of change in education at local, national, and international levels. The outcome, we believe, served to reinforce our argument that the strike was an example of a patriarchy being perpetuated by women on women in the field of education.

Example Three:
It is sometimes helpful to use social science concepts to illuminate an aspect or aspects of an exposition. In our book *Piety and Privilege. Catholic Secondary Schooling in Ireland and the Theocratic State, 1922–67* (2021), for example, we found it helpful to draw on Goffman's notion of a 'total institution' when considering how religious orders involved in teaching in Ireland found reassuring the encouragement that the authorities at the Second Vatican Council (1962–65) gave to their members to reflect on the ideas and works of their founders. The purpose of that exercise was to establish the features of their way of life that should be discarded as they went about trying to reconstitute themselves. Nevertheless, change for some, and especially for older members of religious orders, was traumatic since they had lived for decades in circumstances approximating Goffman's notion of a 'total

institution', the definition of which is 'a place of residence and work where a large number of like-situated individuals cut off from the wider society for an appreciable period of time together lead an enclosed formally administered round of life'. In the case of nuns, many had for decades, in Goffman's terms, led a life separated from the basic social arrangements in modern Western society whereby the individual tended 'to sleep, play and work in different places with different co-participants, under different authorities and without an overall rational plan'.

Example Four:
In *Teacher Preparation in Ireland: History, Policy and Future Directions* with Teresa O'Doherty (2017), we devoted a considerable part of our overall exposition to the teacher education curriculum. Underpinning it was a notion that academic fields of study are sites of contestation where different interest groups struggle for influence and power. In adopting this notion, we took our lead from Hargreaves' (1989, p. 56) view that academic fields of study, including in the higher education sector, are 'more than groupings of intellectual thought. They are social systems too. They compete for power, prestige, recognition and reward'. While we recognised that this position had been adopted in various ways in exploring the history of school subjects, we considered that it could equally be applied to the study of the history of how education studies as a distinct field of study has been constructed.

We saw value also in the position that in order to develop a historical perspective, curriculum history should be studied at both the pre-active and interactive level. To engage in the study of curriculum history at the pre-active level is to focus on the plans or syllabi that outline what is included in a course or programme. It involves studying not only the structures and patterns within documents, but also identifying the various individuals and interest groups who were involved in their production, and the nature and extent of their influence within a context that consisted of social, political, economic, philosophical, and technological influences.

A study of the interactive curriculum (which we did not undertake) demands that there be a focus on the interactions that take place in classrooms, lecture theatres and other learning sites, thus examining how the curriculum was mediated by lecturers and students. This, we held, was equally important work. From the outset, however, we deemed that it could only be addressed in a very general way in our book and that it was worthy of a separate project to be undertaken at another time.

Example Five:
Recently in our introduction to our edited work, *A Cultural History of Education in the Modern Age* (Harford and O'Donoghue, 2020b), we outlined trends in education internationally at the end of the nineteenth century. To that end we drew upon a cogent framework developed by political scientists for considering developments in education in any place at any moment in history, as well as over time. It consists of three interrelated properties of education institutions at levels. Those properties are 'access to education', 'the process of education', and 'the structure of an education system'.

To examine the history of access to education requires that one focus on the strategies and measures that influenced, promoted, or hindered participation. To examine the history of the process of education requires that one focus on the inner workings of the heart of any education system. This can relate to what went on in individual classrooms and schools. It also includes considering the physical and instructional environment and the nature of the curriculum and instruction that prevailed. To examine the history of the structure of an education system requires that one interrogate issues related to its local, national, and international contexts; the details of its governance and funding; and the articulation mechanisms guiding cross-sectoral links.

7.5 Areas Awaiting Investigation

From the outset we made clear our view that students of education can gain value from conducting investigations in the history of education because of their potential to provide understanding on their antecedents. We hold in particular that it is hardly possible to have a full understanding of a present-day issue in education and be fully equipped to try to solve it intelligently without having a sound knowledge of its background development. Engaging in projects in the field also helps one generate a detector system for piercing 'smoke screens' and refuting false information regarding some event in the past. Adopting this approach is particularly important currently in Ireland so that one can be constantly vigilant in cases where there may be a misuse, a raiding, or a distortion of the past.

In their outstanding review of writing in the history of education in Ireland up to 2015, Kelly and Hegarty (2017) argue that it took until the twenty-first century for those specialising in the field to cast off an introspective insularity that had defined it for a century. Following that, they list a very wide range of work completed in such a vein. Nevertheless, much remains to be undertaken. The remainder of this section indicates a range of areas deserving attention. It is by no means comprehensive.

Rather, it is offered not just by way of indicating topics one might address but also as a prompter for cogitation on what else might be possible.

Regarding access to education in Ireland

While a certain amount is known about who attended school over the last 150 years, much more needs investigation. Broad trends on the situation nationally have been uncovered but we are much less informed about regional variations regarding all levels of the education system. A totally under-researched area relates to the students who crossed the Border daily between the Republic of Ireland and Northern Ireland in each direction (a practice that is still widespread). We have no idea of the numbers involved, who are those who engaged in the practice and why? Equally, we have many silences on a similar cohort whose families lived on one side of the Border, yet they boarded in schools on the other. What we do know, however, is that the movement was not one just of Protestant children from the South going North. In particular, because certain Catholic dioceses are located on both sides of the Border and because the authorities of some of those established their diocesan secondary colleges on one side of it and other located it on the other side, Border-crossing was necessary for some who wished to attend them. For too long there has been a tendency to ignore the fact that while particular Catholic religious teaching orders specialised in the education of students from particular social class backgrounds, there were exceptions, as with the exclusive, albeit small, number of schools run by the Irish Christian Brothers and the Presentation Brothers.

Regarding curriculum

A certain amount of research has been undertaken on the history of the curriculum, including the history of school subjects in Ireland over the decades. Unfortunately, it has not been complemented by similar work on the curriculum of the various faculties, departments and schools in the nation's universities and other institutions of higher education. Regarding the schooling sector, so much of 'the hidden curriculum' has been unexplored. For example, we know very little about such matters as the following:

- The perspectives promoted in different kinds of schools on what it was to be Irish.
- The nature of bullying and other forms of child-abuse, the extent of it, and attitudes to it by students and authorities.

- The extent to which Catholics and Protestants may have formed enduring friendships as a result of rubbing shoulders on the playing fields.
- The nature and extent of home schooling at primary and post-primary school level.
- The officially declared functions of school uniforms and the actual messages that those who wore them sent out to the population.

Regarding teaching and learning

We are still very much in the dark on the following matters:

- The perceived characteristics of a 'good teacher' and by implication, 'a bad teacher'.
- The official position on corporal punishment, the various forms it took, the extent to which it was used, resistance (if any) from students, parents, and certain teachers, and if any individuals other than teachers executed it with the knowledge and co-operation of the authorities in a school.
- Student resistance on a range of issues, what those issues were, how it was carried out, levels of success and attitudes of parents, teachers, and others.
- The pedagogical practices used in schools at different levels, for various learning areas, and amongst various social classes, and what variations obtained.
- The pedagogical practices and assessment practices used in universities and higher education institutions and how they differed across academic disciplines.

Regarding leadership

- What was the nature of the relationships that the authorities of schools had with teachers (both religious and lay people)?
- How was school policy formulated?
- How was it communicated?
- How was the annual school timetable, including the allocation of 'free days', drawn up?
- What relationships did schools' authorities and teachers have with parents and how did that change overtime?
- What views were there towards streaming in schools and was it ever resisted?

Regarding participants

We know very little about the experience of being an 'actor', either female or male, in the education system over the last 150 years. As suggested already, work on this could commence with life story research undertaken with a wide range of individuals and then be used to help one to seek out primary source material such as written accounts of the time, diaries, school magazines, circulars, letters, etc. Amongst those in need of investigation are:

- Students of all ages, backgrounds across the full range of schools that existed.
- The authorities of all types of schools.
- Teachers, including those who taught in various types of schools.
- Junior and senior public servants within the national Department of Education and the Vocational Education Committees.
- Inspectors of schools at all levels.
- Students in all types of school.
- University students and students in other types of further and higher education across all disciplines.
- University academics at all levels and all types of teaching personnel in other institutions of further and higher education.

7.6 Conclusion

Historical research in education offers the novice researcher the capacity to better understand any seminal issue/topic in the field of education. Reading the present through the lens of what we know about the past in education allows us to properly interrogate and understand issues and debates, appreciating the nuances and complexities of consensus and conflict, continuity and change across time and space.

Suggested Reading

Harford, J. (2008). *The Opening of University Education to Women in Ireland* (Dublin and Portland OR: Vallentine Mitchell/Irish Academic Press).

Harford, J. (ed.) (2018). *Education for All? The Legacy of Free Post-Primary Education* (Oxford: Peter Lang).

O'Donoghue, T., and Harford, J. (2016). *Secondary School Education in Ireland: Memories and Life Histories, 1922–1967* (London and New York: Palgrave Macmillan).

O'Donoghue, T. and O' Doherty, T. (2019). *Irish Speakers and Schooling in the Gaeltact, 1900 to the Present* (London and New York: Palgrave Macmillan).

References

Abrams, L. (2014) The transformations of oral history, in S. Berger and B. Niven (eds.) Writing the history of memory, pp 88–107, (London: Bloomsbury Press).

Harford, J., and O'Donoghue, T. A. (2020a). 'Challenging the dominant Church hegemony in times of risk and promise: Carysfort women resist' in *Gender and Education*, 3(3), pp 372–384.

Harford, J., and O'Donoghue, T. (eds.) (2020b). *A cultural history of education in the modern age: 1920 to the present* (London: Bloomsbury).

Hargreaves, A. (1989) Curriculum and Assessment Reform, p. 56, (Toronto: OISE Press).

Hyland, A., and Milne, K. (1987). *Irish educational documents*, Vol. 1 (Dublin: Church of Ireland College of Education).

Hyland, A., and Milne, K. (1992). *Irish educational documents*, Vol. 2 (Dublin: Church of Ireland College of Education).

Hyland, A., and Milne, K. (1995). *Irish educational documents*, Vol. 3 (Dublin: Church of Ireland College of Education).

Kelly, J., and Hegarty, S. (2017). 'Introduction: The writing of Irish history', in J. Kelly and S. Hegarty (eds) *Schools and schooling, 1650–2000: New perspectives on the history of education*, pp 13–33 (Dublin: Four Courts Press).

O'Donoghue, T., and Harford, J. (2022). 'Investigating the potential of cultural-historical activity theory for studying specific transitions in the history of education', in *Paedagogica Historica*, 58(2), pp 180–195, DOI: 10.1080/00309230.2020.1822886.

O'Donoghue, T., and Harford, J. (2021). *Piety and privilege. Catholic secondary schooling in Ireland and the theocratic state, 1922–67* (Oxford: Oxford University Press).

O'Donoghue, T., Harford, J., and O'Doherty, T. (2017). *Teacher preparation in Ireland: History, policy and future directions* (Biggley, UK: Emerald Publishing).

Parkes, S. M. (2010). *A guide to sources for the history of Irish education, 1780–1922* (Dublin: Four Courts Press).

CHAPTER 8

The 'Method' of Philosophy? Thinking, Reading, and Writing

Áine Mahon and Emma Farrell, School of Education, University College Dublin

8.0 Introduction

This chapter demystifies the process of engaging with educational issues from a philosophical perspective. It considers how writing in a philosophical vein differs from more empirical approaches and elucidates why a student of education might wish to read and write philosophically. Threaded throughout the chapter is an understanding that philosophy of education is an iterative approach that involves thinking, reading, and writing. As such, the chapter foregrounds the various textual and visual resources that students of education might draw upon and it presents philosophical engagement as a mode of close and careful reading.

Drawing also on the seminal work of Fulford and Hodgson (2016), our contribution explores important methodological distinctions including 'writing-as-product' and 'writing-as-process' as well as 'writing-for-research' and 'writing-as-research'. As these authors point out, in philosophy of education 'writing is the research, not just something tagged onto the end of the real work of research, of data collection and data analysis' (Fulford and Hodgson, 2016, p. 151). In philosophy of education, the craft of writing takes centre stage.

A word of encouragement here for the novice researcher: When considering a philosophical approach, there are particular worries that a student might have. They might worry that their lack of background in academic philosophy presents a significant barrier. They might be concerned that philosophy is an abstract discipline and doesn't speak directly to the everyday concerns of educators. Or perhaps they might worry that philosophy is just writing and that its lack of an obviously discernible, easy-to-follow method is a barrier for those wishing to present their work as serious research. To these and related worries, we would contend that philosophy of education, in fact, offers a particular freedom and a particular mode of empowerment for student researchers. Philosophical approaches to education can be uniquely responsive, purposeful, and powerful, and such approaches can be made just as sensitively and meaningfully by those with a background in teaching/education as those with a prior knowledge of philosophy.

In order to offer students a working example of what philosophy of education might look like – both in its process and in its product – we explore our recent experience of co-authoring a journal article at the intersection of philosophy, education, and mental health. A short extract from this article is reproduced, together with a detailed commentary on its key reading and writing practices in addition to the intellectual convictions that initially inspired the piece. We hope that this commentary will offer a helpful insight into the key reasons why a student or any academic researcher might wish to approach a question philosophically.

We begin and end the chapter with two fictionalised dialogues. These dialogues capture some of the most pressing questions that are typically raised for beginning researchers in the philosophy of education. Our choice of the dialogue format is a practical one, as it brings to light many of our own professional experiences in working with postgraduate students of Education, but it carries also theoretical or even meta-philosophical importance. In foregrounding the importance of dialogue in this way, we acknowledge the long-standing importance in any philosophical endeavour of mutual interaction, of frank speaking, and of the authentically expressive. Michel Foucault's term for this expressiveness is 'parrhesia' (a term he develops from the Ancient Greeks to denote both the risks and the gifts of active truth-telling) while Stanley Cavell will write of 'passionate utterance' (a term he contrasts with the realm of the performative to foreground the role of vulnerability in human encounter).[1] With the importance of frank and open expression very much in mind, we turn now to Dialogue 1.

8.1 Dialogue 1

CHARACTERS

Stephen, M.Ed. Year 2 Student (Teacher of English and Religion)

Áine, Assistant Professor in Education (specialising in Philosophy of Education)

The scene takes place in Áine's office in UCD.

The 'Method' of Philosophy? Thinking, Reading, and Writing

SCENE
Áine is in her office, sitting at her desk. It is a sunny afternoon in late October, and she is enjoying the opportunity to catch up on reading. There is a knock at the door. Stephen enters.

Stephen: Hi Áine, how are you? Are you free now?

Áine: Hi Stephen, of course. Come on in. *[Áine and Stephen shake hands. He takes a seat in the chair opposite hers].*

Stephen: I just wanted to talk to you about my M.Ed. dissertation. The research proposal isn't due for a few more weeks but I've been mulling over some ideas.

Áine: Of course, Stephen, delighted to chat. What are you thinking?

Stephen: Well, I was really interested in the lecture last year on Teacher Identity. I've been thinking about the early career teacher and how they can be really torn between being an actor and being an authentic self – you know, you have to share a certain amount with your students in order to build a sincere relationship with them, but you can't share too much either.

Áine: That's right Stephen. That's something we all struggle with, I think.

Stephen: Well, I'd like to write my dissertation about this struggle for identity and the related notions of authenticity and sincerity in teaching. I studied a bit of philosophy at undergrad and am really interested in what the existentialists have to say about the whole issue. Sartre's idea of 'bad faith' definitely corresponds with some of the attitudes I've seen in my staffroom! I'd like to explore these ideas further in my M.Ed. dissertation.

Áine: That's great, Stephen. I'd love to supervise a project along those lines.

Stephen: The problem is Áine – and I don't mean to say the wrong thing here – over the past semester I've been taking two modules in research methods, and we've been told that we need to identify a research paradigm for our initial proposal. And I'm just a bit confused. If I'm taking a philosophical approach, where does my project fit? I presume it doesn't meet the criteria for quantitative research? So, is it qualitative, or is it mixed methods? The lecturer says that I need to pick one of them so that I can fill out the 'Research Design' and 'Methodology' sections. I know that I won't be conducting surveys or interviews if I'm doing philosophy but what I'm confused about is how exactly I go about gathering data to analyse? If they're not conducting surveys or in-depth interviews, or analysing policy, what is it that philosophers of education actually do?

Áine: Well philosophy is a bit different from other approaches in the Social Sciences. It doesn't involve the gathering of data. It's more theoretical than that. It involves close and careful reading of texts; those texts can be written by other philosophers, but they can also include things like poetry or fiction or work in children's literature or even in film. Mostly, philosophy is about paying attention to particular concepts and ideas and engaging with those concepts in a deep and extended way.

Stephen: Right. I'm not sure I follow, Áine. Could you give me an example?

Áine: Well, in terms of your interest in Teacher Identity, you'd be exploring questions like: Is there such a thing as an authentic self? How might this self be constructed in dialogue with the other? To what extent does taking up a professional persona involve suppressing aspects of the personal? And, maybe most importantly from an educational point of view: Where is the personhood from which good teaching comes? These types of questions can't be answered by observation or experiment, and I'm not sure you'd get very far by asking teachers or parents for their perspectives either.

Stephen: So, you think I'd be better off going down the philosophy route?

Áine: From what you've said Stephen, it does seem that you're more interested in the conceptual side of things. A research dissertation in this vein would involve the ability firstly to isolate the key concepts in question (and you've already mentioned 'the Self', 'the Other', 'Authenticity', 'Sincerity') and the ability, secondly, to stay with those concepts as you position yourself critically in the ongoing philosophical conversation about them. The work of Sartre is definitely a good place to start here but I would also encourage you to look at the work of Parker Palmer.

Stephen: But you can't tell me whether this is qualitative or quantitative as an approach?

Áine: Your research won't involve fieldwork or engaging with data. You won't be able to tick the 'qualitative' or 'quantitative' box because your work isn't empirical to begin with.

Stephen: Right. So, I won't be doing any real research?

Áine: You will, Stephen. It's just a different type of research.

Stephen: Ok. [Stephen pauses]. Thanks, Áine. I might have to think about this a bit more. *Áine and Stephen say their goodbyes. Stephen exits the office.*

In the scene presented above, some of the difficulties that philosophers face when asked to describe their 'method' or their 'methodology' are brought to the fore. The dialogue is partly fictionalised but it is partly based on our own experiences supervising students in departments of Education. It is often the case that these students are deeply interested in philosophical ideas but that they struggle to reconcile the discipline of philosophy with the language of research methods more generally. There can be a perception, as with the fictionalised Stephen above, that philosophy of education is not 'real research' or that reading and writing about concepts does not constitute a serious approach to problems encountered while teaching and learning. Paul Standish has described the question of method in philosophy as 'a vexed one' (Standish, 2009, p. ii), while Richard Smith has warned of fundamental difficulties in articulating any fixed procedures for philosophy. In his own words, 'in doing philosophy we need to be aware of the awkwardness of thinking in terms of having a method, still more any kind of 'methodology" (Smith, 2009, p. 437).

Interestingly, in his most recent book on educational research, Gert Biesta has identified a 'strong convergence' towards a narrow number of messages which together 'construct a kind of "common sense"' of what it means to do research about or in the classroom (Biesta, 2020, p. 2). According to Biesta, there are certain orthodoxies of educational research that are passed on to postgraduate students of education: students must locate their work within a research paradigm; they must choose between quantitative, qualitative, or mixed approaches; they must articulate the epistemological and ontological assumptions underlying their research question; they must identify an appropriate theoretical framework etc. Because philosophy of education does not always answer to these orthodoxies it is understandable why students of education are tempted to steer clear of a philosophical approach.

In this chapter, we aim to demystify the process of engaging with educational issues from a philosophical perspective. We aim to elucidate why a student of education might wish to read and write philosophically, and we aim to establish why certain educational questions benefit most from a philosophical engagement.

We turn now to a concrete example. In our own academic work, we have recently co-authored a journal article at the intersection of philosophy, education, and mental health. Offered below is a brief introduction to this piece, followed by a short extract from the article itself, and an extended consideration of its reading and writing practices. We are particularly keen to illustrate those practices that distinguish the piece from other disciplinary approaches in education, and to explore again the distinction between 'empirical' and 'non-empirical' (or theoretical) approaches.

In general, we offer the extract below as a touchstone for what philosophy of education might look like. It constitutes a single instance, but it might also stand for something greater. It should not be taken as definitive or exemplary, rather, it is intended to illustrate opportunities, pathways, and possible points of departure.

8.2 A Touchstone for Philosophy of Education: Our Article in Context

The extract below is taken from a co-authored journal article exploring alternative ways of thinking and talking about youth mental health. The paper focuses particularly on the experiences of students in Higher Education in Ireland. From a philosophical standpoint, it foregrounds the work of contemporary American philosopher, Cora Diamond. Diamond is not typically viewed as a philosopher of education, but she has written extensively and powerfully on ethics in general and on human experiences of mental anguish in particular. Our article turns to Diamond's writings as a body of work that might bring an illuminating set of concepts to discourses of mental health in Ireland and more broadly.

Our main concern with this piece was to show how mental health as a phenomenon has become dominated by certain vocabularies and certain ways of thinking. And the problem with these vocabularies and ways of thinking is that they crowd out or make very difficult alternative conceptions of the human. Specifically, we sought to demonstrate that mental health is too often understood in terms of a medicalised vocabulary where 'vocabularies of distress' are invariably 'vocabularies of deficit' (Gergen, 1990). These vocabularies pathologise the individual and radically simplify a broad array of emotional and behavioural challenges. They exemplify a narrowing in how we describe, diagnose, and respond to experiences of distress. We argue in the piece that such narrowing raises significant conceptual as well as ethical concerns.

To counteract such narrowing, a central aim of our article was to open up a set of pressing, if often-avoided questions: In general, what would it mean for our understanding of mental health if we were to step away from the dominant medical model? What would it mean for the participating students if their individual experiences had not been responded to in terms of diagnosis and medication? What would it mean for us not to reduce complexity to simplicity but to sit with what Diamond terms 'difficulties of reality'? The following extract is taken from Section I of the paper – on 'Difficulty'.

EXTRACT

UNDERSTANDING STUDENT MENTAL HEALTH: DIFFICULTY, DEFLECTION, AND DARKNESS [2]

1. Difficulty

People were completely misunderstanding the way I was communicating, and I think it just, not that I got a little bit lost, but just things weren't heard and especially when you go into a therapy session and you have people who already have ideas about who you are because you have an eating disorder, it cuts you off, you stop. [...] I had one therapist who refused to believe that I wasn't abused. She said, 'until you can admit it, you are never going to get better'. She would give me books about not remembering being abused and I was like 'But I wasn't fucking abused'. (Kate)

I didn't understand what it was, I didn't understand what was going wrong and although you know, my parents, my mother was always very, 'You can always ask us anything,' and stuff, I would have still been an embarrassed child and you grow up in the west of Ireland, Catholic Ireland, you're kind of just taught to be that way even if you don't want to be and I didn't really know how to understand what was going on myself. (Ella)

Borderline personality disorder, that's my favourite. I'm like, 'You literally give that to everyone' (Lauren)

[...] For the philosopher Cora Diamond, the capacity to identify and to name has a profoundly important role in human life because a rich conceptual life enables a rich understanding of personal experience. To possess or to command a concept that is meaningful to your own biography and that locates that biography within a broader community of understanding inscribes your experience within a shared linguistic practice. Finding our concepts makes public the private and salvages community from isolation. Specifically, in 'Losing Your Concepts', Diamond outlines two ways in which conceptual articulacy may fail. Such failure may manifest either in the misexpression of one's thoughts or in a complete lack of expression, either in 'misnamed' or in 'unnamed' experiences (Diamond, 1988, p. 259). In the experiences of Ella and Lauren above, we find instances of the former ('She would give me books about not remembering being abused and I was like "but I wasn't fucking abused"'; 'Borderline personality disorder, that's my favourite. I'm like "you literally give that to everyone"') and a consequent turning to anger, to cynicism or to a gallows humour. Perhaps it is in the experience of Ella that the latter (the grappling with unnamed experience) comes most obviously to the fore: 'I didn't understand what it was, I didn't understand what was going wrong', she says. [...]

In her emphasis on our involvement with language as a necessarily communal practice, Diamond is of course deeply indebted to the later Wittgenstein. Rejecting the prevailing picture of language as representation, or the idea that there is an objective connection between words and world, Wittgenstein (1953) argues that language does not link us to the external world per se but that language links us to each other. Words gather meaning not statically but in practice where such meaning is determined by context, by human 'language games', human 'criteria', human 'forms of life'. Thus, Diamond follows Wittgenstein in his call that we return to our everyday and existing contexts and that we stop worrying about some kind of transcendent or metaphysical perspective.

One of the key aspects in Diamond's interpretation of Wittgenstein is its profoundly moral inflection. If Wittgenstein denies the possibility of a private language and urges instead that private utterances make sense only against a public framework of understanding, then Diamond interrogates what this denial might mean for the individual within the community. This moral inflection of Wittgenstein's work is expressed most powerfully in Diamond's 2003 essay, 'The Difficulty of Reality and the Difficulty of Philosophy'. It is in this context that her acknowledgment of epistemological limitation combines with a profound emphasis on vulnerability and animality, and on the fleshiness and woundedness of our embodied selves.

What Diamond wishes to foreground in this paper is the human experience of conceptual failure. She wishes to draw attention to a cluster of experiences where everyday concepts falter or lose traction on encountering the inexplicably beautiful or the inexplicably horrifying. This is more than an absence (of language or understanding). It is an incidence of exile where we are driven out or literally 'dis-ordered' from our structures of signification. Such disorder is profoundly painful and profoundly isolating as it evicts us from everything and everyone that we thought we knew. In Diamond's words:

> What interests me there is the experience of the mind's not being able to encompass something which it encounters. It is capable of making one go mad to try, to bring together in thought what cannot be thought. [This is] a difficulty that pushes us beyond what we can think. To attempt to think it is to feel one's thinking become unhinged. [...] the difficulty, if we try to see it, shoulders us out of life, is deadly chilling (2003, p. 12).

In the most straightforward sense, 'difficulty' involves a sundering between concept and reality. It involves breakdown in its very literal sense. What interests Diamond philosophically in her range of examples (and these examples are literary rather than medical: a poem by Ted Hughes; a lecture series by J.M. Coetzee; a memoir by Ruth Klüger; a story by Mary Mann) are those moments of uncoupling, or disconnection, or cleavage – those moments of conceptual collapse – when clarity gives way to bewilderment and comfort, or habitat collapses to pain. 'I mean that they can give us the sense that this should not be, that we cannot fit it into the understanding we have of what the world is like. It is wholly inexplicable that it should be, and yet it is' (Diamond, 2003, p. 13).

We suggest that Diamond's concept of difficulty is particularly intriguing in its illumination of the gap between experience and concept. Highlighted continually in her writing is the profoundly disappointing aspect of language – the inadequacy of its communicative potential – and this disappointment is strikingly present in the accounts of these students struggling to attach words and meanings to their experience. Ashley, for example, describes unsuccessful efforts to communicate with a mental health practitioner armed with a professional framework of understanding: 'you go in and you desperately want someone to help so bad that you can't communicate what's going on so they can't understand and then they can't get there'. For Millie: 'It was all, kind of, just one big jumble in the head that I was just trying to figure out, but I couldn't. [...] When I was going through it, I couldn't actually grasp what was going on. I didn't even really know how to explain it because it wasn't like, oh I feel sick or something.'

The experiences of Ashley and Millie go to the very heart of human life. These are experiences that demand understanding (a particular phenomenon is so affecting that we are desperate to make sense of it) and yet jeopardise intelligibility (our failure to make sense of a particular phenomenon threatens our sense-making capacities in general). In Diamond's work, we are alerted to these very disappointments and failures. She foregrounds the very real possibility that we might feel, at times, insurmountably unknown – even unknowable – and thus painfully distant from other people.

[...] What would it mean for us, when faced with accounts of distress, not to reduce complexity to simplicity – but to sit with difficulties of reality? What would it mean for the students encountered through these interviews if individual experience had not been deflected or avoided? This, perhaps, is what Diamond encourages us to consider when she invites us to think about 'what it would be not to be deflected as an inhabiting of a body (one's own, or an imagined other's) in the appreciating of a difficulty of reality' (Diamond, 2003, p.13). Such an appreciation would recognise the difficulties we are experiencing, not as individual deficiencies, but as metaphysical finitudes. It would recognise our students' experiences of distress as indicators not of personal but of human limitation. In this way, to parse Diamond as well as Cavell, what we are invited to consider is not knowledge but acknowledgment. What we are invited to face up to are the impossibilities of fully understanding ourselves as well as each other, the terror this presents, and the need for constant deflection of the difficult and the unknowable. We are invited to be compassionate in the face of all that we cannot quite understand. [...]

8.3 Reading and Writing Practices in This Extract

The extract you have just read includes a number of features that typify work in the philosophy of education in addition to a number of features that push the boundaries of what philosophy of education might look like. No doubt this boundary-pushing is at least partly a result of the interdisciplinary nature of the piece, with the first author (Farrell) coming to the discussion with particular expertise in youth mental health and the second author (Mahon) coming with a background in contemporary Anglo-American philosophy. Uniting the authors is our commitment to philosophical thinking more broadly and our conviction that the discipline of philosophy has a distinctive role to play in making sense of human experience.

Our extract opens with what is usually referred to as qualitative data: we include the detailed responses of a number of participating interviewees in order to understand their personal experience of a particular phenomenon. More specifically, our data is based on the narrative landscapes of a number of third-level students in Ireland, who shared their experiences as part of a hermeneutic phenomenological study into the lived experience of mental health difficulties (Farrell, 2017). Our approach, then, might be described as 'empirical', at least in the sense that it is rooted in and proceeds from direct observation of human experience.

The empirical dimension of our piece is worthy of critical commentary given that philosophical research (as explored earlier in this chapter) is typically defined as 'non-empirical'. Indeed, it is often distinguished from other approaches in the Social Sciences by its attention to the theoretical, the conceptual, or the abstract. Philosophers do not collect data in the traditional sense, we are told. Rather, the sources for philosophers are primarily textual. Philosophers read and respond to the work of other philosophers and sometimes they read and respond to literary or cinematic texts.

However, it is important to clarify that these practices of reading and writing are quite distinctive. What is involved is not simply a reviewing or a narrating of work that has already been carried out. We might make a comparison here with a typical Social Sciences literature review which seeks to summarise the current state of knowledge in a particular area. Part of the ambition of such a review is to synthesise work already done in order to identify gaps in the current state of knowledge and so, perhaps, to formulate one's research question accordingly. Reading and writing in a philosophical vein is different.

Perhaps most distinctively, such reading and writing involves a careful attention to language and a fresh consideration of concepts and ideas. To take an example from our piece, what exactly Cora Diamond means by 'a difficulty of reality' is not something that can be summarised in a sentence or two before moving on to her next idea. Rather, this is a concept that might be interpreted in many different ways, and these multiple meanings and resonances are deeply insightful (or so we would argue) for a novel appreciation of what it means to be human – what it means to be vulnerable, what it means to be exposed, what it means to be struggling with ourselves and those around us. Moreover, a fuller understanding of Diamond's concept involves a consideration of her work in the context of its broader philosophical lineage; in the extract above, we discuss how her philosophy is indebted to the practices and the spirit of the later Ludwig Wittgenstein as well as being importantly in tune with the more contemporary writing of Stanley Cavell.

The purpose in reading Diamond, then, is not to review nor to synthesise nor to summarise but to engage in depth. This mode of close reading is particularly needed given that Diamond's essay relies so heavily on its own original formulations. One can attempt an intelligent gloss at the central concepts of the essay – difficulty, deflection, woundedness, exposure – but always these concepts outstrip our efforts to pin down or to fully understand.

A philosophical engagement with Diamond's work involves utilising both reason and imagination in bringing clarity to thought. For this reason, it is typical of philosophers not to review all the research in a particular expert area but to focus instead on a limited number of sources; you will notice that in the extract above we limit our analysis to two Diamond essays (and in actual fact we focus mostly on one). In general, in the philosophy of education, selected texts are highly significant and are read slowly and sensitively for their multiple meanings and conceptual insights. As Fulford and Hodgson capture this point, 'how [these selected texts] are read – in detail, with a focus on etymology and the particular use of language – is characteristic of work in this field'. Similarly, in terms of practices of writing, in philosophy of education 'writing *is* the research, not just something tagged onto the end of the real work of research, of data collection and data analysis' (Fulford and Hodgson, 2016, p. 148). We would add to these points that in the philosophy of education, we read and write in order to work through conceptual confusion. We read and write in order to figure out what we are thinking. This is necessarily a patient, deliberate, painstaking, and sometimes a painful process.

8.4 Dialogue 2

CHARACTERS

Stephen, Doctoral Candidate in Education (Teacher of English and Religion)

Áine, Assistant Professor in Education (specialising in Philosophy of Education)

The scene takes place in UCD.

SCENE

One year later and Áine is again in her office, waiting for Stephen to arrive. Stephen has completed his M.Ed. programme and is now in the process of applying for Ph.D. funding. There is a knock at the door. Stephen enters.

Stephen: Hi Áine, how are you? Thanks a million for taking the time to see me.

Áine: Hi Stephen, of course. Come on in. *[Áine and Stephen shake hands and he takes a seat].* I was delighted to read your completed dissertation over the summer, Stephen. It's a wonderful piece of work.

Stephen: Thank you so much Áine. It really allowed me to explore the deeper questions I've always had about the life of the teacher.

Áine: That's fantastic Stephen. Tell me, how are the Ph.D. funding applications going?

Stephen: Well, not great to be honest. That's what I wanted to talk to you about today.

Áine: Go ahead. Hopefully I can help.

Stephen: Well, I'm just struggling to answer some of the questions on the form. Firstly, there's a really detailed section that requires candidates to explain the 'impact' of their work. Now I know that 'impact' broadly refers to the contribution your research can make to society and the economy, but I'm not sure if the contributions of my work can be so easily identified. Building on my M.Ed. thesis, I'm intending to explore in much more detail the related ideas of Authenticity, Identity, and Integrity in the context of Early Career Teaching (again with primary reference to existentialist philosophy) but my thesis won't be 'putting forward solutions' or 'influencing educational policy' or even 'improving practice'. It's a philosophical exploration of what should be meaningful in our teaching careers.

Áine: I can definitely see why completing a section on 'Research Impact' is challenging for the type of work you're proposing Stephen! Any other issues?

Stephen: Well, there's a bit towards the end of the form where I have to detail the Ph.D. schedule. They're asking for 'milestones' and 'deliverables' for completion of the proposed research. These have to be visualised in a Gantt project planner. I just … I'm not sure how I can do this. From my M.Ed. experience, philosophy is not a linear process. There doesn't seem to be a straightforward trajectory from designing your research question to seeking ethical approval to collecting and then analysing your data etc. It's more the case that you begin with an intuition, you read in the area, you identify some key concepts, and then you go back to reading even more. To be honest I don't think I really figured out my research question until I was writing my conclusion.

Áine: Stephen I completely identify with that process, just as you have described it. Often in philosophy, what is important and meaningful can only reveal itself in a gradual way; the philosopher Stanley Cavell would say that philosophical thinking involves being responsive rather than being assertive. You could say that there's a certain element of immersing yourself in the reading, of really sitting with the material for an extended period of time, before it can make sense to you. A friend of mine says that in philosophy you have to let things 'percolate', like small particles passing through a sieve, and there's a certain degree of resistance that you have to become comfortable with.

Stephen: Well, it's a relief to hear that these are issues for philosophy more broadly, and it's not just me that's the problem! I'll take another look at the form this weekend.

Áine: Ok Stephen. Happy to work on it with you over the coming weeks.

Stephen: Thanks, Áine. I'll keep in touch. *Stephen exits the office.*

As identified by Stephen in the exchanges above, the procedures of philosophy don't always align with the empirically-orientated frameworks of the contemporary research university. This lack of fit can impact on how philosophy of education is situated within postgraduate modules in Research Methods (as we saw in our opening dialogue) but it can also disorientate doctoral candidates seeking to articulate and justify their work for the purposes of research funding. Such disorientation can be a significant road block at an early and formative stage of the research process, and can certainly cause researchers to question again whether philosophy is the intellectual pathway for them. As Pirrie, Manum, and Necib (2020) have recently written, there are in fact distinctively damaging consequences – especially in the context of doctoral work – to this obsession with linear and measurable progress, and with this thinking of 'time's arrow' as unstoppable and unidirectional: 'In short, time's arrow wounds', they argue. 'It can put pressure on relationships. There are "milestones" to be reached and "progress reports" to complete if the "student journey" is to proceed smoothly [...] and these mechanisms make us prisoners of measured time' (p. 149).

The presumption, then, that doctoral work 'progresses' exactly along the lines of departmental guidance documents and graduate student handbooks can in fact be a very unhelpful one. With these complexities in mind, we return to some of the motivating questions articulated at the outset of this chapter: Why might a student of education wish to read and write philosophically? And are there certain educational questions that benefit particularly from a philosophical engagement?

It is important to articulate again that philosophy is primarily conceptual. It deals with ideas, notions or abstractions that can seem free-floating, nebulous, or impossible to pin down. At its heart it is committed to this conceptual work, to an unpicking, tinkering or an engineering of ideas. What is truth? What is beauty? What does it mean to be fair? For the 'thinking teacher' (Standish, 2010, p. 8) who invovles themselves in this conceptual work, their thinking is engaged and sharpened. They unpick, they untangle, and they resist what has been given before. This of course is where the long-standing image of the Socratic gadfly comes in: the figure that refuses to cede to platitudes or accepted wisdoms.

8.5 Conclusion

One of the biggest challenges with these conceptual questions, of course, is that they cannot be answered by observation or experiment alone. If we are interested in the essence of truth, or beauty, or fairness, we cannot grasp this essence in empirical or evidence-based ways. We cannot simply observe or experiment with the world to find out the answer. In Standish's words, research in the philosophy of education involves a move 'from considering how things are to how they ought to be, addressing the normative/philosophical as distinct from the descriptive/sociological' (Standish, 2010, p. 7). Here we might think again of our fictionalised Stephen who is interested above all in 'what should be meaningful' in any teacher's career. Biesta articulates this distinction between the normative and the descriptive in the following way: 'Rather than asking what education produces, we should be asking what education means. And rather than asking what education makes, we should be asking what education makes possible' (Biesta, 2017, p. 13).

The point to be emphasised here is that sometimes, in thinking deeply about educational matters, we need to dwell just a little bit longer at the theoretical level. This is because the matters we assume as straightforwardly empirical are sometimes fully fraught with philosophical conundrums. In our personal and professional lives, we can be genuinely hampered by hasty generalisations, by assertions lacking evidence, by naïve ideas about knowledge and reality and – in the particular case of teaching – by unexamined notions of the purpose and value of education.

To take one final example: An early career teacher is very interested in the teaching of religion in post-primary schools in Ireland. She wants to write her dissertation in this area. One way she might approach this question is empirical. She might design questionnaires and interviews with teachers working in the field to ascertain their attitudes to the teaching of their subject; she might prioritise the perspectives of actual practitioners and communicate her findings textually as well as visually. But another way she might approach the problem is philosophical. Choosing to stay at the normative rather than the descriptive level, this teacher-researcher asks: Should teachers teach religion in post-primary schools? What are the links between religious instruction and moral education? Should every child have the right to explore a spectrum of religious traditions, even if that same exploration directly contravenes the wishes of their parents? What is religion? What is morality? What is education?

These types of questions cannot be resolved by an empirical approach. They cannot be meaningfully addressed by research models involving data collection and data analysis. And so, they call for philosophy. They call for a careful examination of the very assumptions and the very reasoning that underpin our everyday practice. They invite and reward a conceptual consideration which involves by its very nature a certain measure of stepping back, of reading slowly, of paying careful attention to language and idea, and of thinking together with relevant philosophical and literary resources. In this cautious and excavatory mode, novel and imaginative pathways of thinking are opened up – and the power of philosophical thinking can do justice to the deeply important questions of the educator – and become a rich area for the novice researcher to explore.

Recommended Readings

Bridges, D., and R. Smith (eds.) (2007). *Philosophy, Methodology, and Educational Research* (London: Blackwell).

McNamee, M., and Bridges, D. (eds.) (2002). *The Ethics of Educational Research* (Oxford: Blackwell).

Ruitenberg, C. (2009). 'Introduction: The Question of Method in Philosophy of Education', in *Journal of Philosophy of Education*, 43(3), pp 315–323.

Smeyers, P. and Smith, R. (eds.) (2014). *Understanding Education and Educational Research* (Cambridge: Cambridge University Press).

References

Biesta, G. (2017). 'What if? Art education beyond expression and creativity', in C. Naughton, G. Biesta, and D. Cole (eds.), *Art, Artists and Pedagogy: Philosophy and the Arts in Education* (London: Routledge).

Biesta, G. (2020). *Educational Research: An Unorthodox Introduction* (London: Bloomsbury).

Diamond, C. (1988). 'Losing Your Concepts', in *Ethics*, 98(2), p. 255.

Diamond, C. (2003). 'The Difficulty of Reality and the Difficulty of Philosophy' in *Partial Answers*, 1(2), p. 1.

Farrell, E. (2017). *Losing the plot: a hermeneutic phenomenological study of the natue and meaning of psychological distress amongst third level students in Ireland*, Ph.D. (University of Dublin, Dublin). (11127)

Fulford, A., and Hodgson, N. (eds.). (2016). *Philosophy and Theory in Educational Research: Writing in the Margin* (London: Routledge).

Gergen, K. (1990). 'Therapeutic Professions and the Diffusion of Deficit' in *The Journal of Mind and Behavior*, 11(3/4), p. 353.

Pirrie, A., Manum, K., and Necib, S. E. (2020). 'Gentle Riffs and Noises Off: Research Supervision Under the Spotlight' in *Journal of Philosophy of Education*, 54(1), pp 146–163.

Smith, R. (2009). 'Between the Lines: Philosophy, Text and Conversation', in *Journal of Philosophy of Education*, 43(3), pp 437–449.

Standish, P. (2009). 'Editorial', in *Journal of Philosophy of Education*, 43(4), pp iii–iv.

Standish, P. (2010). 'What is the Philosophy of Education?', in R. Bailey (ed.), *The Philosophy of Education: An Introduction* (London: Continuum), pp 4–19.

Wittgenstein, L. (1953) *Philosophical Investigations* (Cambridge: Cambridge University Press).

Acknowledgments

In writing this chapter, Áine Mahon would like to acknowledge the work of her own doctoral students in Philosophy of Education as well as the work of those she has had the privilege to examine or to read in recent years. The creativity and courage of this writing has been absolutely central to her conception of what Philosophy of Education is or what it might be. Thanks, especially, are due to Elizabeth O'Brien and Rowan Oberman (University College Dublin); Adrian Skilbeck and Alison Brady (University College London); Claire Skea (University of Edinburgh); Naziya O'Reilly (Leeds Trinity University); and John McCall (Edge Hill University). And thank you to Paul Jenner (Loughborough University) for the image of philosophical thinking as 'percolation'!

Notes

1. For more on 'parrhesia' and 'passionate utterance', particularly in the context of Initial Teacher Education, please see Fulford's excellent article, Amanda Fulford (2012), 'Conversations: risk, passion and frank speaking in education', *Ethics and Education*, 7(1), pp 75–90.

2. This extract is taken from Emma Farrell and Áine Mahon (2021), 'Understanding Student Mental Health: Difficulty, Deflection, and Darkness', *Ethics and Education*.

CHAPTER 9

Using Technology in Your Research Project

Enda Donlon, Institute of Education, Dublin City University, Ireland

9.0 Introduction

In 1943 Thomas Watson, the then-chairman of IBM, famously proclaimed, 'I think there's a world market for maybe five computers.' Given the size and complexity of computers at that time, Watson would be forgiven for underestimating just how much computers, and subsequently mobile technologies such as smartphones and tablets, would become part of life today. With regard to academic undertakings, it is now likely that the novice researcher will, to some extent, employ digital technologies when engaging in at least some of the various processes associated with conducting research and compiling their findings. With that in mind, this chapter broadly overviews some of the ways that technology can be used by students to help them plan, manage, and undertake their research project. We will begin, however, by considering some of the key factors to be aware of in choosing and using the various technological tools for research which may be at your disposal.

9.1 Device-Based and Cloud-Based Software

There are, generally speaking, two ways in which we can access and utilise software. The first is device-based (sometimes referred to as 'local') software, which simply means that the software itself is installed on a particular device, such as a computer or tablet. The second is cloud-based software, which means that the software is not installed on the device you are using, but rather is available as an online service which you are accessing via your device through a web browser and an internet connection (this is sometimes referred to as 'Software as a Service', or SaaS). An example of cloud-based software is Google Docs, which is word-processing software that is accessed online through a web browser such as Chrome or Firefox.

Both approaches have their advantages and disadvantages. Device-based software does not usually rely on an internet connection and so can be used at any time and location, but obviously requires access to that specific device in order to use it; cloud-based applications, on the other hand, can be accessed from multiple devices and locations once you have an internet connection to facilitate this. Device-based software tends to be linked to specific operating systems and devices (such as Microsoft Windows, Mac OS and Linux) and can function differently across these operating systems or not be available for some at all, while cloud-based software simply requires a web browser and internet connection to be used and will function in the same manner across most devices. Device-based software is often more powerful in terms of functionality and the range of options for use, but the trade-off is that it tends to require increasingly more powerful devices to run and can sometimes occupy large amounts of storage space. Cloud-based approaches are often more streamlined and simplified in terms of functionality but can be utilised on older or lower-specification devices. And finally, device-based software usually saves its files to the local device or portable storage such as a USB drive (or requires an additional solution to move or mirror this to a cloud-based storage location), whereas cloud-based solutions tend to save their work in the cloud.

With great power comes great responsibility

As the functionality, availability and general ease-of-use of software, apps and services has increased for use within research, so too have the governing factors that determine what options you can use and what factors need to be in place to use them effectively. In particular, Research Ethics processes and procedures now play an increasingly central role with regard to the use of digital tools for research purposes (please see Chapter 2 for a discussion on conducting ethical research). It is now not uncommon for Research Ethics processes within institutions, for instance, to enquire about what steps and measures a researcher is taking to ensure that data captured for research purposes is being securely stored and protected, and to require that appropriate measures are put in place to ensure this. Compliance with data protection legislation (primarily the European Union's General Data Protection Regulation, or GDPR) is also a factor that all researchers, both novice and experienced, must be aware of, and it is now standard for institutions to have procedures in places (sometimes linked to Research Ethics applications, sometimes separate) to ensure that research data is appropriately sourced, stored, accessed, used, and in many cases, discarded after use.

The significance of these factors cannot be overstated, and it is important to be aware of the requirements, guidelines, and options available within your own institution before you begin using digital tools for research purposes. The remainder of this chapter should be read with these factors in mind; while several options are presented in some cases as to the tools and services that might be considered for a particular purpose during your research project, your own institution may have specific recommendations, requirements and restrictions about which ones can be used, and it is important to become aware of these and, where necessary, to be in compliance with them.

9.2 Backup and Version Management

Accounts of losing written work certainly pre-date the use of digital technologies. One well-known example comes from John Steinbeck, who had the unfortunate experience of finding that the first draft of his classic novel *Of Mice and Men* had been eaten by his dog, Toby. 'Two months' work to do over again', Steinbeck lamented, 'there was no other draft', although he reflected good naturedly that 'the poor little fellow may have been acting critically'. More recently, experiences and accounts of losing work are usually associated with technological failures such as the document or storage drive becoming corrupted or the device no longer working, or of the device itself being lost or stolen. Needless to say, this is the last thing you want for your research project and so it is best to have strategies in place from the outset in order to help minimise the chances of this happening.

There are a few simple principles that we can follow to help keep our work safe. Perhaps most obviously, it is important to frequently save the document or file you are currently working on in case of system crashes or power cuts. If you are using Microsoft Word, a simple shortcut for this is to press 'Ctrl' and 'S' together if using a Windows device, or 'Cmd' and 'S' together if using a Mac device – try to get into the habit of doing this frequently. If you are using Google Docs or Word for the Web (Microsoft's online version of Word) your work is automatically being saved every few seconds (in fact, you may have noticed that there is no 'save' button for these tools as one is not needed).

It is also beneficial to keep versions of your work as you go. In addition to having multiple backups to call upon if needed, keeping versions also means that you can go back to an earlier draft to retrieve some content that you have since dropped but subsequently reconsidered and decided it might again be useful for your project, whereas if you are simply working from one live document to which you are adding and deleting content as you go, this is more difficult and sometimes impossible. You can use any naming convention that is logical to you for this process, but one simple format is to append the current date to the filename of the document (e.g.,

'Sociology Essay 16May21') to make it easy to identify if you are searching through a number of these version files. These steps are particularly relevant if you are using device-based word-processing software like Microsoft Word or Apple's Pages. Cloud-based options like Word for the Web and Google Docs will keep a version log of changes which you can then consult or revert to if needed, although some people find it helpful to still follow a manual process such as that outlined here in order to access earlier versions and drafts of work.

Increasingly, we tend towards cloud storage mechanisms for storing work via services such as Google Drive, Microsoft OneDrive, and Dropbox. These services can be accessed via a web browser or can be added to your device as a drive or folder, bringing the benefit that you simply save your work to this location on your computer as you normally would, and the work will automatically be synchronised or stored in your remote cloud storage (you will need to install an application, such as Google Drive for Desktop, the Microsoft OneDrive app, or the Dropbox software to avail of this functionality). These services come with several of the advantages discussed earlier in this chapter, such as the ability to access your work from a device other than your primary one if you need to, and in most cases the ability to share your work with others if you wish to. If your institution utilises Google or Microsoft cloud-based services for email and storage (which we'll refer to herein as a Google or Microsoft ecosystem) you likely have generous – possibly unlimited – cloud storage space, making this a particularly helpful option for storing all digital files associated with your research project.

Mind mapping and planning

An activity that some students find helpful with regard to their research project is to visually map out ideas and thoughts, possible structures, and so on. One of the most common formats for this is a 'mind map' and while this can of course be done with paper and pen, many digital options also exist for this purpose. One such option is Bubbl (https://bubbl.us), a cloud-based service which can be used without creating a user account (although there are advantages to having one). Other online options for mind mapping include Coggle (https://coggle.it) and Miro (https://miro.com/). Each of these services will allow you to make a limited number of maps for free before needing to purchase a licence to avail of more maps and more advanced features, but in many cases the free offering will be sufficient for your needs. There are also many device-based software options for mind mapping, such as XMind (https://www.xmind.net) and FreeMind (http://freemind.sourceforge.net/).

Those who prefer more flexibility around structures and layouts might opt instead for Padlet (https://padlet.com). Padlet facilitates multiple layouts for structuring content, including a freeform 'canvas' which will allow you to place posts (notes) wherever you wish on the Padlet board, a 'grid' structure to arrange content in rows, and a timeline to place content along a horizontal line. In addition to text, posts can include multimedia and links to websites. The free version of Padlet will currently allow you to save up to three boards.

9.3 Research Project Management

Completing an academic assignment, particularly a large one like a thesis (either undergraduate or postgraduate), consists of many smaller parts that collectively combine to result in the finished product. One option to help you organise and keep track of this is Trello (https://trello.com), a web-based project management application which uses the Kanban visual method for managing tasks. Imagine taking a sheet of paper (which represents your project – for instance, a thesis) and dividing the page into columns. Each column gets a name, such as 'to do', 'in progress', and 'finished' (or any phased structure to your liking). Using post-it notes, you would add tasks to the 'to do' column first, then move each to the 'in progress' column as you undertake it, before finally moving it to the 'finished' column when it is completed. That's effectively what you can do with Trello, which consists of boards (the page), lists (the columns) and cards (the post-it notes). The cards can include lots of additional features, like checklists, due-dates, hyperlinks to websites, images, and so on. Trello enables you to list and track all tasks associated with your research project, and many people find a great sense of satisfaction in moving cards through the various lists until their project is completed. The free version of Trello will currently allow you to save up to three boards.

Focus keeping

Motivating yourself to research and write can be a challenge for even the most experienced researchers. One popular approach to help with this is the Pomodoro technique, which, in short, consists of 25-minute bursts of time on a particular task (such as writing) followed by a short break (five minutes) before undertaking another 25-minute burst (these 25-minute bursts are known as pomodoros). After a number of these iterations, a longer break takes place. The Pomodoro technique has given rise to a multitude of apps and online services designed to help structure the process. On your phone or tablet, simply search your app store for 'pomodoro' or 'tomato timer' to find some options. On your computer there are a number of online services to avail of, such as the 'tomato timers' available at https://tomato-timer.com and http://www.tomatotimers.com. The Pomodoro technique doesn't work for everybody, but many do find the structure and rhythm of the process to be beneficial.

9.4 Reference Management Software

The correct use of references is one of the most important hallmarks of academic writing and is simultaneously one that can prove challenging for students right through from undergraduate to doctoral level. One option for consideration is to employ dedicated software which has been designed to assist with this important task, usually referred to as Reference Management Software (RMS). At their basic level, RMS packages will enable you to store bibliographical details of books, journal articles, conference papers, and other formats, in an atomised manner (so for instance, a separate field for author(s), a separate field for title of the work, and so on). The software then combines these details according to the requirements of the academic style your institution requires and enables you to add them to your document in both citation and bibliographic formats.

In more recent times, the functionality of these applications has expanded significantly beyond storing bibliographical details and formatting these according to prescribed academic styles. Many will now, for instance, interface with online databases of bibliographical information, so that you can quickly import the relevant details to the software without needing to enter the details manually (browser plugins also exist for many of these packages, allowing you to 'grab' references off the page you are viewing on the screen and import them to the RMS). Many packages will also enable you to store a PDF of the document to which the bibliography entry relates, and in some cases these can be highlighted and annotated with your own notes. All packages will allow you to choose from multiple citation styles (such as APA, Chicago, MLA) and to switch between these as often as you wish. There are many options to choose from but some of the more well-known options that you may wish to consider are now outlined.

Endnote is one of the longest-established and best-known options for reference management. It is a commercial offering and thus may not be accessible to everyone; however, some institutions make Endnote available to students and staff, and so it is worth checking if this is the case for you. Options exist for using Endnote as both device-based and cloud-based software. If you don't have access to the full version of Endnote, you could explore Endnote Basic, a free cloud-based version which is more limited in functionality but nevertheless provides many of the core features. Further details can be found at https://www.endnote.com

Zotero has become the tool of choice for many students employing reference management software, not least because of its attractive price tag (free) and high levels of functionality. Zotero currently offers 300MB of cloud storage for free, to which you can synchronise your reference database for backup and to use across multiple devices, with more storage available to purchase if you need it. Further details can be found at https://www.zotero.org

Paperpile is a cloud-based solution for reference management that was originally developed to work with Google Apps, and so continues to be particularly powerful for those who employ Google Docs for word-processing. Paperpile requires an annual subscription but provides an academic licence option at a reduced cost for those using the service for educational purposes. Further details can be found at https://paperpile.com

Mendeley was created with an emphasis on collaboration and social interaction for research, and for many people that remains one of the key attractions to using this service. It is particularly disposed to sharing your research with other people and likewise seeing what citations others are compiling in their Mendeley libraries. Mendeley can be used as a free service, with a premium option to increase storage space. Further details can be found at https://www.mendeley.com

An important factor to consider is how these RMS packages interface with the word-processing tool that you are using, so that you may incorporate material from your RMS directly into your document. If you are using a desktop tool for writing, then check that your chosen RMS can integrate with this. The most common option here is, of course, Microsoft Word, and most packages come with a plugin for Word that will allow you to 'pull' references directly from your RMS into your document (for instance, EndNote, Zotero, Paperpile, and Mendeley all facilitate this). If you are using Pages (on Mac OS) then Endnote offers an option for this. If you are opting instead to use a cloud-based word-processing option, most likely Google Docs or Word for the Web, then you'll need to check that your RMS software can dialogue with this (usually through a browser plugin/addon/extension). Paperpile offers a particularly seamless solution for Google Docs (via Google Chrome) and Zotero also integrates well with Google Docs, while Mendeley is compatible with Word for the Web.

Reference management software can be hugely helpful when undertaking your research project, particularly in the late stages when you need to produce your final bibliography. However, even for the most experienced researchers, it is advisable to manually check the bibliography that has been produced for any errors that may have slipped through. This can be alleviated by taking appropriate care when you are first adding the bibliographical reference details to the database. There's an old adage about data entry that says, 'garbage in, garbage out', which essentially means that if the wrong information is entered, or information is entered incorrectly or poorly, then the outputted results will reflect this. With this in mind, it is well worth taking the time to make sure the correct fields are being used and the correct details entered so that your outputted bibliography is as accurate as possible.

9.5 Sourcing Research Participants and Assistance via Social Media

While many people will know and use social media for staying connected with friends and family, it can also be a helpful tool to the novice researcher. In particular, it can prove to be a useful gateway to obtaining help and assistance, such as getting answers to questions from experienced practitioners in the field, and recruiting participants to undertake surveys and interviews. Thomas (2017) weighs the advantages and disadvantages to using social media to help gather data. The benefits include an increased range and diversity of people who can become involved in the research, and that it enables participants to become involved in the research when it is convenient for them. On the other hand, such an approach can exclude those who are not already using that social network, and of course, it requires the researcher to be familiar with how it works, and also that this approach can be quite public (which may not be to everyone's liking).

One good example of this is Twitter, which uses hashtags (#) to group tweets together so that interested parties can track or follow tweets which include that particular hashtag. One of the best known examples of this in education is the hashtag of #edchat, which is used broadly by educators who wish to engage in 'Twitter chats' around educational issues, with more localised versions of this existing at national levels, such as #edchatie for Ireland and #ukedchat for the UK (see Carpenter, Tani, Morrison, and Keane, 2020 for a good exploration of the use of education-related hashtags on Twitter). Hashtags also exist for individual subjects, topics (for instance, #InclusiveEducation), and educational events. Similarly, Facebook is home to a multitude of groups and pages around different educational disciplines and topics where you'll also be able to draw upon expertise and participants.

9.6 Online Surveys

One of the most common approaches to gathering data is the survey, be that qualitative, quantitative, or mixed in nature (please see Chapters 4 and 5 for discussions on quantitative and qualitative research methods). Increasingly, internet-based surveys have gained popularity over traditional paper-based formats for a number of reasons. By comparison, they are usually more cost-effective in terms of production (printing), dissemination and return (particularly if this was to be undertaken by post), and extraction/compilation of data (if this had to be manually inputted from paper-based questionnaires into data analysis software). They are usually relatively easy to set up and distribute, and in most cases the submitted data can either be analysed (to some extent) using the software used to produce the questionnaire or downloaded for analysis with additional software. Denscombe (2017) gives a good overview of the general design options for web-based questionnaires. These include:

- A range of pre-existing designs and templates to choose from, either 'as is' or to adapt. Usually you can choose background colour, fonts and layouts, as well as insert logos and other features to personalise the questionnaire.
- A variety of question types, such as single option (radio button), multiple choice (checkboxes and drop-down menus), rank-order questions, and open-ended textboxes.
- Options for ordering questions, such as a set layout, or randomised order, or a branching structure (whereby the respondent's answer determines where they go next in the questionnaire).
- Response options, such as making chosen questions mandatory or to leave questions as optional.

There are many options available to you for constructing and disseminating an online survey. Two of the simplest and most accessible solutions are Google Forms and Microsoft Forms; this is particularly the case if you are based in an institution which uses either the Google or Microsoft ecosystem as it means you probably already have access to the relevant Forms option. By comparison to more advanced survey design software, these options make it relatively simple to create a basic survey and distribute it to invited participants; these surveys are also easy to use from a participant's perspective, and the submitted responses can be downloaded to a Google Sheet or Excel spreadsheet for further analysis. They will also generate basic visual representations, such as pie-charts and bar-graphs, from the responses submitted for the survey.

Those who require a more advanced option (or who do not have access or permission to use the options above) should check if their institution makes any particular online survey software available to students and staff;

for instance, one particular package that is becoming increasingly popular in higher education is Qualtrics (https://www.qualtrics.com/). Qualtrics is a powerful survey software, offering over a hundred question types and with in-built analysis tools. If you don't have access to it through your institution, Qualtrics offers a free account option which (at time of writing) allows you to have one active survey with a choice of eight question types and to receive up to 100 responses.

9.7 Conducting Interviews and Focus Groups via Videoconferencing

Alongside questionnaires, interviews and focus groups are among the most popular approaches used by novice researchers to gather data. In recent times the use of synchronous ('real-time' or 'live') videoconferencing facilities to conduct these interviews has grown in popularity for a number of reasons. It largely negates the financial and time commitments associated with travel for interviews to take place, and indeed it makes the possibility of interviewing international participants significantly more achievable, as well as offering both interviewer and interviewees the convenience to engage in the interview from locations that are mutually convenient for all involved (including their own homes, if they so wish). On the other hand, use of synchronous videoconferencing requires adequate equipment and sufficient and stable internet connectivity for all involved in order for it to function properly, and the absence of these can cause a range of frustrating problems, such as difficulty connecting to the session, calls dropping, screens freezing, and audio lag, all of which can potentially impact negatively on the interview process. Technical problems can occur with hardware such as microphones and webcams and of course, appropriate safeguards must be observed in order to maintain security and participant privacy.

There are many options to choose from if you wish to use a synchronous meeting platform to conduct interviews or focus groups. At the time of writing, one of the most popular options is Zoom (https://zoom.us) which gained an enormous following during the Covid-19 pandemic due to its relative ease of use. Zoom has a number of features which are particularly helpful for interview purposes, such as the ability to record the meeting and the ability to turn on 'closed captioning' to generate a live transcript that can then be downloaded in text format, giving you a head start in terms of transcribing the interview. See Archibald et al. (2019) for a good overview of using Zoom for qualitative data collection.

Additional popular options include Microsoft Teams (https://www.microsoft.com/microsoft-teams/) and Google Meet (https://meet.google.com/). As we have seen elsewhere in this chapter, these options are particularly attractive if your institution uses either the Google or Microsoft ecosystem as they will already be available to you, will integrate well with other tools within that ecosystem, and are also likely to receive better levels of support within your institution. Other options include Webex (https://www.webex.com/) and, one of the longest established videoconferencing platforms of all, Skype (https://www.skype.com/en/). See Lobe, Morgan and Hoffman (2020) for a brief overview of the platforms mentioned here, along with some of the advantages and disadvantages to using each.

Transcription of interviews

Within the general area of qualitative research, a debate often occurs about whether one should transcribe their own interview recordings or outsource the recordings to a professional transcriber. For those who opt to transcribe their own interviews, they have full control over the formatting of the transcript, they have familiarity with any discipline-specific terms that might be used, and perhaps most importantly, transcribing one's audio presents a valuable opportunity to become more acquainted with the data. On the other hand, the process of transcription can be quite time consuming and frustrating, particularly for those who are not adept at typing at a fast rate. Outsourcing to a professional transcriber can greatly speed up the process and allow the researcher to begin analysis quicker; however, transcription can prove costly, particularly if there is a lot of it to be done, and sometimes the transcriber might miss the significance of a key point or misunderstand the pronunciation of a discipline-specific term or word.

Not surprisingly, there are also software options to assist with the transcription of interviews. 'Dragon Naturally Speaking' has a well-established reputation for accurate transcription and features available to assist with this; Dragon is a commercial package and can be found at https://www.nuance.com/dragon.html. It is also possible to find cloud-based services that will automate the transcription work for you, such as Otter (https://otter.ai). The outputs from an Otter transcription are impressive: it will add timestamps to the transcript and differentiate between speakers, and it will link the transcript to the audio file (so for instance, if you wish to hear the exact audio attached to a particular section of the interview, you can jump directly to that audio via the transcript). Otter is a commercial service with more limited options for the free account holder (such as limits on the number of audio files you can import and monthly transcription quotas) but you may find that these limits are sufficient for your project. As outlined earlier, however, it is critical that you establish that your institution permits the use of such third-party services, and if so, what stipulations might apply (for instance, with regard to informed consent for participants).

Recently, something of a middle-ground has emerged as a number of word-processing packages have incorporated voice recognition and dictation options. In Microsoft Word, for instance, the 'dictate' option gives access to a powerful voice transcription facility. When this is activated and the 'dictate' dialogue box is 'listening', speak as clearly as possible and at a moderate pace; you'll see the words you speak converted to text on the screen. The transcription won't always be perfect, there will likely be some mistakes and errors, but for the most part you'll usually find that the transcription is quite accurate. You can add punctuation and formatting by saying such things as 'comma', 'full stop', 'new paragraph', and so on. With regard to transcribing a recorded interview, you can either play the audio file from a separate device (such as your smartphone or an MP3 recorder) that you hold in range of the computer's microphone, or else play the file directly on the computer with the volume turned up. Either way, you'll see Microsoft Word endeavouring to transcribe the audio verbatim. When you see the results, you'll understand why this approach might be best described as a middle ground between manually transcribing the audio yourself and outsourcing it to a professional transcription service. It will almost certainly be much faster than the speed at which many people could transcribe the audio, you'll get to hear the actual voices and their emphasis, and you'll also have that opportunity to get to know your data a bit better. It will, however, probably contain some errors that you'll need to fix, and it will be without some formatting (you'll find, for instance, that some full stops will usually be missing).

If you are using Word for the Web you'll have another option, which is to upload the audio file (such as .mp3 or .wav) for transcription. While there are even more advanced and helpful features available using this option, there are also limits on the file size and how much audio you can have transcribed in a set timeframe. Those who use Google Docs will notice that it too has a dictation facility, which it calls 'voice typing'. Currently, this facility works very well for direct voice-to-text transcription but will usually not work for playing back a recorded audio file; workarounds have been suggested for this, such as speaking aloud the recorded interview as you listen to it via headphones.

9.8 Data Analysis Software

It is often said that computers or software don't analyse data: people do. Nevertheless, another important (and one of the most frequent) use of digital technologies for research purposes is that of analysis of the data obtained, be that qualitative or quantitative in nature (again, please see Chapters 4 and 5 for further detail on these).

Braun and Clarke (2013) overview the various advantages and disadvantages to using software packages for analysis of qualitative data (often known as CAQDAS – computer-assisted qualitative data analysis software). Among the advantages they list (see their book, *Successful Qualitative Research: a practical guide for beginners,* for the fuller discussion) are that the use of such software can increase the organisation of data, coding and analysis, that it can increase efficiency and make the processes of coding and analysis quicker, that it can help increase rigour with regard to coding and analysis, and that it is helpful for managing large data sets. On the other hand, the cost of purchasing such software can be problematic as it is often expensive, it may not be possible to spend the necessary time learning how to properly use new software in a relatively time-limited project, and the temptation may occur to over-code or to use features of the programme not necessary for your analysis.

There are many options to choose from for CAQDAS, with some of the better-known ones being NVivo (https://www.qsrinternational.com/), ATLAS.ti (https://atlasti.com), MAXQDA (https://www.maxqda.com/), and QDA Miner (https://provalisresearch.com/). These packages are increasingly powerful and have evolved over time to incorporate a range of functions with regard to organising, analysing, querying, structuring, and displaying data (see Cohen, Mannion and Morrison (2018) for a good list of these functionalities). Generally speaking, however, CAQDAS software is not inexpensive, and you should check with your institution to see if it has arrangements in place to make any of these (or other) CAQDAS packages available to students. For those who do not have access to such an option, or may just prefer a more simplified approach, you may wish to try QDA Miner Lite, a free but more limited version of the commercial QDA Miner software package. While not equipped with as many features as some of the other packages listed here, QDA Miner Lite will enable you to undertake many of the fundamental tasks associated with qualitative data analysis software, such as importing documents, applying codes to segments of text, and adding comments (or memos) to coded segments.

Discussions around using software for analysis of quantitative data tend to be more decisive. This is mainly because of the quantity of data commonly associated with such projects, and also because analysis of quantitative data usually depends upon the application of statistical formulae which, while not impossible to do without using software, is certainly more cumbersome to do without it. In this regard, the question is often not whether you will use software if undertaking quantitative analysis, but rather, what software you will use.

There is little doubt that the best-known software package for quantitative analysis is SPSS (https://www.ibm.com/analytics/spss-statistics-software).

There are many advantages to using SPSS for quantitative analysis. The popularity of SPSS within educational research circles means that user guides, supports and resources to assist with using it are plentiful. SPSS can handle huge amounts of data, and has been steadily developed and updated (at the time of writing SPSS is on its 28th version) with the effect that the functionality and interface have continued to develop over time. However, as is often the case with powerful software for data analysis, the cost can prove prohibitive for the individual novice researcher and so you should check with your institution to see if it makes SPSS available to students and staff (many institutions do). It is also sometimes suggested that the use of SPSS may be excessive for small-scale research projects and that the levels of analysis often expected of such projects can be achieved with more readily available software such as Microsoft Excel or Google Sheets; indeed, many general research methods books and guides will tend towards Excel when considering more basic quantitative analysis for this very reason. In this regard, it is recommended to establish the types of statistical analysis you will need to undertake before making decisions about whether to employ more advanced analysis packages like SPSS, or whether these outcomes might be achieved using simpler and more easily-available spreadsheet software.

For those who wish to pursue a free or open-source option, one of the better-known dedicated packages for statistical analysis is PSPP (https://www.gnu.org/software/pspp/) which, according to its website, is 'designed as a free replacement for SPSS' (although the range of features and functionalities is more limited in PSPP). Increasingly, R is gaining popularity as a 'free software environment for statistical computing and graphics' (https://www.r-project.org/). The learning curve for installing and using R is, however, steeper and so as this time is less likely to be the first choice for novice researchers undertaking a relatively small-scale research project, although current indications are that this will gain more prevalence for statistical analysis in the future.

All of the software options listed above for both qualitative and quantitative analysis are device-based. If your preference is for a cloud-based software as a service approach, you may wish to explore Dedoose (https://www.dedoose.com/); Dedoose is a commercial offering which requires a monthly fee, but unlike many subscription services it only charges for those months in which the user logs in and uses the platform. The afore-mentioned ATLAS.ti also has a web-based version of its software, accessible via the ATLAS.ti homepage at https://atlasti.com, and as mentioned earlier in this chapter, Qualtrics (https://www.qualtrics.com/) comes with in-built functionality for analysis of data (including the ability to import data that was not captured using a Qualtrics survey).

Grammar guidance

It goes without saying that you want to produce and submit academic work that is as error-free as possible. The word-processor that you are using to write your document will provide some assistance with this, such as highlighting what it considers to be incorrect spelling or grammatical errors. There are, however, additional services that you can avail of to further assist in this regard, with probably the best-known of these being Grammarly (https://www.grammarly.com/). Grammarly is, according to its website, an artificial intelligence powered application which suggests corrections to grammatical mistakes and helps make writing more understandable. The free version of Grammarly (which requires signup and login) will highlight what it considers to be issues with spelling, grammar, and punctuation, while the premium commercial version offers additional features such as tone adjustment, plagiarism detection, and additional word choice suggestions. Grammarly can be accessed in a number of ways, including a desktop app, an add-in for Microsoft Word, and a browser extension/plug-in which means it can be utilised in services accessed via a web browser such as Google Docs and Word for the Web. Several studies have investigated the use of Grammarly by students and the effects of its usage on their writing. One small-scale investigation by Cavaleri and Dianati (2016), for instance, found that students considered their use of the service had improved their writing and understanding of grammatical concepts and rules, and that students can benefit from Grammarly's individual instruction and the self-access nature of the tool; the authors also caution however that while such services are helpful, they should not be viewed as a panacea for grammatical guidance and that students should carefully consider each suggestion in light of sometimes flawed recommendations.

9.9 Conclusion

This chapter has broadly overviewed some of the ways in which technology can assist in planning, undertaking, and completing your research project. The topics and options outlined above are by no means conclusive, but rather serve as a starting point from which you can investigate further. One of the best pieces of advice for any novice researcher is to make yourself aware of the supports, workshops, guides and tutorials on offer from your own institution (in particular, the library) with regard to the use of digital technologies for research; these resources are always superb and well worth engaging with. Ultimately, however, while technology can assist in many ways with the execution of your research project, the more important consideration is not what the technology itself can do, but rather what you do with the technology. As the Hollywood editor and director Walter Murch once said, 'the word processor is a better tool than a quill pen because you can do so much more with it, but on the other hand, what you have to say and how you say it is the ultimate determination'.

Recommended Reading

Dawson, C. (2019). *A–Z of Digital Research Methods* (London: Routledge).

Paulus, T. M., and Lester, J. N. (2021). *Doing Qualitative Research in a Digital World* (London: SAGE).

Speare, M. (2018). 'Graduate student use and non-use of reference and PDF management software: An exploratory study', in *The Journal of Academic Librarianship*, 44(6), pp 762–774, doi:10.1016/j.acalib.2018.09.019

Corbett, B., and Edwards, A. (2018). 'A case study of Twitter as a research tool', in *Sport in Society*, 21(2), pp 394–412, doi:10.1080/17430437.2017.1342622

References

Archibald, M. M., Ambagtsheer, R. C., Casey, M. G., and Lawless, M. (2019). 'Using Zoom videoconferencing for qualitative data collection: Perceptions and experiences of researchers and participants', in *International Journal of Qualitative Methods*, 18(?), https://doi.org/10.1177/1609406919874596

Braun, V., and Clarke, V. (2013). *Successful Qualitative Research: A Practical Guide for Beginners* (London: SAGE).

Carpenter, J., Tani, T., Morrison, S., and Keane, J. (2020). 'Exploring the landscape of educator professional activity on Twitter: An analysis of 16 education-related Twitter hashtags', in *Professional Development in Education*, 48(5), pp 784–805, https://doi.org/10.1080/19415257.2020.1752287

Cavaleri, M. R., and Dianati, S. (2016). 'You want me to check your grammar again? The usefulness of an online grammar checker as perceived by students', in *Journal of Academic Language and Learning*, 10(1), A223–A236, http://journal.aall.org.au/index.php/jall/article/view/393

Cohen, L., Manion, L., and Morrison, K. (2018). *Research Methods in Education*, 8th edn (New York: Routledge).

Denscombe, M. (2017). *The Good Research Guide: For small-scale social research projects*, 6th edn (London: Open University Press).

Lobe, B., Morgan, D., and Hoffman, K. A. (2020). 'Qualitative data collection in an era of social distancing', in *International Journal of Qualitative Methods*, 19, https://doi.org/10.1177/1609406920937875

Thomas, G. (2017). *How to do your research project: A guide for students* (London: SAGE).

CHAPTER 10

Taighde trí Ghaeilge (Doing Your Research through Irish)

Clíona Murray, Scoil an Oideachais agus Niall Mac Uidhilin, Acadamh na hOllscolaíochta Gaeilge, OÉG

Gluais & Giorrúcháin

Teideal	Nod
An tAonad um Oideachas Gaeltachta	AOG
An Chomhairle um Oideachas Gaeltachta & Gaelscolaíochta	COGG
Comhchreat Tagartha na hEorpa um Theangacha *(Common European Framework of Reference for Languages)*	CTET *(CEFR)*
An Bunachar Náisiúnta Téarmaíochta don Ghaeilge *(The National Terminology Database for Irish)*	FCÁT
Polasaí don Oideachas Gaeltachta 2017 – 2022	POG
An Roinn Oideachais agus Scileanna	ROS
Straitéis 20 Bliain don Ghaeilge	S20

10.0 Réamhrá

Déanann an chaibidil seo plé ar thaighde cleachtóir-bhunaithe i réimse na Gaeilge. Tá sí dírithe ar an múinteoir-taighdeoir atá ag iarraidh tabhairt faoi thaighde trí mheán na Gaeilge nó i gcomhthéacs a bhaineann leis an nGaeilge. Tugtar forléargas ar dtús ar stair agus staid reatha na Gaeilge sa chóras oideachais. Tugtar roinnt nodanna ansin maidir leis na téarmaí agus na heochairfhocail a bheidh áisiúil don taighdeoir chun an litríocht sa réimse seo a thuiscint agus a chuardach. Tá an chéad rannóg eile dírithe ar thuiscint chomhthéacsúil an mhúinteora-taighdeora. Déantar plé achoimrithe ar na príomhphointí eolais i ngach ceann de na trí chomhthéacs scolaíochta – scoileanna Gaeltachta, scoileanna lán-Ghaeilge lasmuigh den Ghaeltacht, agus scoileanna lán-Bhéarla – agus tugtar intreoir ghairid ar na curaclaim bhunscoile agus iarbhunscoile. Ar deireadh ansin, tugtar smaointe don mhúinteoir-taighdeoir ar conas an taighde agus an cleachtas a nascadh. Déantar cur síos ar chúpla réimse coitianta taighde, ardaítear roinnt saincheisteanna a eascraíonn ón litríocht taighde agus tugtar blaiseadh ar na cineálacha ceisteanna taighde ar féidir tabhairt fúthu.

Dar ndóigh, níl scóip sa chaibidil seo le gach gné den taighde trí Ghaeilge a phlé go mion. Is éard atá inti ná ábhar machnaimh don taighdeoir atá ag tosú ar thionscnamh a dhearadh. Seachas liosta críochnúil tagairtí, luaitear roinnt príomhshaothar taighde agus beartais oideachais tábhachtacha ionas gur féidir leis an taighdeoir breis léitheoireachta a dhéanamh orthu siúd atá ábhartha dá chomhthéacs taighde féin. Áit a bhfuil teacht ar shaothar taighde trí Ghaeilge, tugtar an tagairt sin agus moltar don taighdeoir na saothair seo a úsáid mar threoir ar conas tabhairt faoin scríbhneoireacht acadúil trí Ghaeilge.

10.1 An Ghaeilge sa Chóras Oideachais

Stair agus cúlra

Cuireadh tús le córas na scoileanna náisiúnta sa bhliain 1831 nuair a bhí tuairim is 23% de phobal na hÉireann ina gcainteoirí dúchais Gaeilge. Níor tugadh aitheantas ar bith don Ghaeilge go dtí 1878 agus is i 1907 a tugadh an Ghaeilge isteach mar ábhar scoile den chéad uair, go príomha de bharr iarrachtaí Chonradh na Gaeilge. Nuair a bunaíodh an Stát i 1922 rinneadh iarracht dháiríre polasaithe athbheochana teanga a fhorbairt. Ó 1948 ar aghaidh ligeadh na maidí le sruth go dtí gur cuireadh roinnt gníomhaíochtaí sa siúl le casadh na mílaoise nua. Léiríonn Tábla 10.1 cuid de na móreachtraí seo.

Tábla 10.1: Móreachtraí i leith na Gaeilge sa Chóras Oideachais.

Bliain	Móreachtraí i Leith na Gaeilge sa Chóras Oideachais
1920í – 1940í	Bunú an tSaorstáit; Gaeilge fógartha mar 'theanga náisiúnta'; Foilsítear iliomad polasaithe athbheochan teanga i réimsí an Oideachais, na Gaeltachta, na Státseirbhíse agus caighdeánaithe teanga.
1950í	Titim mhór i líon na scoileanna tumoideachais taobh amuigh den Ghaeltacht; An Caighdeán Oifigiúil foilsithe.
1960í	Athrú ar rialacha maidir le ceapadh múinteoirí bunscoile; Dúntar na Coláistí Ullmhúcháin; Níl mórán scoileanna fágtha atá ag feidhmiú trí Ghaeilge sa tír.
1970í + 1980í	Iarrachtaí á ndéanamh ag tuismitheoirí scoileanna lán-Ghaeilge a bhunú taobh amuigh den Ghaeltacht – bunú na heagraíochta Gaelscoileanna le 16 Ghaelscoil (1973); Tacaíochtaí Stát sa Ghaeltacht – m.sh. bunú Údarás na Gaeltachta & Raidió na Gaeltachta.

Bliain	Móreachtraí i Leith na Gaeilge sa Chóras Oideachais
1990í	Bunú An Foras Pátrúnachta; Bunú Teilifís na Gaeilge / TG4; Foilsítear An tAcht Oideachais (1998) a thugann freagrachtaí do scoileanna sa Ghaeltacht maidir le caomhnú na teanga; Bunaítear An Chomhairle um Oideachas Gaeltachta agus Gaelscolaíochta (COGG); Foilsítear Curaclam cumarsáideach na mbunscoileanna (1999).
2000í	Foilsítear go leor taighde faoin nGaeilge agus faoin nGaeltacht a chuidíonn le réiteach Straitéis 20 Bliain don Ghaeilge (*S20*) (2010),
2010í	Spreagann *S20* athbhreithniú iomlán ar ról na teanga sa chóras oideachais (curaclaim, polasaithe, srl.), sa Ghaeltacht (26 cheantar ag réiteach pleananna teanga, srl.) agus go náisiúnta (breis seirbhísí poiblí trí Ghaeilge, srl.). *Foilseacháin thábhachtacha: Straitéis 20 Bliain don Ghaeilge; Acht na Gaeltachta; Sonraíocht nua don tSraith Shóisearach; Polasaí don Oideachas Gaeltachta; Curaclam Teanga na Bunscoile; Dréachtshonraíocht nua don Ardteist.*

Staid reatha na Gaeilge sa chóras oideachais

Múintear an Ghaeilge mar chroí-ábhar i mbunscoileanna agus in iarbhunscoileanna uile na tíre ach déanann na polasaithe oideachais agus na curaclaim idirdhealú idir trí chomhthéacs éagsúla bunaithe ar theanga na scoile agus timpeallacht teangeolaíochta an phobail:

1) Scoileanna Gaeltachta – scoileanna lán-Ghaeilge sa Ghaeltacht atá aitheanta faoin bPolasaí Oideachais Gaeltachta [POG] (ROS, 2016)
2) Gaelscoileanna/Gaelcholáistí – scoileanna lán-Ghaeilge lasmuigh den Ghaeltacht
3) Scoileanna lán-Bhéarla – na scoileanna eile sa tír (tá líon beag i gceantair Ghaeltachta laga)

Is in Acht Oideachais 1998 a rinneadh idirdhealú den chéad uair idir scoileanna bunaithe ar theanga teagaisc na scoile. Ó dhearcadh an oideachais lán-Ghaeilge tugadh Scoileanna T1 ar an dá chineál scoil lán-Ghaeilge agus Scoileanna T2 ar na scoileanna lán-Bhéarla. Tá an t-idirdhealú sin á chur i bhfeidhm de réir a chéile ó shin. Úsáideann an litríocht taighde na téarmaí cainteoir T1 (cainteoir dúchais[1] T1) agus cainteoir T2 (foghlaimeoir T2) nuair atá plé á dhéanamh ar theoiricí foghlama teanga agus réimsí gaolmhara. Bíonn cainteoirí T1 Gaeilge agus cainteoirí T2 Gaeilge ag freastal ar Scoileanna T1. Cruthaíonn sé seo dúshláin sna ceantair láidre

Gaeltachta ach go háirithe mar go mbíonn múinteoirí ag iarraidh freastal ar raon leathan riachtanas ó thaobh cúrsaí forbairt teanga de. Léiríonn Tábla 10.1 go bhfuilimid i lár tréimhse forbartha le polasaithe á dtógáil ar Straitéis 20 Bliain don Ghaeilge 2010 – 2030 [*S20*]. Léirigh taighde a rinneadh roimh fhoilsiú na straitéise go raibh caighdeán na teanga ag meath sa chóras oideachais (Harris, Forde, Archer, Nic Fhearaile & O'Gorman, 2006) agus mar theanga phobail sna ceantair Ghaeltachta (Ó Giollagáin, Mac Donnacha, Ní Chualáin, Ní Shéaghdha & O'Brien, 2007). Chuidigh an *S20* leis an státchóras a thuiscint go raibh gá le hathbhreithniú ar an gcóras oideachais i leith teagasc/sealbhú na Gaeilge ón luath-oideachas go dtí deireadh na meánscoile agus go raibh gá le leanúnachas idir na curaclaim a aithníonn go bhfuil gach páiste ag staid éagsúil i sealbhú a c(h)éad, dara teanga nó tríú teanga fiú.

I measc torthaí an athbhreithnithe seo foilsíodh Polasaí don Oideachas Gaeltachta 2017 – 2022 (2016), sonraíocht nua don tSraith Shóisearach, curaclam teanga nua don bhunscoil (2019) agus dréachtshonraíocht nua don Ardteist. Níl mórán fianaise bailithe go fóill ar éifeachtaí na bpolasaithe nua agus is réimse é seo ina mbeadh neart deiseanna taighde torthúla.

Liosta eagraíochtaí

Is fiú don taighdeoir a bheith ar an eolas faoi na heagraíochtaí a bhíonn ag plé leis an oideachas trí Ghaeilge. Tá go leor taighde curtha i gcrích ag cuid acu agus is fiú go mór cuairt a thabhairt ar a láithreáin gréasáin. I measc na n-eagraíochtaí a bunaíodh thar na blianta tá Gaelscoileanna Teo. (1973, Gaeloideachas ó 2014) a dhéanann ionadaíocht ar na scoileanna T1; An Chomhairle um Oideachas Gaeltachta agus Gaelscolaíochta (COGG) (1998) a fhreastalaíonn ar riachtanais oideachais na scoileanna lán-Ghaeilge trí chomhairle agus acmhainní a chur ar fáil agus taighde a choimisiúnú; An Foras Pátrúnachta (1993) a fheidhmíonn mar phátrún ar fhormhór na scoileanna T1; An Fóram Gaeloideachais Bhoird Oideachais & Oiliúna Éireann (2010) a thacaíonn le scoileanna lán-Ghaeilge atá faoi phátrúnacht na mBord Oideachais & Oiliúna; An tAonad um Oideachas Gaeltachta (AOG) (2016) a dhéanann comhordú ar chur i bhfeidhm an POG.

10.2 Téarmaí Cuardaithe

Ba cheart go gcuideodh an t-eolas comhthéacsúil thuasluaite le taighdeoir tabhairt faoin tóraíocht sa litríocht taighde. Teastaíonn liosta téarmaíochta iomlán trí Ghaeilge agus trí Bhéarla le cinntiú gur cuardach cuimsitheach atá ann. Léiríonn Tábla 10.2 roinnt téarmaí féideartha ag brath ar chomhthéacs an taighde. Tabhair faoi deara nach téarmaí comhchiallacha iad na téarmaí gaolmhara. Luaitear iad le deis a thabhairt don taighdeoir fáil amach faoi chuid de na comhthéacsanna éagsúla ar fud an domhain. Mar shampla, d'fhéadfadh alt faoi mhúineadh 'teanga oidhreachta' i Meiriceá a bheith spéisiúil ach níor mhór don taighdeoir in Éirinn luacháil a dhéanamh ar na cosúlachtaí/difríochtaí idir an comhthéacs sin agus a chomhthéacs féin.

Tábla 10.2: Téarmaí Cuardaithe Féideartha

Téarma + téarmaí gaolmhara	Term + related terms
aisiompú teanga; athbheochan teanga; athneartú ~; cothú ~; saibhriú ~;	reversing language shift; ~ revival; ~ revitalisation; ~ maintenance; ~ enrichment;
aistriú teanga; bás ~;	language shift; ~ death;
beartas teanga	language policy
cainteoir teanga 1 (T1); cainteoir teanga (T2); ~ dúchais; ~ nua;	first language (L1) speaker; second language (L2) ~; native ~; new ~;
dátheangachas; ~ suimitheach; ~ dealaitheach; ~ cothrom; ~ éagothrom; ilteangachas	bilingualism; additive ~; subtractive ~; balanced ~; unbalanced ~; multilingualism
feasacht teanga	language awareness
pleanáil teanga; ~ shealbhaithe; ~ chorpais; ~ stádais;	language planning; acquisition ~; corpus ~; status ~;
mionteanga; teanga neamhfhorleathan; ~ faoi bhagairt; ~ i mbaol; ~ oidhreachta;	minority language; lesser-used ~; threatened ~; endangered ~; heritage ~;
sealbhú teanga	language acquisition
tumoideachas; lán-tumadh; páirt-tumadh;	immersion education; total ~; partial ~;

10.3 Comhthéacs an Chleachtais

Tá an curaclam teanga ag bogadh i dtreo an leanúnachais ag gach leibhéal den chóras oideachais, mar a léirítear i bhFíor 10.1, le snáitheanna coiteanna cosúil leis an bhfeasacht teanga agus scileanna cumarsáide. Aithnítear sna hathruithe ar churaclam teanga na bunscoile agus na hiarbhunscoile go bhfuil riachtanais éagsúla ag pobail scoile éagsúla i leith na Gaeilge. Tá dhá leagan ar leith den churaclam Gaeilge forbartha don dá chomhthéacs scoile (T1 agus T2) suas go dtí leibhéal na Sraithe Sóisearaí. Tá an dá leagan atá á bhforbairt don Ardteist ag dul trí phróiseas comhairliúcháin faoi láthair.

Fíor 10.1: Fís nua do sholáthar churaclaim teanga comhtháite (ROS, 2019)[2]

Na trí chomhthéacs scolaíochta

<u>Comhthéacs T1 – Scoileanna Gaeltachta</u>

Aithnítear 3 chatagóir Gaeltachta de réir an sciar cainteoirí laethúla atá sa cheantar: Catagóir A – os cionn 67% den phobal; Catagóir B – 33% – 66% den phobal; Catagóir C – faoi bhun 33% den phobal (Ó Giollagáin et al., 2007). Aithníodh sa *S20* gur ghá an Ghaeilge a neartú sna suíomhanna leochaileacha sochtheangeolaíocha seo. Toisc go bhfuil scoileanna ar cheann de na suíomhanna is tábhachtaí chun meath teanga a mhoilliú agus a thiontú, cuireadh próiseas comhairliúcháin agus taighde ar bun chun polasaí teanga do na ceantair seo a fhorbairt.

Foilsíodh an POG sa bhliain 2016. Is í an phríomhaidhm atá ag an bPolasaí ná a chinntiú go gcuirtear oideachas ardchaighdeáin agus ábhartha trí mheán na Gaeilge ar fáil do mhuintir na Gaeltachta, chun tacú le húsáid na Gaeilge mar phríomhtheanga an phobail sna ceantair sin. Cruthaíodh AOG taobh istigh den ROS le cur i bhfeidhm an Pholasaithe a chomhordú. De réir an *Scéim Aitheantais Scoileanna Gaeltachta* a foilsíodh mar chuid den POG, tá 11 chritéar teanga-bhunaithe le comhlíonadh ag scoil leis an stádas *Scoil Ghaeltachta* a bhaint amach. Tá 115 bhunscoil agus 29 n-iarbhunscoil páirteach sa scéim sa seacht gceantar Gaeltachta.

<u>Comhthéacs T1 – Scoileanna lán-Ghaeilge</u>

Is scoileanna iad seo atá lonnaithe lasmuigh den Ghaeltacht agus a leanann múnla an tumoideachais. Go coitianta, glaoitear Gaelscoileanna ar na bunscoileanna agus Gaelcholáistí ar na hiarbhunscoileanna. Is earnáil í an ghaelscolaíocht ina bhfuil borradh mór i líon na scoileanna, go háirithe ag leibhéal na bunscoile. Faoi láthair, tá 150 bunscoil agus 47 n-iarbhunscoil i gceist (thart ar 8% de scoileanna na tíre). I ndiaidh stocaireachta a léirigh go raibh éileamh ann don scolaíocht lán-Ghaeilge, tá coinníoll anois i dtreoirlínte pleanáil scoile go gcaithfear an leibhéal soláthair trí mheán na Gaeilge sa cheantar a chur san áireamh nuair atá pátrún á roghnú do bhunscoileanna nua.

I roinnt cásanna ag leibhéal na hiarbhunscoile is aonad nó sraith atá sa Ghaelcholáiste laistigh de scoil lán-Bhéarla. De bharr na ndeacrachtaí a bhíonn ann leis an tumoideachas a chur chun cinn in aonaid mar seo, tugadh isteach múnla nua i 2021 ina mbeidh aonaid lán-Ghaeilge nasctha le Gaelcholáistí neamhspleácha seachas le scoileanna lán-Bhéarla. Is 'satailít' faoi choimirce Gaelcholáiste eile a bheidh i gceist leis na haonaid lán-Ghaeilge seo.

Comhthéacs T2 – Scoileanna lán-Bhéarla

Déantar staidéar ar an nGaeilge mar chroí-ábhar sna bunscoileanna agus sna hiarbhunscoileanna lán-Bhéarla (seachas daltaí a bhfuil díolúine faighte acu). Mar sin féin, léiríonn figiúirí an daonáirimh maidir le labhairt na Gaeilge nach labhraíonn mórán foghlaimeoirí an teanga tar éis dóibh an scoil a fhágáil (CSO 2017). Tá an croí-stádas seo ag an nGaeilge mar gurb í an chéad teanga oifigiúil sa Bhunreacht agus aithnítear sa *S20* an ról agus an fiúntas atá ag an nGaeilge agus an leibhéal tacaíochta atá ag teastáil sa chóras lán-Bhéarla:

> Chun na críche seo, déanfar infheistíocht fheabhsaithe i bhforbairt phroifisiúnta agus i dtacaíocht leanúnach do mhúinteoirí mar aon le i soláthar téacsleabhar agus acmhainní, agus i dtacaíocht do mhodhanna nuálacha teagaisc agus foghlama. (*S20*, lch. 21)

Tá an bhéim a leagtar ar ghnéithe éagsúla den teanga agus den ábhar athraithe thar na blianta, ag bogadh ó churaclam dírithe ar thraschur agus an teanga scríofa i dtreo an bhéim a leagtar faoi láthair ar chumas cumarsáide agus scileanna litearthachta inaistrithe.

Tháinig ardú leanúnach ar líon na ndaltaí sna scoileanna lán-Bhéarla a lorg díolúine ón nGaeilge ó na 1990í ar aghaidh agus faoi 2018 bhí díolúine faighte ag 9% den daonra iarbhunscoile. Rinneadh comhairliúchán poiblí ar na coinníollacha maidir le díolúintí i 2019 agus cuireadh polasaí leasaithe i bhfeidhm i 2020. Faoin bpolasaí seo, is féidir le dalta díolúine a fháil ar chúiseanna a bhaineann le riachtanais speisialta oideachais agus leis an achar ama atá caite ag an dalta sa tír.

An Ghaeilge sa bhunscoil

Foilsíodh dhá leagan de churaclam teanga nua na bunscoile dírithe ar scoileanna lán-Ghaeilge agus ar scoileanna lán-Bhéarla (ROS, 2019). Tá na spriocanna comhtháite céanna acu do T1 agus T2 na scoile seachas go bhfuil moltaí breise sa cheann T1 (Gaeilge) do na scoileanna Gaeltachta. Leagtar béim mhór sa dá leagan ar bhuntáistí an dátheangachais agus spreagtar aistriú scileanna ó theanga amháin go teanga eile. Aithnítear freisin go bhfuil go leor páistí nach iad an Ghaeilge ná an Béarla a T1 agus go bhfuil cothú teanga bhaile an pháiste ríthábhachtach.

Is curaclam tumoideachais é an curaclam T1. I gcás na Scoileanna Gaeltachta, tá tréimhse lán-tumtha luath riachtanach don chéad dá bhliain scolaíochta, rud a chuireann múineadh an Bhéarla siar go dtí tús Rang 1. Moltar an cur chuige céanna do na Gaelscoileanna ach go mbeadh sé seo pléite agus aontaithe ag páirtithe leasmhara na scoile ar dtús. Tá moltaí sainiúla ann do na scoileanna Gaeltachta maidir le cén chaoi is fearr an éagsúlacht líofachta sa seomra ranga a láimhseáil agus an saibhriú teanga a chur chun cinn le 'cuidiú le líon na ndaoine a labhraíonn Gaeilge sa Ghaeltacht a mhéadú' (ROS, 2019).

Ceann de na forbairtí is suntasaí sa churaclam nua ná na contanaim dul chun cinn a leagann amach aistear forbairt teanga inmholta do gach páiste dá T1 agus dá T2. Cuirtear contanam ar fáil do gach toradh foghlama a bhaineann leis na 3 ghné forbartha teanga – *cumarsáid*, *tuiscint* agus *fiosrú / úsáid* le haghaidh gach ceann de na 3 mhórshnáithe sa churaclam – *Teanga ó Bhéal*, *Léitheoireacht* agus *Scríbhneoireacht*.

Léiríonn Fíor 10.2 leagan amach contanaim samplach – 'Cur síos, tuar agus machnamh' don Teanga Ó Bhéal (T1). Is féidir suas le 4 thoradh foghlama a shonrú (le haghaidh 4 chéim na scoile) agus 11 mhionchéim dul chun cinn (a-k, sonraí fágtha ar lár) a shonraíonn aistear forbairt teanga tipiciúil don pháiste i ngné amháin den Teanga. I gcás an churaclaim T1, is féidir tréithe breise a shonrú dírithe ar dhaltaí T1.

Fíor 10.2: Leagan amach contanaim dul chun cinn i gCuraclam Teanga na Bunscoile (T1) (ROS, 2019)

Tá an curaclam teanga do na scoileanna T2 mórán mar a chéile leis an gceann T1 ach go bhfuil babhtáil déanta ar thorthaí foghlama an T1 agus an T2.

An Ghaeilge san iarbhunscoil

Déantar iarracht múnla tumoideachais a chur i bhfeidhm sna hiarbhunscoileanna T1 (Scoileanna Gaeltachta aitheanta agus Gaelcholáistí). Ní éiríonn le gach scoil an múnla seo a chur i bhfeidhm go foirfe, áfach, mar gheall ar ghanntanas múinteoirí ábhar atá sách líofa sa Ghaeilge. Ó thaobh mhúineadh na Gaeilge de, leantar an tsonraíocht T1 ag leibhéal na Sraithe Sóisearaí agus ansin an tsonraíocht chomónta don Ardteist (atá i lár athbhreithnithe faoi láthair).

Aithníonn sonraíocht T1 na sraithe sóisearaí an tábhacht a bhaineann le 'eispéireas foghlama teanga saibhrithe' a chur ar fáil do chainteoirí dúchais agus foghlaimeoirí i scoileanna T1. Is iad forbairt, saibhriú agus buanú scileanna teanga atá mar aidhmeanna na sonraíochta. Tá trí shnáithe chomhtháite sa tsonraíocht: *cumas cumarsáide, feasacht teanga agus chultúrtha*, agus *féinfheasacht an fhoghlaimeora*, mar a léirítear i bhFíor 10.3. Tagann na torthaí foghlama a bhaineann leo le leibhéal B2 ar an CTET.

Tá na snáitheanna céanna i sonraíocht T2 na sraithe sóisearaí ach go dtagann na torthaí foghlama sa tsonraíocht seo le leibhéal A2-B1 ar an CTET. Aithnítear gur minic a bhíonn foghlaimeoirí T2 spleách go hiomlán ar an seomra ranga Gaeilge mar nach bhfuil pobal teanga Gaeilge ar fáil go héasca dóibh. Leagtar béim, mar sin, ar naisc a chothú leis an bpobal teanga ionas go dtiocfaidh forbairt ar dhearcthaí na ndaltaí i leith na teanga agus go n-aithneofar í mar theanga bheo. Tá sé mar aidhm ag an tsonraíocht tacú le daltaí deiseanna úsáide teanga a aimsiú, teacht ar eiseamláirí dílse teanga agus páirt a ghlacadh i bpobal na Gaeilge.

Fíor 10.3: Snáitheanna sa tSraith Shóisearach (mar an gcéanna sna sonraíochtaí T1 agus T2) (ROS, 2015a)

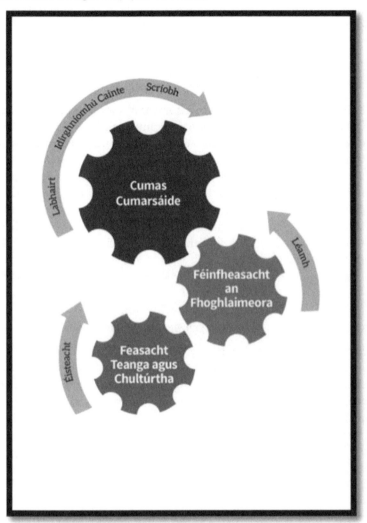

Tá athbhreithniú á dhéanamh faoi láthair ar shonraíocht na hArdteiste. Tógann na dréachtshonraíochtaí ar an bhfoghlaim sa chontanam teanga ón mbunscoil ar aghaidh agus tá sonraíochtaí ar leith ann do na suíomhanna T1 agus T2. Bíodh is go n-aithnítear gur forbairt dhearfach atá ann sonraíocht T2 a bheith ar fáil chun freastal ar riachtanais na bhfoghlaimeoirí i scoileanna lán-Bhéarla, tá ceisteanna ardaithe maidir leis an leibhéal ionchais, go háirithe mar nach bhfuil Bonnleibhéal ann a thuilleadh, leibhéal a thug deis d'fhoghlaimeoirí nach mbeadh ar a dtoil tabhairt faoin nGnáthleibhéal. Tá ceisteanna ann faoin tsonraíocht T1 chomh maith mar go maítear go mbeidh dúshláin ann daltaí a mhealladh i dtreo na sonraíochta sin mar go bhfuil dearcadh ann go mbeadh breis oibre i gceist léi.

10.4 Taighde agus Cleachtas a Nascadh

Mar mhúinteoir-taighdeoir, is gá smaoineamh faoi na cineálacha téamaí taighde atá ábhartha don chomhthéacs ina bhfuil tú ag obair. Tugtar forléargas sa rannóg seo ar dhá réimse taighde atá ábhartha do gach comhthéacs – *An Tumoideachas agus an Fhoghlaim Chomhtháite Ábhair agus Teanga* agus *An Sealbhú Teanga agus Scileanna Teanga* – ansin pléitear roinnt deiseanna taighde a bhaineann le comhthéacsanna ar leith. Léargas ar roinnt féidearthachtaí taighde atá anseo seachas liosta críochnúil nó plé cuimsitheach. Beidh na caibidlí eile sa leabhar seo úsáideach chun modheolaíochtaí agus cuir chuige oiriúnacha a roghnú chun tabhairt faoin taighde i réimse na Gaeilge.

Réimsí taighde

<u>An tumoideachas agus an fhoghlaim chomhtháite ábhair agus teanga</u>

Is réimse laistigh den oideachas dátheangach agus ilteangach é an tumoideachas a tháinig chun cinn i gCeanada sna 1960í le tumoideachas sa bhFraincis. I suíomh tumoideachais, déantar an teagasc agus an fhoghlaim ar fad trí mheán na sprioctheanga. Go hiondúil is í an scoil an príomhshuíomh teagmhála leis an sprioctheanga, is é sin le rá nach í an sprioctheanga sa scoil tumoideachais príomhtheanga cumarsáide an phobail i gceantar na scoile. Tagann daltaí isteach sa chóras tumoideachais ar chomhchaighdeán (srianta) sa sprioctheanga agus is é an dátheangachas suimitheach atá mar aidhm leis an gcóras, sa mhéid is go mbeadh sé mar chuspóir go ndéanfaí forbairt ar T1 agus T2 an dalta araon i rith a t(h)réimhse scolaíochta. Leantar cur chuige cumarsáideach agus idirghníomhach sa tumoideachas chun sealbhú teanga agus scileanna cumarsáide an dalta a fhorbairt. Dar ndóigh, le go mbeadh tumoideachas éifeachtach, tá gá le múinteoirí le hardscileanna teanga sa sprioctheanga.

Ceann de na dúshláin i suíomhanna tumoideachais ná gur minic a fheictear sealbhú neamhiomlán sa sprioctheanga agus go mbíonn éifeacht ag an idirtheanga agus trasnaíl teanga ar an teanga a shealbhaítear, go háirithe maidir le scileanna ginchumais, feasacht teanga, cruinneas agus foghraíocht. D'fhéadfadh go mbeadh scileanna cumarsáide na ndaltaí srianta mar go mbíonn an teagasc dírithe ar theanga riachtanach an ábhair, le heaspa béime ar theanga chomhlántach. Forbraíodh múnla chun dul i ngleic leis an dúshlán seo ina mbeadh béim staidéartha ar fhoghlaim an ábhair agus ar shealbhú na teanga araon: an Fhoghlaim Chomhtháite Ábhair agus Teanga [FCÁT/CLIL] (Coyle, Hood & Marsh 2010). Tá sé mar chuspóir san FCÁT go mbeadh múinteoirí ní hamháin in ann an t-ábhar agus teanga an ábhair a theagasc ach a bheith in ann bearnaí teangeolaíocha a aithint agus tabhairt faoi fheasacht teanga na ndaltaí a fhorbairt.

Mar chuid den *S20*, tá scéim phíolótach curtha ar bun ag an ROS maidir le páirt-tumadh a chur i bhfeidhm i scoileanna lán-Bhéarla ina mbeadh líon beag ábhar (m.sh. an corpoideachas) á theagasc trí mheán na Gaeilge ag úsáid an mhúnla FCÁT. Tá treoir maidir le modheolaíochtaí FCÁT a úsáid i mbealach atá ailínithe le curaclam teanga na bunscoile don Ghaeilge curtha ar fáil ag an CNCM.

Topaicí/ceisteanna taighde féideartha

- Conas is féidir liom modheolaíochtaí FCÁT a úsáid chun leas na ndaltaí sa seomra ranga Eolaíochta i suíomh tumoideachais?
- Cén éifeacht atá ag an tréimhse luath-thumtha ar scileanna teanga labhartha naíonán i suíomh T1?
- Iniúchadh ar úsáid FCÁT chun an corpoideachas a theagasc trí mheán na Gaeilge i suíomh T2.
- Conas is féidir le múinteoir Gaeilge na Chéad Bhliana tacú le daltaí atá ag aistriú ó shuíomh bunscoile T2 go suíomh iarbhunscoile T1?

Sealbhú teanga agus scileanna teanga

Thar na blianta tá forbairt tagtha ar na modheolaíochtaí teagaisc is coitianta sa seomra ranga le tacú le daltaí a gcuid scileanna teanga a fhorbairt agus a fheabhsú agus aithnítear anois gur fearr modheolaíochtaí atá bunaithe ar chumarsáid idirghníomhach seachas ar an traschur díreach. Tuigtear gur féidir foghlaim ón mbealach ina ndéanann páiste sealbhú ar a c(h)éad teanga chun cur chuige éifeachtach a fhorbairt don fhoghlaimeoir teanga, áit a bhfuil béim ar leibhéal oiriúnach ionchuir sa sprioctheanga atá dílis agus cruinn, chomh maith le neart cleachtadh cumarsáide idirghníomhach. Tá tábhacht ar leith ag baint le scafláil teanga a thugann aghaidh ar an zón neasfhorbartha chun tacú leis an bhfoghlaimeoir tabhairt faoin gcleachtadh seo agus bogadh i dtreo an neamhspleáchais agus an fhéinriar foghlama.

Dar ndóigh, beidh éagsúlachtaí áirithe ann sa chur chuige a thógann tú ag brath ar an suíomh ina bhfuil tú ag obair agus cúlra teanga na ndaltaí sa suíomh sin. É sin ráite, caithfear aird staidéartha a thabhairt ar fhorbairt scileanna teanga na ndaltaí i suíomhanna T1 agus T2 araon. Is éard atá i gceist leis na scileanna teanga ná na scileanna ginchumais (labhairt agus scríobh) agus na scileanna gabhchumais (éisteacht agus léamh), ar a dtugtar freisin uaireanta na scileanna táirgeacha agus gabhálacha. Anuas air sin, is féidir an cúigiú scil a áireamh, an idirchumarsáid, a úsáideann scileanna ginchumais agus gabhchumais araon. Tá an curaclam teanga don Ghaeilge i suíomhanna T1 agus T2 dírithe ar fhorbairt na scileanna teanga seo ar fad agus caithfear mar sin a bheith cinnte go bhfuil na scileanna á gcomhtháthú sna gníomhaíochtaí teagaisc agus foghlama. Is féidir na torthaí foghlama atá faoi na snáitheanna éagsúla sa churaclam teanga agus na tuairiscíní ar na hinniúlachtaí éagsúla sa CTET a úsáid chun cabhrú leat sa phleanáil.

Tá tuiscint ann anois chomh maith go bhfuil scileanna teanga inaistrithe ó theanga go teanga, ach go háirithe i dtaobh na feasachta teanga. Mar a fheicfidh tú sa churaclam teanga, leagtar béim ar fhorbairt na feasachta teanga ionas gur féidir le foghlaimeoirí a gcumais litearthachta agus a gcuid scileanna teanga a fhorbairt i ngach réimse den churaclam. Ní hamháin mar sin gur ag díriú ar scileanna teanga na ndaltaí sa Ghaeilge a bheadh an múinteoir Gaeilge, ach ag tacú le daltaí a gcuid scileanna teanga inaistrithe a fhorbairt. Anuas air sin, ní mór do mhúinteoirí i suíomhanna T1 cuimhneamh agus iad ag teagasc ábhar seachas an Ghaeilge gur ceart aghaidh a thabhairt ar fhorbairt teanga na ndaltaí chomh maith le teagasc an ábhair, mar a luaitear sa rannóg thuas ar an tumoideachas agus an FCÁT.

Topaicí/ceisteanna taighde féideartha

- Conas is féidir liom scileanna idirchumarsáide teanga na ndaltaí a fhorbairt i rang Gaeilge i suíomh T2 trí úsáid na drámaíochta?
- Cé na straitéisí teagaisc atá éifeachtach chun scileanna gabhchumais a fhorbairt i measc naíonán i suíomh T1?
- Conas is féidir liom scileanna ginchumais a fhorbairt trí rannpháirtíocht ó bhéal a spreagadh sa rang Gaeilge T2?

Deiseanna taighde comhthéacsúla

<u>Taighde sa Ghaeltacht</u>

Tá éagsúlachtaí móra idir na cineálacha Scoileanna Gaeltachta atá ann agus idir na cineálacha daltaí a fhreastalaíonn orthu. Scoileanna beaga tuaithe is ea go leor acu, go háirithe i gceantair Chatagóir A. Is minic, go háirithe sna bunscoileanna, go mbíonn páistí ó bhlianta difriúla istigh in aon seomra ranga. Cruthaíonn sé seo go leor dúshlán do mhúinteoirí ó thaobh riachtanais éagsúla na bpáistí a shásamh. Go traidisiúnta, chuir go leor scoileanna níos mó béime ar riachtanais na bpáistí T2 de bharr go raibh Gaeilge líofa ag na cainteoirí T1 ach éilíonn an POG go ndíreofaí ar fhorbairt teanga na gcainteoirí T1 freisin. Teastaíonn tacaíocht ó mhúinteoirí le straitéisí idirdhealaithe (taighde-bhunaithe) a fhorbairt le cinntiú go ndéanann gach páiste dul chun cinn sa seomra ranga Gaeltachta, rud atá geallta sa POG.

Bíonn imní ar go leor de na scoileanna beaga go ndúnfar iad nó go n-iarrfar orthu comhnascadh le scoileanna eile mar gheall ar thitim an daonra sna ceantair ina bhfuil siad. Más gá do scoileanna Gaeltachta comhnascadh, ba cheart go gcuideodh treoirlínte an POG leo a chinntiú go mbeidh an cur chuige teangeolaíoch céanna á leanúint acu.

Bíonn go leor dúshlán ag baint le hacmhainní teagaisc sna scoileanna T1 agus sna Scoileanna Gaeltachta ach go háirithe. Tá amhras léirithe go minic ag muintir na Gaeltachta faoin gcineál Gaeilge (atá bunaithe ar an gCaighdeán Oifigiúil) a fheictear go hiondúil sna hacmhainní a chuirtear ar fáil do na scoileanna. Tugtar 'Gaeilge na leabhar' ar an gcineál Gaeilge a fheictear sna téacsleabhair agus bíonn idir fhoireann agus dhaltaí ag streachailt leis an réim teanga atá in úsáid. Beidh daltaí áirithe a thuigeann ábhar níos fearr ina gcanúint féin agus daltaí eile a bheidh ag streachailt leis an ábhar mar go bhfuil sé i nGaeilge chasta. Úsáideann múinteoirí cuir chuige éagsúla le hiarracht a dhéanamh na riachtanais éagsúla seo a shásamh. Tá tús curtha le blianta beaga anuas le hacmhainní a réiteach ar bhonn canúna, go háirithe ag leibhéal na bunscoile, agus tá fáilte mhór curtha roimh an bhforbairt seo.

Ábhar imní is ea an sóisialú trí Bhéarla atá ag tarlú i measc óige na Gaeltachta. Cuireadh an milleán faoi seo go minic ar thionchar na meán. Cé gur buntáistí móra iad an dátheangachas agus an t-ilteangachas ag leibhéal an pháiste aonair, ní i gcónaí gur chun leas na mionteanga ag leibhéal an phobail iad. Caithfear a bheith coinsiasach freisin faoi pháistí T1 (mionteanga) nach bhfuil an teanga baile sealbhaithe go hiomlán acu faoin am a thosaíonn siad ar scoil. Tá siad i mbaol an 'dátheangachais éagothrom', áit a n-éiríonn níos fearr le sealbhú na mórtheanga ar scoil ná an mhionteanga sa mbaile. Déanann go leor taighde ar mhionteangacha idirdhealú idir na buntáistí a thugann an dátheangachas don pháiste aonair agus an baol a chruthaíonn an dátheangachas don mhionteanga féin ag leibhéal an phobail.

Tá deiseanna taighde a bhaineann le cur chun cinn na Gaeilge sa phobal – ról atá le comhlíonadh ag scoil ar bith a bhaineann stádas mar *Scoil Ghaeltachta* amach. Aithnítear an Scoil Ghaeltachta mar ionad teanga-bhunaithe fíorthábhachtach sa POG agus sna pleananna teanga atá á bhforbairt i 26 cheantar Gaeltachta ar fud na tíre. Tá an Foras Taighde ar Oideachas (FTO) ag comhoibriú leis an Aonad Oideachais Gaeltachta chun meastóireacht ilbhliantúil ar an Scéim Aitheantais Scoileanna Gaeltachta a chur i bhfeidhm.

Topaicí/ceisteanna taighde féideartha

- Conas is féidir liom labhairt na Gaeilge a chur chun cinn lasmuigh den seomra ranga?
- Cén chaoi is fearr tacú le cainteoirí dúchais a n-inniúlacht sa Ghaeilge (labhartha/éisteachta/léitheoireachta/scríofa) a fheabhsú?
- Cé na héifeachtaí atá ag cur i bhfeidhm an POG ar an scoil/ceantar?
- Céard iad na slite ar féidir liom comhoibriú le múinteoirí ábhar le hacmhainní eolaíochta/gnó/srl. níos fearr a chur ar fáil?

Dearcthaí i leith na Gaeilge

In ainneoin go bhfuil croí-stádas ag an nGaeilge sa churaclam scoile agus go gcaitheann daltaí thart ar 1500 uair an chloig ag foghlaim na teanga, léiríonn daonáireamh 2016 go mbíonn titim shuntasach i líon na gcainteoirí gníomhacha ó aois 18 ar aghaidh (i.e. ní leanann foghlaimeoirí na teanga á húsáid tar éis dóibh an scoil a fhágáil) (CSO 2017). Bíodh is go bhfuil dearcadh dearfach ag móramh den phobal i leith na Gaeilge, tá rátaí úsáide na teanga fós ag titim, lasmuigh agus laistigh den Ghaeltacht.

Ceann de na téamaí a thagann chun cinn go minic ná an gaol láidir atá idir dearcthaí i leith na Gaeilge mar ábhar scoile agus caighdeán teagaisc na Gaeilge, i scoileanna lán-Bhéarla ach go háirithe. De réir an staidéir *Growing Up In Ireland,* léiríonn daltaí bunscoile agus iarbhunscoile níos lú suime sa Ghaeilge ná sna croí-ábhair eile sa churaclam. Léirítear meonta níos dearfaí i leith na Gaeilge mar theanga i suíomhanna T1 ná i suíomhanna T2. É sin ráite, níl an dearcadh i leith na Gaeilge mar ábhar scoile chomh dearfach céanna, go háirithe i scoileanna Gaeltachta. Is i nGaelscoileanna agus i nGaelcholáistí a bhíonn na dearcthaí is dearfaí i leith na Gaeilge mar ábhar scoile ach ní leanann úsáid ghníomhach na Gaeilge an treocht dhearfach agus bíonn rátaí sách íseal d'úsáid na teanga lasmuigh den scoil agus i ndiaidh do dhaltaí an scoil a fhágáil.

Tá an gaol seo idir dearcthaí agus úsáid ar cheann de na cúiseanna go bhfuil béim sna curaclaim atá á bhforbairt le déanaí ar scileanna cumarsáide a láidriú, ar phobal teanga a neartú agus ar an teanga bheo a chur chun cinn. Beidh le feiceáil sna blianta amach romhainn cén tionchar a bheidh ag na hathruithe seo agus is cinnte go bhfuil neart deiseanna saibhre taighde faoin réimse seo.

Topaicí/ceisteanna taighde féideartha

- Cén tionchar atá ag an bhfoghlaim thascbhunaithe ar dhearcthaí daltaí iarbhunscoile T2 i leith na Gaeilge?
- An bhfuil éifeacht ag polasaí teanga sa seomra ranga ar mheonta i leith na Gaeilge i ranganna T1?
- Conas is féidir na meáin cumarsáide a úsáid chun nasc a chruthú leis an teanga bheo i seomra ranga T2?

Caighdeán teagaisc agus oiliúint múinteoirí

Luann tuarascálacha cigireachta na Roinne agus taighde neamhspleách go bhfuil gá le feabhas i gcaighdeán agus i modheolaíochtaí teagaisc na Gaeilge go ginearálta agus go bhfuil nasc láidir idir caighdeán teagaisc, inniúlacht teanga an mhúinteora agus suim na ndaltaí sa Ghaeilge. Ceann de na dearcthaí ba choitianta sa chomhairliúchán ar dhíolúintí ón nGaeilge ná nach mbeadh an t-éileamh céanna ar dhíolúintí dá ndéanfaí forbairt agus feabhas ar mhodheolaíochtaí teagaisc agus dá mbeadh curaclam níos ionchuimsithí agus níos tarraingtí ar fáil.

Tá gaol láidir chomh maith idir caidreamh dearfach múinteoir-dalta sa rang Gaeilge agus suim na ndaltaí san ábhar. Tá tábhacht ar leith leis an gcaidreamh seo i gceantair faoi mhíbhuntáiste. Mar shampla, maíonn O'Sullivan et al. (2019) go mbíonn eispéireas diúltach foghlama sa Ghaeilge ag a lán daltaí i scoileanna lán-Bhéarla DEIS agus gur ionchais ísle múinteora agus modheolaíochtaí teagaisc mí-oiriúnacha is cúis le seo.

Ceann de na deacrachtaí is mó a luaitear maidir le scoileanna T1 ná earcú múinteoirí bunscoile agus múinteoirí ábhar le Gaeilge d'ardchaighdeán. Anuas air sin, tá riachtanais ar leith ag múinteoirí i scoileanna Gaeltachta maidir le Forbairt Ghairmiúil Leanúnach (FGL) agus ní shásaíonn na seirbhísí tacaíochta gairmiúla atá ar fáil na riachtanais sin. Dá bharr seo, tá feabhas sna réimsí FGL agus Oiliúint Tosaigh Múinteoirí (OTM) dírithe ar scoileanna T1 mar cheann de chuspóirí an *S20* agus an POG agus tá cláir nua trí Ghaeilge d'ábhar oidí agus do mhúinteoirí tosaithe anois in Institiúid Marino (céim 4 bliana) agus i gColáiste Mhuire gan Smál (iarchéim 2 bhliain), chun cur leis an iarchéim MGO in Ollscoil Éireann Gaillimh.

Dearcadh a mhaireann fós ná go ndéanann scoileanna lán-Ghaeilge freastal ar mhuintir mheánaicmeach amháin, bíodh is gur fianaise starógach a bhíonn mar bhunús leis an dearcadh seo go minic. Tá rochtain ar scoileanna lán-Ghaeilge i gceantair faoi mhíbhuntáiste, áfach, agus tá líon na scoileanna sin ag fás go leanúnach. Rinneadh staidéar ar an 13 Ghaelscoil atá sa scéim DEIS chun iniúchadh a dhéanamh ar ghnóthachtáil agus rannpháirtíocht agus is fiú do mhúinteoirí sa chomhthéacs sin aghaidh a thabhairt ar na saincheisteanna a ardaítear, go háirithe maidir le scileanna litearthachta agus uimhearthachta a fhorbairt (Ní Chlochasaigh, Shiel & Ó Duibhir, 2020).

Mar mhúinteoir-taighdeoir, ba cheart féachaint go machnamhach ar do chleachtas féin chun aghaidh a thabhairt ar roinnt de na dúshláin a ardaítear maidir le modheolaíochtaí teagaisc. Tá neart deiseanna forbartha sa taighde cleachtóir-bhunaithe chun cur le cumas an mhúinteora a bheith in ann freastal ar riachtanais na ndaltaí i gcomhthéacs a c(h)leachtais.

<u>Topaicí/ceisteanna taighde féideartha</u>

- Iniúchadh ar an mbuíonteagasc mar straitéis chun cur le rannpháirtíocht agus gnóthachtáil sa rang Gaeilge.
- Cé na deiseanna FGL atá ar fáil do mhúinteoirí ábhar i suíomh tumoideachais?
- Conas is féidir liom an difreáil a úsáid chun scileanna ginchumais a chur chun cinn i rang de chaighdeán measctha i suíomh T2 i gceantar faoi mhíbhuntáiste?
- Cé na straitéisí teagaisc atá éifeachtach chun tacú le daltaí a scileanna uimhearthachta a fhorbairt i nGaelscoil i gceantar faoi mhíbhuntáiste?

<u>Polasaithe oideachais agus leasuithe sa churaclam</u>

Mar atá luaite cheana, tá go leor polasaithe oideachais nua foilsithe agus leasuithe déanta do na curaclaim mar thoradh ar an *S20*. Níl mórán taighde déanta go fóill ar cén éifeacht atá acu seo ar an eispéireas sa seomra ranga do mhúinteoirí agus do pháistí. Tá go leor deiseanna ann don mhúinteoir-taighdeoir le hanailís a dhéanamh ar chur i bhfeidhm na n-athruithe seo i seomraí ranga sna comhthéacsanna éagsúla.

> *Topaicí/ceisteanna taighde féideartha*
> - Conas atá foireann teagaisc na Gaeilge i suíomh scoile T1 ag cur sonraíocht T1 ag leibhéal na Sraithe Sóisearaí i bhfeidhm?
> - Cén éifeacht atá ag critéir theangabhunaithe an *Scéim Aitheantais Scoileanna Gaeltachta* ar chur chuige teagaisc an mhúinteora i suíomh bunscoile T1?
> - Cén chaoi a bhfuil mé ag baint leasa as an gcuraclam teanga nua?

10.5 Conclúid

Tá forléargas tugtha sa chaibidil seo ar na príomhphointí a bhaineann le taighde ar an nGaeilge sa chóras oideachais. Más ag tabhairt faoin gcineál taighde seo atá tú, is féidir na pointí agus nodanna a luaitear sa chaibidil seo a úsáid mar ábhar machnaimh agus tú ag roghnú topaice agus ag dearadh ceiste. Maidir le cuir chuige agus modheolaíochtaí taighde, cuimhnigh gurb iad na prionsabail chéanna atá tábhachtach i ndearadh taighde trí Ghaeilge agus atá in aon teanga eile. Mar sin, beidh na caibidlí eile sa leabhar seo áisiúil duit mar stiúir ar conas do cheist a bheachtú, tabhairt faoin léirmheas litríochta agus modheolaíocht a dheáradh.

Ceann de na moltaí is tábhachtaí maidir leis an taighde trí Ghaeilge ná go gcaithfear a bheith machnamhach agus airdeallach ar chomhthéacs an taighde agus ar do ról féin sa chomhthéacs sin. Agus tú ag dearadh do thionscnamh taighde mar sin, smaoinigh go cúramach faoi na saincheisteanna atá ag teacht chun cinn i gcomhthéacs do chleachtais féin agus féach cá suíonn na ceisteanna sin i measc na réimsí taighde níos leithne a luaitear anseo agus in áiteanna eile. Tosaigh leis na heochairthéacsanna atá luaite anseo againn chun tús a chur leis an taighde. Dar ndóigh, toisc gur forléargas atá anseo seachas plé cuimsitheach, beidh ort breis léitheoireachta a dhéanamh chun tógáil ar an méid atá luaite sa chaibidil.

Léitheoireacht mholta

Coyle, D., Hood, P., agus Marsh, D. (2010). *Content and Language Integrated Learning* (Cambridge: Ernst Klett Sprachen).

Dunne, C. (2020). *Learning and Teaching Irish in English–medium Schools. Part 2: 1971 —present* (Baile Átha Cliath: An Chomhairle Náisiúnta Curaclaim agus Measúnachta), https://ncca.ie/media/4797/learning-and-teaching-irish-in-english-medium-schools-1971-present-part-2.pdf

Ó Duibhir, P., Ní Chuaig, N., Ní Thuairisg, L., agus Ó Brolcháin, C. (2015). *Soláthar Oideachais trí Mhionteangacha: Athbhreithniú ar thaighde idirnáisiúnta* (Baile Átha Cliath: An Roinn Oideachas agus Scileanna), https://www.education.ie/ga/Preas-agus-Imeachta%C3%AD/Imeachta%C3%AD/Molta%C3%AD-Polasa%C3%AD-Oideachas-Gaeltachta/Soláthar-Oideachais-tr%C3%AD-Mhionteangacha_Athbhreithniú-Ar-Thaighde-Idirnáisiúnta_2015.pdf

Roinn Oideachais agus Scileanna (2016). *Polasaí don Oideachas Gaeltachta 2017–2022*, https://www.education.ie/ga/Foilseacháin/Tuarascálacha-Beartais/Polasai-don-Oideachas-Gaeltachta-2017-2022.pdf

Tagairtí

Central Statistics Office. [CSO] (2017). *Gaeilge agus an Ghaeltacht*, https://www.cso.ie/en/releasesandpublications/ep/p-cp10esil/p10esil/gag/

Harris, J. agus Ó Duibhir, P. (2011). *Múineadh Éifeachtach Teangacha: Sintéis ar thaighde. Tuarascáil taighde 13* (Baile Átha Cliath: An Chomhairle Náisiúnta Curaclaim agus Measúnachta), https://ncca.ie/media/2713/muineadh_eifeachtach_teangacha.pdf

Harris, J., Forde, P., Archer, P., Nic Fhearaile, S., agus O'Gorman, M. (2006). *Irish in Primary Schools: Long-term national trends in achievement* (Baile Átha Cliath: An Roinn Oideachais agus Eolaíochta).

Ní Chlochasaigh, K., Shiel, G., agus Ó Duibhir, P. (2020). *Iniúchadh ar an Tumoideachas do Dhaltaí i Scoileanna Lán-Ghaeilge i gCeantair Mhíbhuntáiste* (Ollscoil Chathair Bhaile Átha Cliath agus An Foras Taighde ar Oideachas), https://www.erc.ie/wp-content/uploads/2020/08/An-Tumoideachas-3.pdf

Ó Duibhir, P., Ní Chuaig, N., Ní Thuairisg, L., agus Ó Brolcháin, C. (2015). *Soláthar Oideachais trí Mhionteangacha: Athbhreithniú ar thaighde idirnáisiúnta* (Baile Átha Cliath: An Roinn Oideachas agus Scileanna), https://www.education.ie/ga/Preas-agus-Imeachta%C3%AD/Imeachta%C3%AD/Molta%C3%AD-Polasa%C3%AD-Oideachas-Gaeltachta/Soláthar-Oideachais-tr%C3%AD-Mhionteangacha_Athbhreithniú-Ar-Thaighde-Idirnáisiúnta_2015.pdf

Ó Giollagáin, C., Mac Donnacha, S., Ní Chualáin, F., Ní Shéaghdha, A., agus O'Brien, M. (2007). *Staidéar Cuimsitheach Teangeolaíoch ar Úsáid na Gaeilge sa Ghaeltacht: Príomhthátal agus Moltaí* (Baile Átha Cliath: Oifig an tSoláthair:).

O'Sullivan, K., Bird, N., agus Burns, G. (2019). 'Students' experiences of the teaching and learning of Irish in designated disadvantaged schools', *International Journal of Education, Culture and Society*, 4(5), lgh 87–97, DOI: 10.11648/j.ijecs.20190405.13

Rialtas na hÉireann. (2010). *Straitéis 20 Bliain don Ghaeilge 2010–2030* (Baile Átha Cliath: Oifig an tSoláthair).

Roinn Oideachais agus Scileanna. (2015a). *Sonraíocht Ghaeilge na Sraithe Sóisearaí*, https://curriculumonline.ie/Junior-cycle/Junior-Cycle-Subjects/Gaeilge/Course-overview/?lang=ga-ie

Roinn Oideachais agus Scileanna (An Chigireacht) (2015b). *Athbhreithniú ar an Oideachas sa Ghaeltacht: Athbhreithniú ar an litríocht náisiúnta*, https://www.education.ie/ga/Preas-agus-Imeachta%C3%AD/Imeachta%C3%AD/Molta%C3%AD-Polasa%C3%AD-Oideachas-Gaeltachta/Athbhreithniú-ar-Litr%C3%ADocht-Náisiúnta_Oideachas-sa-Ghaeltacht-2015.pdf

Roinn Oideachais agus Scileanna. (2016). *Polasaí don Oideachas Gaeltachta 2017–2022*, https://www.education.ie/ga/Foilseacháin/Tuarascálacha-Beartais/Polasai-don-Oideachas-Gaeltachta-2017-2022.pdf

Roinn Oideachais agus Scileanna. (2019). *Curaclam Teanga na Bunscoile* (Baile Átha Cliath: An Roinn Oideachais agus Scileanna).

Notaí

1. Tá go leor easaontais faoin téarma 'cainteoir dúchais' sa litríocht taighde.
2. 'An Luath-Óige' atá i gceist seachas 'An Luath Óige' (earráid sa bhunleagan).

CHAPTER 11

Practitioner Research

*Emma Farrell, School of Education, University College Dublin,
Shane D. Bergin, School of Education, University College Dublin and
Declan Fahie, School of Education, University College Dublin*

11.0 Introduction

Let us assume that you have identified some aspect of your professional practice in your classroom that is puzzling you. Why, for example, do pupils seem more engaged with maths lessons after they've had a break outside in the yard? Or can technology help improve student engagement with mathematics? Perhaps you have read about a technique in a teacher journal or an online discussion forum and wonder how it might apply to your own professional practice? At this point you have taken the first step in practitioner research i.e., you, as a practitioner, have identified an educational issue that warrants attention.

In this chapter we define practitioner research and guide prospective researchers through all the pathways and potential pitfalls associated with effective practitioner research in education settings. With a particular emphasis on dissemination, this chapter seeks to encourage educators not only to 'do' practitioner research, but to share their findings with others. It is this sharing that distinguishes practitioner research from personal enquiry or reflective practice and reminds us of the social nature of research activity. Written with the busy teacher in mind, we seek to make this chapter as practical as possible and draw on a range of illustrative examples of practitioner research from our own practice and those kindly shared by students and colleagues we've worked with. We hope that this chapter provides the guidance and reassurance required to step into practitioner research as well as acts as a resource to which to return at all stages across the professional lifecycle.

11.1 What Is Practitioner Research?

> Practitioner research in education is systematic enquiry in an educational setting carried out by someone working in that setting, the outcomes of

which are shared with other practitioners (Menter, Dely, Hulme, Lewin, and Lowden, 2011, p. 3)

Menter and colleagues' definition offers a succinct and straightforward description of practitioner research as well as an overview of its five key elements:

1. Enquiry: The word 'research' carries many meanings and, as can been seen throughout this book, comes in many forms. Common to all, however, is a sense of enquiry. A desire to 'find out' or investigate. To develop new knowledge or understanding.
2. Systematic: Research is systematic in that there is order to the nature of the enquiry – it begins with a clear rationale and follows a predefined approach or method that can be described and defended.
3. Practitioner: Practitioner research, in contrast to the other forms of research in this book, is uniquely carried out by someone who is also 'practicing' i.e., a practicing teacher or other professional. It is usually assumed that the research is being carried out within the practitioner's own practice or setting, although groups of researchers can come together to take part in collaborative practitioner research.
4. Educational setting: The term 'educational setting' ought to be taken in its broadest sense to include research in the classroom, staff room and other education settings, research with parents or other members of the wider community and even research that considers education policy in practice.
5. Sharing outcomes: Sharing the outcomes of learning, whether informally or more formally in publications or at conferences, is what separates research from reflection or personal enquiry.

In this chapter we explore these key elements and examine, not only what is practitioner research but why one would choose this approach and how one would go about doing practitioner research for their education research project. In addition to the why and the how, we explore how a practitioner researcher might share their findings so that others might benefit from, and respond to, the research that has been undertaken.

11.2 Why Do Practitioner Research?

While readers of this book are likely reading with their education dissertation in mind, practitioner research is not only an effective approach to research but facilitates higher quality teaching, professional development across the career span and an opportunity for whole school improvement.

Practitioner research supports:

- Quality teaching: Research highlights, time and again, that the single most important within-school factor that determines educational experience and outcomes is the quality of teaching (Hattie, 2009; McKinsey and Co., 2007). Educators who are research-engaged are known to possess 'a better understanding of their practice and ways to improve it' (McLaughlin, Black-Hawkins, and McIntyre, 2004, p. 5). Practitioner research, therefore, offers educators, at all stages of their career, the opportunity to reflect on and improve their own education practice which in turn leads to higher quality teaching and learning experiences and outcomes.
- Initial teacher education: Recent decades have seen a growing emphasis on 'teaching as a research and evidence-based profession' (Hargreaves, 1996). However, early education research was criticised as poorly conducted and poorly communicated (Hargreaves, 1996; Tooley and Darby, 1998). Teacher education in Ireland offers student teachers the opportunity to become research literate and research engaged at an early stage in their career development. Practitioner research is a particularly effective approach with which to become familiar at an initial career stage as it can both 'enlighten current practice and inform future practice' (Middlewood, Coleman, and Lumby, 1999, p. x). In Ireland, the Teaching Council's initiative CROÍ (Collaboration and Research for Ongoing Innovation) is designed specifically to support the development of a professional culture of evidence-based and research informed practice. The Teaching Council is committed to the concept of the 'teacher-as-researcher' and provides a range of online resources, webinars and, critically, research funding to support teachers and student teachers in developing their own expertise and confidence in the area of research engagement (for more details see www.teachingcouncil.ie/en/research-croi-/)
- Personal or collaborative continuing professional development (CPD): If teaching truly is a 'research and evidence-based profession' as Hargreaves (1996, p. 1) suggests, research, in its various forms represents a central component of any educator's commitment to professional learning and skills development. While at times, as Newman (2004, p. i) suggests, 'professional development is seen as something to be endured rather than enjoyed', practitioner research offers practitioners the opportunity

to exercise critical appraisal and analysis skills appropriate to their setting and career stage.
- Whole school/education setting improvement: The Department of Education requires all schools to engage in School Self-Evaluation (SSE) (see www.schoolself-evaluation.ie). This involves regular, collaborative, evidence-based reflection on the school's activities in order to assess effectiveness and, ultimately, improve the quality of the teaching and learning it provides. It is a dynamic process which is predicated on the school's commitment to systematic reflexivity. However, it is neither casual nor ad hoc; the self-evaluation must be informed by good quality data (evidence) which is then assessed rigorously/dispassionately before appropriate action(s) is taken. In essence, School Self-Evaluation is practitioner research in action, and key to its success is an understanding of, and familiarity with, key research skills as well as an acknowledgment of the power of both the individual and the collective to shape and influence school practice for the better.

While there are undoubtedly many benefits to practitioner research, it is not without its challenges. Ellis and Loughland (2016), in their excellent comparative study of practitioner research in New South Wales and Singapore, identify time, training and culture as some of the key challenges. They found that teachers face significant time pressures that limit opportunities for research and reflection, both alone and with colleagues. Our experience of teaching research methods to student teachers confirms their second finding that teachers report a lack of knowledge about research and often feel ill-equipped and lacking in confidence to conduct research in their classrooms. Thirdly, while a culture of research in a school, particularly in schools with informed and supportive school leadership, supports practitioner research, the absence of a culture of research posed a significant challenge to the conduct of practitioner research. All of these challenges reflect the reality that culture change takes time. Practitioner research is a relatively new concept in most Irish schools and the most effective way to create a culture of research in schools is to do research in schools. We hope that this chapter, and indeed this book, offers practitioners at all career stages the confidence to integrate practitioner research into their own practice, classrooms, and schools.

11.3 How to Do Practitioner Research

Practitioner research is distinguished from the other approaches in this book, more by the person doing the research, and the context in which it is done, than the process followed, or the methods adopted. As such, the 'how' of practitioner research is not dissimilar to the 'how' of education research more generally. Practitioner research begins with choosing and refining your research question (as described by Fahie, Bergin and Farrell in Chapter 1); considering the ethical implications of the research (as described by Leavy in Chapter 2); and selecting a methodology and method that will best enable you to generate the information required to answer your research question.

Formulating a research question is perhaps the most important part of any practitioner research project – one that requires careful consideration and troubleshooting. A clear and manageable research question guides a researcher both in terms of knowing what you are looking for but also being realistic about what it is possible to see or determine within your particular timeframe and confines. All too often eager researchers embark and collect data only to discover that what they've collected tells them very little about the subject they set out to examine. A clear research question helps to (a) crystallise the focus of your research, (b) set the parameters (in focusing on X, I am not interested in Y), (c) determine the methodology and methods by which you gather and analyse evidence, and (d) enable you to draw conclusions at the end. Even the most experienced researcher will have done research only to discover a large and unnegotiable gap between their research question and the data they've collected. The best way to avoid this is to ensure that the data you are collecting is relevant to your research question. This is best achieved with a clear research question.

Once you have clarified your research question, your research will likely benefit from a review of literature in order to understand what is already known on a subject (see McDaid, Chapter 3). For example, you may wish to employ a particular pedagogical technique that requires you to first become familiar with that technique and its literature base. Or you may wish to examine the origins, say, of inclusive education practices in Ireland. Regardless of how exhaustive, or not, your literature review may be, it is important to provide some context and a rationale for your research. Why do this research? Why your practice/classroom? Why now? Your research may benefit from a reflexive component. As researchers, indeed as human beings, we all carry prejudice. Our values, beliefs, and factors such as our socioeconomic status, gender, age and ethnicity, all predispose us to a particular way of viewing the world. In fact, one of the most frequent criticisms levied at practitioner research is that it is biased (Ellis and Loughland, 2016).

> There is no neutrality. There is only greater or less awareness of one's biases.

And if you do not appreciate the force of what you're leaving out, you are not fully in command of what you're doing (Rose, 1985, p. 77).

Effective practitioner research requires careful consideration of 'what you're leaving out' as Rose puts it. For example, if the practitioner researcher leading the second research study outlined in Table 11.1 below has a particular interest in drama, they might consider how their own enjoyment of drama might influence what they see in terms of its effectiveness in improving student understanding of Shakespeare's characters. Or, in offering feedback to a colleague, a teacher might be aware that their feedback is influenced by their conceptualisation of 'good teaching', how they prefer to teach, rather than whether or not the type of teaching being demonstrated is supporting student learning. It is only when armed with an awareness of our prejudice that we can best defend against its inimical influence in our research.

Once you have determined your research question and reviewed the available literature you will need to select the most appropriate approach or methodology, and associated methods, by which to gather information or evidence. You may, for example, adopt an empirical approach and use quantitative forms of data to answer your question (see Chapter 4). Or perhaps you may wish to adopt an interpretative or constructivist approach for which qualitative methods might be most suitable as a way of gathering data (see Chapter 5).

The most important consideration in selecting which method to choose from for practitioner research is not which method is best but rather which method best enables you to generate the kind of data or evidence you need to answer your research question. Therefore, 'fitness for purpose' should be your main consideration in selecting an approach or method and your supervisor will be able to support you in determining which approach or methods will best serve you in answering your research question. One tip we offer prospective researchers is to find a study with a similar aim or research question to your own, even if the subject matter is entirely different, and carefully study the methodology. One effective way of avoiding what doesn't work, is to find what does work and apply that to your own practice, classroom, or question. Producing original research doesn't involve developing a novel or unique method but rather applying an existing method to your classroom, practice, students, or school.

While your choice of methodology and method will determine what you do, being systematic, as we discussed earlier in the chapter, is essential to effective practitioner research. This means maintaining comprehensive records; labelling and organising data accurately; carefully following a pre-defined protocol for analysis; and adhering to the standards of trustworthiness and rigour of your field so that you can clearly explain (or defend) what you did, why you did it and how you drew your conclusions. Once your data is generated, analysed and refined, what remains, as Shulman (1993, p. 7) puts it, is 'an artefact, a product, some form of community property that can be shared, discussed, critiqued, exchanged, built upon'. This sharing of research forms the focus of the remainder of the chapter.

Table 11.1: Examples of practitioner research outlines

Research questions	Method	Evidence/data	Tools/resources
How is the concept of 'well-being' understood by primary school parents?	Literature search	Literature	Peer-reviewed literature, books, reports, and government publications
	Interviews with parents	Qualitative data	Interview schedule
Can the use of drama activities help develop students' understanding of the characters in *Macbeth*?	Observation	Qualitative and quantitative data	Observation schedule
	Student feedback	Qualitative and quantitative data	Questionnaire (open and closed questions)
			Verbal feedback from students
How does using a problem-based-learning approach in practical (lab) science classes affect students' understanding of the nature of science?	Literature search	Literature	Peer-reviewed literature, books, reports, and government publications
	Student feedback	Qualitative and quantitative data	Questionnaire (co-constructed with student advisory groups)
	Student advisory groups		Student advisory groups (representing one control and one non-control group)

11.4 Sharing Practitioner Research

Sharing your research is what distinguishes practitioner research from reflection or evaluation. While your primary motivations for conducting research may be to improve your practice as an educator in an area of interest and to write an excellent thesis, the benefits of disseminating your work to various groups cannot be understated. This section explores formal and informal routes for the novice education researcher to do this.

Academic publications

Academic publications are the lifeblood of academic scholarship. Articles are peer-reviewed by experts ensuring claims made by the authors meet the highest academic standards. And while the majority of articles within these publications will be written by experienced researchers, all journals will gladly accept submissions from those new to research and those who are practitioner researchers.

If you are interested in submitting your research to an academic journal, the following points may help as a guide:

- Talk to your thesis supervisor about your interest. They will be well-placed to suggest i) whether the thesis findings are of a sufficient standard for publication, ii) how to translate a thesis into an article, and iii) what journals might be interested in your work. They may also be interested in working with you to write the article. If you are happy to work together, have a conversation about what that means in terms of sharing the writing, authorship, and any cost of publication.
- Consider carefully which journal you are going to submit your work to. Every journal will have a particular readership; you need to find a journal where your work will be of interest to the readers. To begin, it might be helpful to look at the journals you have referenced frequently in your thesis and identity those that publish articles like yours. Visit the journal website and read the 'about this journal' section. It is important that your article falls within the scope of the journal. If you are unclear, you might ask your thesis supervisor for their advice or write an email to the editor of the journal.
- Having chosen an academic journal, you will need to produce a manuscript that conforms with their 'instructions for authors'. These will typically outline the sections your article should have, the word count limit, and any style-guide requirements (paying particular attention to the reference style).
- Journal articles are much shorter than theses. Do not be surprised if you are asked to write a document of no more than 3,000 – 6,000 words. Do not be tempted to find a journal that accepts longer

pieces to avoid editing your thesis. Read a few articles from your journal of choice to get a sense of what you need to write. While writing is a slow and iterative process, the pace offers opportunity to deepen your understanding of the issue at hand.
- Once you have a completed manuscript, you can begin the submission process. For most journals, you will need to create an account on their website to upload your manuscript. You will also be asked for the following:
  - The name of the authors and their academic affiliations. If there are multiple authors, make sure the order is agreed before you submit.
  - Keywords that reflect your research area. This helps others find your work when they are searching for published research.
  - A letter to the editor that makes the case for the journal publishing your work. It should be written in a formal style and should i) state what your article is about, ii) state why their journal is a good fit, citing one or two articles they have published on similar topics, and iii) why you believe their readers will be interested in your work.
- Having submitted your article, the journal editor will decide whether, or not, to send your article for peer-review. If the editor rejects the article, you will need to find another journal. If your article is sent for peer-review, you will receive their comments in a few weeks/months (the timeframe depends on the journal). They can recommend that your article: i) is accepted for publication, ii) requires further work that they will review, iii) is not accepted. It's most uncommon for any scholar to have their work accepted without any corrections. While it can be frustrating, the review process helps to improve the work. Each journal sends clear instructions to authors on how to submit corrections to articles. It's also not uncommon for a scholar to have their work rejected by a journal after peer-review, and for them to resubmit to another.
- Once the editor has signed-off on your work, your article will be checked for minor errors (spelling, etc.) and published on-line (and sometimes in print). If issues of copyright and open access arise, talk to your thesis supervisor or university library. It is a huge achievement to have your work published in this way, so make sure to celebrate!

Professional magazines

Education Matters, InTouch, and *Education Magazine* are just some of the widely read publications for educators in Ireland. Most of them welcome articles from practitioners who are research active. As well as being a place for you to describing the findings of your work, they offer a platform for you to write about the experience of doing research and the impacts that it had on you and your practice. Having completed your research project, you should consider publishing a piece in such a magazine.

The first step in this process is to write to the editor and make a pitch for your article. Use clear language; describe your findings in a sentence or two; think about why the article would be a good fit for their magazine. Articles like this tend not to be peer-reviewed. It is therefore important that you ask colleagues to review what you have written before you submit: ask them for critical feedback and try to incorporate their advice into the article, if sensible.

It is important to note that publishing a piece in an academic journal does not preclude you from writing a complementary article in a professional magazine. Indeed, many magazines welcome articles like this, where they might ask you to emphasise the connections between your research and the practical realities of educational practice.

Example 1: Practitioner research in action
Karen noticed an absence of women and girls in the textbooks she used to teach physics to her Leaving Certificate students. She believed that for her female students to have a sense of belonging in physics, they would need female role-models and that the textbook was an obvious place for these. She therefore decided to undertake a systematic study of female representation in textbooks for her final year dissertation.

She began with a literature review on representation in educational materials before systematically analysing gender balance in Leaving Certificate physics textbooks. Karen's research revealed: i) women are significantly under-represented in all physics textbooks (in images and in text), ii) that while government reports have pointed to the importance of gender equality in science subjects, there are no guidelines for publishers to follow in this regard, and iii) that revisions to the physics specification for Leaving Certificate students might include a learning outcome to address the issue e.g., 'students will consider the historic and cultural factors that have limited the participation of women and minorities in physics'.

After completing her dissertation, Karen worked with her supervisor to publish the findings in an academic journal (Pillion and Bergin, 2022). Following publication, Karen shared her findings with the committee of the National Council for Curriculum and Assessment

> (NCCA) that is advising on a reformed physics specification. Karen was invited to present her work to other physics teachers at a conference and has discussed her findings with several textbook authors.

Conferences

Presenting your work at an education conference is an excellent way to share the research with other professionals. This can often lead to collaborations and further research. In Ireland, regular conferences are arranged by The Teaching Council (Féilte), by teacher organisations (often subject specific), by universities, and by other organisations (e.g., Education Studies Association of Ireland (ESAI) or SCoTENS). There are also many international education conferences you might consider (there are too many to list here: speak to your thesis supervisor if you are interested).

Most education conferences will have an open call where you can propose a poster or a talk that will describe your research. You will need to submit an abstract and often a brief paper.

State bodies

Education policy should be based on research. While those creating policy will look to the body of existing research to inform their work, they will also accept submissions from researchers.

If your research is relevant to the work of a state agency, such as the National Council for Curriculum and Assessment, The Teaching Council, etc., contact the relevant office within the organisation. Write a brief letter outlining the research findings and attach any academic paper you have written on the matter (your work will have more impact if the work is published in an academic journal). Most state bodies have numerous committees that work on different issues (many of these committees have several educators sitting on them); a good outcome for you might be that a committee considers your work when formulating related policy.

If your research findings relate to the subject you teach, consider contacting your associated professional body (e.g., Institute of Physics, Royal Society of Chemistry, etc.). If your work concerns your school community, talk to your principal about it and, having consulted the principal, consider sharing your research with the Board of Management or student body. This might be through a talk, a brief report, or by leading a workshop, etc.

Social media

Sharing your work online using Twitter or blogs can extend the reach of your research, generate conversation on the associated issues, and lead to your work having impact. If you are a social media user, you might like to use your own account. If you do not use social media, you might ask your school or university to share the work through their accounts. When Tweeting, composing a thread is a great way to present your work. Open with the title of your work, the people you worked with, and any links you have to publications you have produced. Follow with the claims your research is making. Use images in your Tweets to show any graphs, quotes, etc. that you feel are relevant. While Twitter content is very much a snapshot of people's feelings on various issues, it is best that you present your research in an objective and professional manner.

11.5 Conclusion

Practitioner research supports, not just the initial development of an educator, but the ongoing practice of teaching. Indeed, Stenhouse (1975) described teaching 'as a process in which the teacher learns how to improve his or her teaching'. Practitioner research is essential to this process. In this chapter we described what practitioner research is, how it might be useful not just for teachers at the beginning of their professional careers but throughout their career. We offer some pointers for those who may wish to do practitioner research and offer a detailed insight into how to share your findings with the wider education community. We wish you every success in your research and practice!

Suggested Readings

Menter, I., Dely, E., Hulme, M., Lewin, J., and Lowden, K. (2011). *A guide to practitioner research in education* (Thousand Oaks, CA: SAGE).

Campbell, A. McNamara, O., and Gilroy, P. (eds.) (2004), *Practitioner Research and Professional Development in Education* (London: Paul Chapman Publishing).

See also: https://www.teachingcouncil.ie/website/en/research-croi-/using-research-in-our-school/

References

Ellis, N. J., and Loughland, T. (2016). 'The challenges of practitioner research: a comparative study of Singapore and NSW', in *The Australian journal of teacher education*, 41(2), pp 122–136, doi:10.14221/ajte.2016v41n2.8

Hargreaves, D. H. (1996). *Teaching as a research based profession: possibilities and prospects* (London).

Hattie, J. (2009). *Visible Learning. A Synthesis of Over 80 Meta-analyses Relating to Achievement* (London: Routledge).

McKinsey and Co. (2007). *How the world's best-performing school systems come out on top*, http://www.mckinsey.com/App_Media/Reports/SSO/Worlds_School_Systems_Final.pdf.

McLaughlin, C., Black-Hawkins, K., and McIntyre, D. (2004). *Researching Teachers Researching Schools, Researching Networks: A Review of the Literature* (Cambridge: University of Cambridge/NCSL).

Menter, I. (2011). *A guide to practitioner research in education* (Thousand Oaks, CA: SAGE).

Middlewood, D., Coleman, M., and Lumby, J. (1999). *Practitioner research in education: making a difference* (London: Paul Chapman).

Newman, S. (2004). 'Forward', in A. Campbell, O. McNamara, and P. H. Gilroy (eds.), *Practitioner Research and Professional Development in Education* (London: Paul Chapman Publishing).

Pillion, K., and Bergin, S. D. (2022). 'The representation of women in Irish Leaving Certificate Physics textbooks', in *Physics education*, 57(2), 25017, doi:10.1088/1361-6552/ac4145

Rose, P. (1985). *Writing on women: Essays in a renaissance* (Middletown CT: Wesleyan University Press).

Shulman, L. (1993). 'Forum: Teaching as community property', *Change: The Magazine of Higher Learning*, 25(6), pp 6–7.

Stenhouse, L. (1975). *An Introduction to Curriculum Research and Development* (London: Heinemann).

Tooley, J., and Darby, D. (1998). *Educational research: a critique: a survey of published educational research: report presented to OFSTED* (London).

Index

abstracts 5–6
access to education 106–07
anonymity 10, 21–3, 49, 72, 75–6
Apple Pages 132
arts-based research 14, 25
ATLAS.ti 140–1
audio recording 22–3, 70, 73–4, 89, 98, 138–9

bar charts 57, 136
Belmont Report 16–18
Bubbl 131

case studies 14, 64, 67, 75, 77; design 68–71
Cavell, Stanley 112, 121, 123
census data 14, 4, 987
children, research with 20–1, 24–7, 82–92; challenges 85–7, 89–92; child-led 87; 'collaborative seeing' 88; 'least-adult' role 85–6; methodological approaches 83–4; 'new social studies of childhood' paradigm 82–3; participatory visual methods 87–9; and photography 88–9; 'photovoice' 88; and rights 83; in schools 86
Children's School Lives (*CSL*) study 47
Coggle 131
Commission of Investigation into Mother and Baby Homes 15
confidentiality 10, 17, 22, 24, 49, 74, 76, 90–1
content analysis 66, 68
continuing professional development (CPD) 166–7
conversation analysis 66
corporal punishment 108
correlation analysis 57–8
critical reading 32, 37
cultural sensitivity 27
curriculum history 105, 107

data: administrative 47; analysis 56–61, 68, 77, 139–42; bias 24; central tendency 57; cleaning 56; coding 71; cohort 47; collection/generation 48–56; display 69, 70; extraction 136; frequency 57; handling 23, 27–8, 46; numeric 55; ownership 75; reduction 69–70; storage 77; transcription 77; types 54–6; visualisation 57 *see also* variables
databases 14, 30, 32, 34–6, 47, 100, 133–5
decision trees 60
Declaration of Helsinki 15, 18
Dedoose 141
Diamond, Cora 116–21
discourse analysis 66–7
Dragon Naturally Speaking 138
Dropbox 131

education research 9, 13–14; nature of 2–3; history of 95–109, 166
emic understandings 96
EndNote 36, 133–4
ethical research 13–28, 129; approaches (consequentalist, principlist, critical, virtue) 15–16; and beneficence 17; with children 20–1, 24–7, 89–91; guiding principles (respect for persons, concern for welfare, focus on justice) 16–17; issues 13, 18; with under-represented groups 96
ethics regulation 15, 28
ethnicity 9, 26, 88, 94, 103, 168
ethnography 14, 27, 66, 67, 83, 83–8, 90, 91–2
etic understandings 96

focus groups 9–10, 14, 25, 45, 64, 67, 70–4, 77, 137; of children 87–8; example 69–70; interviews 72–4
focus keeping 132
Foucault, Michel 112
frames 65–6
FreeMind 131
frequency polygons 57

General Data Protection Regulation (GDPR) 76, 129
Google 131, 137–8; Apps 134; Docs 128, 130–1, 134, 139, 142; Drive 131; Forms 54, 136; Meet 137; Sheets 136, 141
Grammarly 142
graphs 57, 175
grounded theory 66–7
Growing Up in Ireland (GUI) study 14, 47, 50, 53, 158

'hidden curriculum' 107–08
histograms 57
historical research 95–109; credibility of sources 100; life v. traditional history 102; oral 100–02; primary sources 98–101, 109; secondary sources 96–100; strategies 97–100

informed (and voluntary) consent 13, 15–16, 18–22, 26–7, 72, 76, 91, 138; and 'assent' 20; forms 21
interpretative phenomenological analysis 66–7
interpretivism 64–65
interviews 8–10, 13–14, 22–3, 27, 45, 64, 66–7, 71–2, 75–7, 80, 84–5, 88–9, 98, 100–02, 119–20, 125, 135, 137, 170; focus-group 25–6, 70–4; open-ended 83; semi-structured 68, 69; software 69; transcription 69, 72, 77, 80, 137–9
Irish language, research through 144–61

jargon 26, 49

language 25, 66, 68–9, 80, 118–19, 121, 126, 148, 173; challenges 21; inclusive 10; minority 40; plain 20, 26, 76
LGBTQI+ people 82, 90, 94
Likert scales 51–2, 54, 55–6
literacy 20–1, 25, 69
literature reviews 30–43, 69, 70, 121, 168, 173; academic journals 34; books 36; drafting 41–2; evaluation 38–9; 'golden thread' 41; headings 41; key words 35; media sources 33–4; paraphrasing 42; plagiarism 42; process 31; product 31; questions to ask 32; reference management software 36; search engines 34; selection 33–6; summarising 37–8; synthesis 39–40; and table of contents 41–2

managing risk 24
MAXQDA 140
medical research 24
Mendeley 36, 134
mental health 77, 115–20
Microsoft 131, 136–8; Excel 136, 141; Forms 54, 136; OneDrive 131; Teams 137; Windows 129; Word 130–1, 134, 139, 142
mind mapping 131–2
Miro 131
mixed methods research 45, 47, 61, 66, 113, 115, 136
Murch, Walter 143

narrative analysis 66, 68, 88
null hypothesis 58, 60
Nuremberg Code 15, 18–19
NVivo 68–9, 140

Otter 138

Padlet 132
Palmer, Parker 114
Paperpile 134
parenting strategies 85
parents, working with 26, 86, 88, 90–1, 114, 165, 170
parrhesia 112, 127

participants 10–11; choosing 75; contacting 16; debriefing 76; exclusion criteria 24; openness with 76; privacy 17, 22, 28; recording 76; rights of 18–19, 22; safety 10, 22–3, 77, 89; selection of 17, 24–5; v. 'subjects' 14; well-being 22–3, 89
'passionate utterance' 112, 127
pedagogical practices 108
philosophy of education 111–27
pie charts 57, 136
Pomodoro technique 132–3
positionality 9, 11
Post-Primary Longitudinal Study (PPLS) 47
power 9–11, 19, 25, 68, 86, 105
practitioner research 164–74; academic publications 171–2, 174; and bias 168–9; conferences 174; definition 164–5; examples 170, 173–4; key elements 165; professional magazines 172–3; self-evaluation 167
privilege 9, 11
process of education 106
Programme for International Student Assessment (PISA) study 46
pseudonyms 22
PSPP 141
published work 2, 4–5, 8, 99, 172, 174; non-peer-reviewed 5–6; peer-reviewed 5–6

QDA Miner 140
qualitative research methods 45, 64–80, 84, 120, 136; definitions 65–8; ethics 75–7; generalisability 79; objectivity 78; observation 74–5; and 'truth' 78
Qualtrics 137, 141
quantitative research methods 45–61, 64, 68, 136, 141; execution stage 48; planning stage 48; regression designs 58–9; reliability 79; validated tools 48; validity 79 *see also* sampling; surveys

questionnaires 24, 52, 71, 73, 125, 136–7, 170

R (software) 141
reading effectively 4–5
research question 17–18, 33; choosing 1–11, 45, 168; examples of creating 7–8
researchers 14; reflexive 78; safety 77
right to withdraw 19, 21, 26–7, 72, 76, 90

sampling 52–3; clustered 52–3; convenience 52–3, 75; non-probabilistic 52–4; probabilistic 53; purposive 52–3, 73, 75; simple random 52–3; snowball 52–4, 75; stratified 52–3; systematic 52–3; targeted 75; voluntary response 52–3
Sartre, Jean-Paul 113–14
school policy 108
self-study 14
Skype 138
social media 53, 57, 135, 175
software: backup 129–31; cloud-based 128–9, 141; data analysis 139–42; device-based 128–9, 139–41; project management 132–3; reference management 133–5; version management 130–1
SPSS 68–9, 140–1
statistical tests 58–61; decision trees 60; p-values 60
statistics 14, 45, 98; descriptive 56–7
Steinbeck, John 130
'Stop-Go' system 26–7
'storying' 23
student advisory groups 170
surveys 14, 48–56; design checklist 52; matrix 51; online 135–7; open-ended 51; piloting 52; questions (checkbox, closed, multiple choice, open) 49–52; rating scales 50; stratified 53 *see also* quantitative research methods

tables of contents 41–2
taighde trí Ghaeilge 144–61

Teaching and Learning International Survey (TALIS) 46–7
Technology 27, 72, 128–143
terminology 6, 14, 66
thematic analysis 8, 66, 69
thesis/academic advisor 1–4, 6–7, 9, 12, 33, 48, 61, 83, 87, 97, 174
'Three Ps' 9–11
transgender children 90, 94
Trello 132
Twitter 53, 135, 175

United Nations Convention on the Rights of the Child 20, 83

variables 54–6; binary 55; categorical 55; continuous 55–6; dependent 57–8; discrete 55; independent 57–8; nominal 55; numeric 55; ordinal 55–6; relationship between 58–9

video conferencing 23, 74, 137
vulnerable people 10–11, 21, 23, 82, 89–92, 94

Warwick wellbeing scale 56
Watson, Thomas 128
Webex 138
Wittgenstein, Ludwig 118, 121
'writing-as-process' 111
'writing-as-product' 111
'writing-as-research' 111
'writing-for-research' 111

XMind 131

Zoom 74, 137
Zotero 36, 134